HOTEL AND PUBLIC RELATIONS

HOTEL AND PUBLIC RELATIONS

M. C. METTI

ANMOL PUBLICATIONS PVT. LTD.
NEW DELHI - 110 002 (INDIA)

ANMOL PUBLICATIONS PVT. LTD.

H.O.: 4374/4B, Ansari Road, Darya Ganj,
New Delhi-110 002 (India)
Ph.: 23278000, 23261597

B.O.: No. 1015, Ist Main Road, BSK IIIrd Stage
IIIrd Phase, IIIrd Block
Bangalore - 560 085 (India)
Visit us at: www.anmolpublications.com

Hotel and Public Relations

ISBN 978-81-261-3239-3

PRINTED IN INDIA

Printed at Mehra Offset Press, Delhi.

Contents

Preface

Public Relations have a great role to play in running successful business of hotels. Public relations are the art and science of managing communication between an organization and its key public ingredients to build, manage, and sustain its positive image. Its successfully management implies to the sound business of hotels in this cut throat competition.

Researches and case studies are a very much important tools to study the ground reality of the hotels and public relations. Studying the research data will benefits all the readers.

As it is the process of aligning the perceptions of targeted audiences (or publics) with the current realities and reasonable prospects of another entity, this book covers all perspective of public relations in dealing day today running of hotel business. Hope the book helps students and research scholars in exploring the secrets of public relations in hotels.

Author

Chapter 1

Introduction

PUBLIC RELATIONS

Public Relation is a powerful form of advertising and the most effective way to get media coverage. Hotel Travel Check offers a variety of press release services to meet your needs. Our expert PR service is an affordable, cost-effective way to "spread the news" to your target audience. Public relations (PR) is the art of managing communication between an organization and its key publics to build, manage and sustain a positive image. One of the earliest definitions of PR was coined by Edward Bernays. According to him, "Public Relations is a management function which tabulates public attitudes, defines the policies, procedures and interest of an organization followed by executing a Programme of action to earn public understanding and acceptance."

Hotel Management Public Relations can be a complicated task when you aren't prepared to maneuver within the industry. According to two American PR professionals Scott M. Cutlips and Allen H. Center, "PR is a planned effort to influence opinion through good character and responsible performance based upon mutual satisfactory two-way communication".

Public relations is the art and science of managing communication between an organization and its key public constituents to build, manage, and sustain its positive image.

Public relations is the process of aligning the perceptions of targeted audiences (or publics) with the current realities and reasonable prospects of another entity.

Public relations is about building public relationships.

Public relations involves:

1. Evaluation of public attitudes and opinions.
2. Formulation and implementation of an organization's procedures and policy regarding communication with its publics.
3. Coordination of communications Programmes.
4. Developing rapport and good-will through a two way communication process.
5. Fostering a positive relationship between an organization and its public constituents.

Examples include:

- Corporations use marketing public relations (MPR) to convey information about the products they manufacture or services they provide to potential customers to support their direct sales efforts. Typically, they support sales in the short and long term, establishing and burnishing the corporation's branding for a strong, ongoing market.
- Corporations also use public-relations as a vehicle to reach legislators and other politicians, seeking favorable tax, regulatory, and other treatment, and they may use public relations to portray themselves as enlightened employers, in support of human-resources recruiting Programmes.
- Non-profit organizations, including schools and universities, hospitals, and human and social service agencies, use public relations in support of awareness Programmes, fund-raising Programmes, staff recruiting, and to increase patronage of their services.
- Politicians use public relations to attract votes and raise money, and, when successful at the ballot box,

to promote and defend their service in office, with an eye to the next election or, at career's end, to their legacy.

Precursors to public relations are found in publicists who specialized in promoting circuses, theatrical performances, and other public spectacles. In the United States, where public relations has its origins, many early PR practices were developed in support of the expansive power of the railroads. In fact, many scholars believe that the first appearance of the term "public relations" appeared in the 1897 Year Book of Railway Literature.

Later, PR practitioners were—and are still often—recruited from the ranks of journalism. Some journalists, concerned with ethics, criticize former colleagues for using their inside understanding of news media to help clients receive favorable media coverage.

Despite many journalists' discomfort with the field of public relations, well-paid PR positions remain a popular choice for reporters and editors forced into a career change by the instability of the print and electronic media industry. PR historians say the first PR firm, the Publicity Bureau, was established in 1900 by former newspapermen, with Harvard University as its first client.

The First World War also helped stimulate the development of public relations as a profession. Many of the first PR professionals, including Ivy Lee, Edward Bernays, and Carl Byoir, got their start with the Committee on Public Information (also known as the Creel Commission), which organized publicity on behalf of U.S. objectives during World War I. Some historians regard Ivy Lee as the first real practitioner of public relations, but Edward Bernays is generally regarded today as the profession's founder. In describing the origin of the term Public Relations, Bernays commented, "When I came back to the United States, I decided that if you could use propaganda for war, you could certainly use it for peace. And propaganda got to be a bad word because of the Germans.. using it. So what I did was to try to find some other words, so we found the words Council on Public Relations".

Ivy Lee, who has been credited with developing the modern news release (also called a "press release"), espoused a philosophy consistent with what has sometimes been called the "two-way street" approach to public relations, in which PR consists of helping clients listen as well as communicate messages to their publics. In the words of the Public Relations Society of America (PRSA), "Public relations helps an organization and its publics adapt mutually to each other." In practice, however, Lee often engaged in one-way propagandizing on behalf of clients despised by the public, including Standard Oil founder John D. Rockefeller. Shortly before his death, the US Congress had been investigating his work on behalf of the controversial Nazi German company IG Farben.

Bernays was the profession's first theorist. A nephew of Sigmund Freud, Bernays drew many of his ideas from Freud's theories about the irrational, unconscious motives that shape human behaviour. Bernays authored several books, including Crystallizing Public Opinion, Propaganda, and The Engineering of Consent. Bernays saw public relations as an "applied social science" that uses insights from psychology, sociology, and other disciplines to scientifically manage and manipulate the thinking and behaviour of an irrational and "herdlike" public. "The conscious and intelligent manipulation of the organized habits and opinions of the masses is an important element in democratic society," he wrote in Propaganda. "Those who manipulate this unseen mechanism of society constitute an invisible government which is the true ruling power of our country."

One of Bernays' early clients was the tobacco industry. In 1929, he orchestrated a legendary publicity stunt aimed at persuading women to take up cigarette smoking, which was then considered unfeminine and inappropriate for women with any social standing. To counter this image, Bernays arranged for New York City débutantes to march in that year's Easter Day Parade, defiantly smoking cigarettes as a statement of rebellion against the norms of a male-dominated society. Photographs of what Bernays dubbed the "Torches of Liberty Brigade" were sent to newspapers, convincing many women to equate smoking with women's rights. Some women went so far as to demand membership in all-male smoking clubs, a highly controversial act at the time.

In 1950 PRSA enacts the first "Professional Standards for the Practice of Public Relations," a forerunner to the current Code of Ethics, last revised in 2000 to include six core values and six code provisions. The six core values are "Advocacy, Honesty, Expertise, Independence, Loyalty, and Fairness." The six code provisions are "Free Flow of Information, Competition, Disclosure of Information, Safeguarding Confidences, Conflicts of Interest, and Enhancing the Profession."

The Industry Today

According to the U.S. Bureau of Labor Statistics, there were approximately 122,000 public relations specialists in the United States in 1998, while there were approximately 485,000 advertising, marketing, and public relations managers working in all industries. Public relations practitioners deliver information through the media to target audiences or, with the advent of the Internet, directly to specific stakeholder groups. Because similar opinions tend to be shared by a group of people rather than an entire society, research may be conducted to determine a range of things such as target audiences, appeal, as well as strategies for coordinated message presentation. PR may target different audiences with different messages to achieve an overall goal. Public Relations sets out to effect widespread opinion and behaviour changes.

Modern public relations uses a variety of techniques including opinion polling and focus groups to evaluate public opinion, combined with a variety of high-tech techniques for distributing information on behalf of their clients, including satellite feeds, the Internet, broadcast faxes, and database-driven phone banks to recruit supporters for a client's cause. According to the PRSA,

"Examples of the knowledge that may be required in the professional practice of public relations include communication arts, psychology, social psychology, sociology, political science, economics, and the principles of management and ethics. Technical knowledge and skills are required for opinion research, public issues analysis, media relations, direct mail, institutional advertising, publications, film/video productions, special events, speeches, and presentations."

Although public relations professionals are stereotypically seen as corporate servants, the reality is that almost any organization that has a stake in how it is portrayed in the public arena employs at least one PR manager. Large organizations may even have dedicated communications departments. Government agencies, trade associations, and other non-profit organizations commonly carry out PR activities.

Public relations should be seen as a management function in any organization. An effective communication, or public relations, plan for an organization is developed to communicate to an audience (whether internal or external publics) in such a way the message coincides with organizational goals and seeks to benefit mutual interests whenever possible.

Specialization

- Property development PR
- Real estate PR
- Retail sector PR
- Agricultural PR
- Food service PR
- Health care PR
- Technology/IT PR
- Public affairs PR

- On-line PR
- Financial/investor relations
- Employee/member communications
- Community PR
- Not-for-profit PR
- Crisis communication PR

As industry consolidation becomes more prevalent, many organizations and individuals are choosing to retain "boutique" firms as opposed to so-called "global" communications firms. These smaller firms typically specialize in only a couple of practice areas and thus, often have a greater understanding of their client's business. And because they deal with certain journalists with greater frequency, specialty firms often have stronger media contacts in the areas that matter most to their clients. Added benefits of smaller, specialty firms include more personal attention and accountability and as well, cost savings. This is not to say that smaller is always better, but there is a growing consensus that specialty firms offer more than once considered.

A number of specialties exist within the field of public relations, including:

- Crisis management
- Reputation management
- Issue management
- Investor relations and labour relations
- Grassroots PR (sometimes referred to as astroturf PR)

Methods, Tools and Tactics

Public relations and publicity are not synonyms. Publicity is the spreading of information to gain public awareness in a product, service, candidate, etc. It is just one technique of public relations as listed here.

Audience Targeting

A fundamental technique used in public relations is to identify the target audience, and to tailor every message to appeal to that audience. It can be a general, nationwide or worldwide audience, but it is more often a segment of a population. Marketers often refer to economy-driven "demographics," such as "white males 18-49," but in public relations an audience is more fluid, being whoever someone wants to reach. For example, recent political audiences include "soccer moms" and "NASCAR dads."

In addition to audiences, there are usually stakeholders, literally people who have a "stake" in a given issue. All audiences are stakeholders (or presumptive stakeholders), but not all stakeholders are audiences. For example, a charity commissions a PR agency to create an advertising campaign to raise money to find a cure for a disease. The charity and the people with the disease are stakeholders, but the audience is anyone who is likely to donate money.

Sometimes the interests of differing audiences and stakeholders common to a PR effort necessitate the creation of several distinct but still complementary messages. This is not always easy to do, and sometimes – especially in politics – a spokesperson or client says something to one audience that angers another audience or group of stakeholders.

Press Conferences

A press conference consists of someone speaking to the media at a predetermined time and place. Press conferences usually take place in a public or quasi-public place. Press conferences provide an opportunity for speakers to control information and who gets it; depending on the circumstances, speakers may hand-pick the journalists they invite to the conference instead of making themselves available to any journalist who wishes to attend.

It is also assumed that the speaker will answer journalists' questions at a press conference, although they are not obliged to. However, someone who holds several press conferences on a topic (especially a scandal) will be asked questions by the press, regardless of whether they indicate they will entertain them, and the more conferences the person holds, the more aggressive the questioning may become. Therefore, it is in a speaker's interest to answer journalists' questions at a press conference to avoid appearing as if they have something to hide.

But questions from reporters – especially hostile reporters – detracts from the control a speaker has over the information they give out. For even more control, but less interactivity, a person may choose to issue a press release.

Press releases

Press release format The typical press release announces that the statement is "For Immediate Release" across the top (some may instead be embargoed until a certain date), and lists the issuing organization's media contacts directly below. The media contacts are the people that the release's issuer wants to make available to the media; for example, a press release about new scientific study will typically list the study's lead scientist as its media contact. The bottom of each release is usually marked with or -30- to signify the end of the text.

Five "W"s and an "H" There are 6 vital facts to convey in the first paragraph of a release to ensure that it doesn't end up in the bin.

- Who
- What
- When
- Where
- Why
- How

A press release is a written statement distributed to the media. It is a fundamental tool of public relations. Press releases are usually communicated by a newswire service to various news media and journalists may use them as they see fit. Very often the information in a press release finds its way verbatim, or minimally altered, to print and broadcast reports. If a media outlet reports that "John Doe said in a statement today that...", the "statement" usually originated in a press release, or a direct quote from an interview with a John Doe.

The text of a release is usually (but not always) written in the style of a news story, with an eye-catching headline and text written standard journalistic inverted pyramid style. This style of news writing makes it easier for reporters to quickly grasp the message. Journalists are free to use the information verbatim, or alter it as they see fit. PR practitioners research and write releases that encourage as much "lifting" as possible.

Many journalists believe it is unethical to copy from a press release—they believe it is a lapse of good judgement (for instance, a direct quote, as in: Senator Smith said, "This is the most fiscally irresponsible bill that the Congress has passed since the Buy Everyone A Mercedes Act." In this case, a journalist may copy the quote verbatim into the story, although ethical reporters prefer to try soliciting an individual quote from the speaker before filing their story). Public relations professionals believe that press releases and other collateral material aid a journalist's job, and it is the job of the journalist to decide whether or not reprinting material verbatim tells the real story.

Since press releases reflect their issuer's preferred interpretation or positive packaging of a story, journalists are often skeptical of their contents. The level of skepticism depends on what the story is and who's telling it. Newsrooms receive so many press releases that, unless it is a story that the media are already paying attention to, a press release alone often isn't enough to catch a journalist's attention.

With the advent of modern electronic media and new technology, press releases now have equivalents in these media_video news releases and audio news releases. However, many television stations are hesitant to use VNR's that appear canned and are not newsworthy.

A New Kind of Press Release—"Optimized" for the Internet

The advent of the Internet has ushered in a new kind of press release known as an optimized press release. Unlike conventional press releases of yore, written for journalists' eyes only, in hopes the editor or reporter would find the content compelling enough to turn it into print or electronic news coverage, the optimized press release is posted on an online news portal. Here the writer carefully selects keywords or keyword phrases relevant to the press release contents. If written skillfully, the press release can rank highly in searches on Google News, Yahoo or MSN News (or the many other minor news portals) for the chosen keyword phrases.

Readers of optimized press releases constitute far more than journalists. In the days before news search engines, a press release would have landed only in the hands of a news reporter or an editor who would make the decision about whether the content warranted news coverage. Although the news media is always privy to online press releases in the search engines, most readers are end-users. Optimized press releases circumvent the mainstream media which is formerly—but no longer—the gatekeeper of the news.

Lobby groups

Lobby groups are established to influence government policy, corporate policy, or public opinion. These groups purport to represent a particular interest. When a lobby group hides its true purpose and support base it is known as a front group.

Astroturfing

Creating an artificial "grassroots" movement is known as astroturfing. A typical example would be the writing of letters to multiple newspaper editors under different names to express an opinion on an issue, creating the impression of widespread public feeling but being controlled by one central entity.

Spin

In public relations, spin is a, sometimes pejorative, term signifying a heavily biased portrayal in one's own favor of an event or situation. While traditional public relations may also rely on creative presentation of the facts, "spin" often, though not always, implies disingenuous, deceptive and/or highly manipulative tactics. Politicians are often accused of spin by commentators and political opponents, when they produce a counter argument or position.

The term is borrowed from ball sports such as cricket, where a spin bowler may impart spin on the ball during a delivery so that it will curve through the air or bounce in an advantageous manner.

The techniques of "spin" include:

- Selectively presenting facts and quotes that support one's position (cherry picking)
- Non-denial denial
- Phrasing in a way that assumes unproven truths
- Euphemisms to disguise or promote one's agenda
- Ambiguity
- Skirting
- Rejecting the validity of hypotheticals
- Appealing to internal policies

Another spin technique involves careful choice of timing in the release of certain news so it can take advantage of prominent events in the news. A famous reference to this practice occurred when UK government press officer Jo Moore used the phrase It's now a very good day to get out anything we want to bury, (widely paraphrased or misquoted as "It's a good day to bury bad news"), in an email sent on September 11, 2001. The furor caused when this email was reported in the press eventually caused her to resign.

Spin Doctor

Skilled practitioners of spin are sometimes called "spin doctors", though probably not to their faces unless it is said facetiously. It is the PR equivalent of calling a writer a "hack". Perhaps the most well-known person in the UK often described as a "spin doctor" is Alastair Campbell, who was involved with Tony Blair's public relations between 1994 and 2003, and also played a controversial role as press relations officer to the British and Irish Lions rugby side during their 2005 tour of New Zealand.

The American radio and television talk-show host Bill O'Reilly, who is often considered a spokesman for conservatism, has called his television show The O'Reilly Factor "The No Spin Zone", emphasizing his own purported dislike of the phenomenon. Some other American talk and radio-show hosts and commentators, such as Keith Olbermann, who maintains an on-going "feud with Bill O'Reilly", and who himself has been tagged with being more liberal in his views, mock O'Reilly's epithet "no spin zone" suggesting his own avoidance of "spin" to be just another instance of spin from "the other side". (Olbermann frequently labels O'Reilly as "The Worst Person in the World" in one of his segments on his own show Countdown, which airs at the same time as The O'Reilly Factor on rival cable network MSNBC.)

Such commentators on politics, despite their prominent roles in mainstream-media journalism, which purports to maintain objectivity, at times and sometimes even often seem engaged in the very phenomenon of spin that they deride. Many such commentators and their featured on-air media consultants, commonly termed "talking heads" or pundits, come to Programmes on radio, television, and in publishing from prior professional careers in public relations and politics, sometimes even as former political campaign directors or speech writers for political figures; for those who do, mastering the "art" of spin has already been an important part of their past work experience, and it may lead not only to their acute understanding and critique of the phenomenon but also to their supreme ability to continue practicing it in ever-more subtle ways.

State-run media in many countries also engage in spin by selectively allowing news stories that are favorable to the government while censoring anything that could be considered critical. They may also use propaganda to indoctrinate or actively influence citizens' opinions.

Meta-semantics

- Meta-semantics is the rapidly growing study of group interactions providing a model for public relations.

Other

- Publicity events or publicity stunts
- The talk show circuit. A PR spokesperson (or his/her client) "does the circuit" by being interviewed on television and radio talk shows with audiences that the client wishes to reach.
- Books and other writings
- After a PR practitioner has been working in the field for a while, he or she accumulates a list of contacts in the media and elsewhere in the public affairs sphere. This "Rolodex" becomes a prized asset, and job announcements sometimes even ask for candidates with an existing Rolodex, especially those in the media relations area of PR.
- Direct communication (carrying messages directly to constituents, rather than through the mass media) with, e.g., newsletters – in print and e-letters.
- Collateral literature, traditionally in print and now predominantly as web sites.
- Speeches to constituent groups and professional organizations; receptions; seminars, and other events; personal appearances.
- The slang term for a PR practitioner or publicist is a "flack."

The Process of Public Relations

Scott Cutlip, Allen Center and Glen Broom describe the public relations process in four steps. The first step is "Defining Public Relations Problems," usually in terms of a "situational analysis," or what public relations professionals call a SWOT analysis (strengths, weaknesses, opportunities, threats). According to Cutlip, Center and Broom, this should answer the question, "What's happening now?" The next step in the public relations process is "Planning and Programming," where the main focus is "strategy," Cutlip, Center and Broom argue that this step should answer the question "What should we do and say, and why?"

The third step in the public relations process is "Taking action and Communicating," also known as "Implementation;" this step should answer the question "How and when do we do and say it?" The final step in Cutlip, Center and Broom's Four-Step Public Relations Process is "Evaluating The Programme," making a final "assessment," which should answer the question "How did we do," this is where public relations professionals make a final analysis of the success of their campaign or communication.

Another process model by Sheila C. Crifasi (2000) uses the acronym "ROSIE" to define a five-step process of "Research, Objectives, Strategies, Implementation and Evaluation." Using another acronym, "ROPES," Dr. Kathleen S. Kelly explains a five-step process through "Research, Objectives, Programme, Evaluation and Stewardship." Wilcox, Ault, Agee and Cameron (2002) define the public relations process through four steps of "Research, Action (Programme Planning), Communication and Evaluation." Center and Jackson (1995) define the process of public relations through four steps: "Fact-finding and data gathering; Planning and programming; Action and communication; Evaluation."

People who are professionals in public relations use different methods for analyzing the results of their work such as focus groups, surveys, and one-on-one interviews. These same methods are used in defining what medium of communication will be used in the process of strategy and what tools will be used in relaying the message, such as press releases, brochures, Web sites, media packs, video news releases, news conferences and in-house publications.

Politics and Civil Society

A tactic used in political campaigns is known as "defining one's opponent". Opponents can be candidates, organizations and other groups of people. In the 2004 US presidential campaign, George W. Bush defined John Kerry as a "flip-flopper," among other characterizations, which were widely reported and repeated by the media, particularly the conservative media. Similarly, George H.W. Bush characterized Michael Dukakis as weak on crime (the Willie Horton ad) and as hopelessly liberal ("a card-carrying member of the ACLU"). In 1996, President Bill Clinton seized upon opponent Bob Dole's promise to take America back to a simpler time, promising in contrast to "build a bridge to the 21st century." This painted Dole as a person who was somehow opposed to progress.

In the debate over abortion, pro-abortion rights groups defined their opponents by defining themselves instead: "pro-choice." Anti-abortion rights groups responded in kind, branding themselves "pro-life." Extrapolating their respective rhetoric, pro-choice groups refer to their opponents as "anti-choice," and pro-life groups refer to their opponents as "anti-life."

More recently, opponents of same-sex marriage in the U.S. have declared that their opponents are not the gay couples suing for the right to marry in various state courts, but rather the judges who rule in their favor. They are now calling them "activist judges," implying that they impose their personal beliefs instead of objectively interpreting the law. This sidesteps the thorny issue of making millions of gay people an "enemy," and instead focuses attention on the much smaller judiciary, who all Americans can ostensibly agree should be prevented from being "activists" on the bench.

Managing Language

If a politician or organization can use an apt phrase in relation to an issue, such as in interviews or news releases, the news media will often repeat it verbatim, thus furthering the message. (This may be considered an example of a meme.)

"New Deal" became a description of President Franklin D. Roosevelt's anti-Depression economic plans, and "states' rights/state sovereignty" became near-code words for anti-civil rights legislation.

Recent examples include: "death tax" for estate tax, "racial preferences" for affirmative action, "faith-based" instead of religious, "climate change" for global warming, and "partial-birth abortion" for pro-choice.

Entertainment and Celebrity

Celebrities tend to be fans of the dictum "any publicity is good publicity". If a celebrity says or does something embarrassing, he or she will often turn it into a strength and make it part of his or her "image." This tactic is used just as much with favorable situations as much as with unfavorable ones.

A current example involves the entertainer Jessica Simpson, who gained nationwide prominence when she wondered aloud on a reality show if "Chicken of the Sea"-brand tuna fish was actually chicken or tuna, garnering her a reputation for being slow-witted. But by the summer of 2004, she was being paid to endorse a brand of breath mints called "Liquid Ice." In the product's television commercial, Simpson replicates her earlier confusion by debating whether the mint is really liquid or ice. So although she was previously ridiculed, she (and her advisers) turned her nationwide embarrassment into a lucrative endorsement deal.

Branching Out

As Oscar Wilde is supposed to have said, the only thing worse than being talked about is not to be talked about at all. Many celebrities seem to take this truism to heart, because when their popularity (and income) wane, they take on new projects that attract media attention. Considering that a celebrity's celebrity is a brand unto itself, many celebrities are under constant pressure to "reinvent" themselves, as a prophylactic against obscurity.

A current trend among American celebrities is the transformation of musicians, comedians, and almost every other sort of performer into children's book authors. Madonna, Jay Leno, Billy Crystal, Ricky Gervais and several other celebrities have recently written children's books, accompanied by much media coverage.

A more traditional way of branching out is the celebrity restaurant. This is especially common among professional athletes, whose time in the spotlight is often limited by the physical demands of their jobs. Basketball player Michael Jordan opened a restaurant in Chicago, and singer Britney Spears opened an ill-fated eatery in New York which closed a few months later.

Male celebrities like Tim Robbins, Sean Penn and Charlton Heston seem to gravitate toward politics, although some female celebrities, such as Susan Sarandon and Barbra Streisand, also become strong political voices.

Younger female celebrities on the other hand are often drawn into the fashion world. Hotel heiress Paris Hilton recently announced that she was starting her own line of jewelry, and Jennifer Lopez has started a line of clothing. And fading star Elizabeth Taylor launched a fragrance called "White Diamonds" several years ago, bringing renewed interest from the media. Britney Spears also kept herself in the public eye when she had her secretive marriage to Kevin Federline and bore his child. Although neither topic has to do with her career, audiences seemed to be just as intrigued to know about her personal life.

Some celebrities have also entered the world of self promotion by establishing other business ventures. St. Louis rapper Nelly's Vokal for men and Applebottoms for Women and Ludacris's "Disturbing the Peace" record company are both examples of celebrities taking public relations into their own hands.

Ethical and Social Issues

Many of the techniques used by PR firms are drawn from the institutions and practices of democracy itself. Persuasion, advocacy, and education are instruments through which individuals and organizations are entitled to express themselves in a free society, and many public relations practitioners are engaged in practices that are widely considered as beneficial, such as publicizing scientific research, promoting charities, raising awareness of public health concerns and other issues in civil society.

One of the most controversial practices in public relations is the use of front groups—organizations that purport to serve a public cause while actually serving the interests of a client whose sponsorship may be obscured or concealed. The creation of front groups is an example of what PR practitioners sometimes term the third party technique—the art of "putting your words in someone else's mouth." PR Watch, a non-profit organization that monitors PR activities it considers to be deceptive, has published numerous examples of this technique in practice. Critics of the public relations industry, such as PR Watch, have contended that Public Relations involves a "multi-billion dollar propaganda-for-hire industry" that "concocts and spins the news, organizes phoney 'grassroots' front groups, spies on citizens, and conspires with lobbyists and politicians to thwart democracy.".

Instances of the use of front groups as a PR technique have been documented in many industries. Coal mining corporations have created environmental groups that contend that increased CO_2 emissions and global warming will contribute to plant growth and will be beneficial, trade groups for bars have created and funded citizens' groups to attack anti-alcohol groups, and tobacco companies have created and funded citizens' groups to advocate for tort reform and to attack personal injury lawyers.

Current issues in ethical and social arenas have been brought to the attention of people from all strata of the population when it was found that more than one journalist with a platform had received money from a Public Relations firm for espousing a certain point of view.

Crisis Management

Crisis management involves identifying a crisis, planning a response to the crisis and confronting and resolving the crisis. Crisis management can be applied in almost any field of endeavor, but it is most commonly used in international relations, political science, business and management. For more about crisis management in international relations.

Many school districts have developed crisis response guides, which identify potential situations such as fires and other disasters, bomb threats, confronting unwelcome visitors, violence (and threats thereof) and the death of a student.

In general terms, the theory of crisis management can be divided into crisis bargaining and negotiation, crisis decision making, and crisis dynamics.

In Management

In business there are three main types of crisis:

- Financial crisis - short term liquidity or cash flow problems; and long term bankruptcy problems
- Public relations crisis - More commonly called "crisis communications," negative publicity that could adversely affect the success of the company
- Strategic crisis - changes in the business environment that call the viability of the company into question - for example the introduction of the automobile was a strategic crisis for buggy-whip manufacturers

Certain preliminary measures need to be taken to prevent a crisis. Companies should always plan ahead and project likely outcomes. They should avoid decisions that have the potential to turn into a crisis. They should know their "worst case scenarios" and have a contingency plan for it.

If prevention has not been successful, then the following six steps should be undertaken immediately:

- Do an objective assessment of the causes of the crisis.
- Determine whether the causes will have a long term effect or whether it will be a short term phenomena.
- Project the most likely course of events.

- Focus all the most capable people (including yourself) on activities that will mitigate or eliminate the problem.
- Look for opportunities - there could be a "silver lining".
- Immediately act to guard cash flow.

If it is a cashflow crisis do not wait for further evidence before acting. Immediately take actions to maintain or increase cash flow.

These could include:

- Accelerating accounts receivable payments even if this requires the granting of discounts
- Decelerating accounts payable payments even if this means losing discounts
- Increasing short term sales
- Maintaining or increasing profit margins on sales if possible
- Reducing expenses:
  - Eliminating non-essential expenses
  - Selling non-mission critical assets
  - Reducing payroll
  - Outsourcing non-mission critical operations
- Renegotiating loans and other debts wherever possible - obtaining interest-only loans or extended payment terms

If it is a public relations crisis, act immediately to prevent or counter the spread of the negative information. Containment may require intense media activities. Use every media available to you to provide a counter argument or question the credibility of the original negative publicity.

Issue Management

In public relations, issue management is the process used to align organizational activities and stakeholder expectations. "Issue Management" means influencing public policy. Issue

Managers work in government affairs, legal affairs, public affairs and regulatory compliance.

The framework of issues management was developed by Chase (1977) as a public relations strategy for industry. According to this objective, issues are critical developments for a company. They begin as demands from special interest groups and may evolve through public debates in the media into political and legislative demands with a potential for harming the company or limiting its ability to act. Issues management, therefore, means the orchestrating of a positive plan for dealing with the issue, rather than merely reacting to it. Any issues - including risk issues - have a life cycle. For example, a risk issue begins to appear in the academic literature and at small conferences without any public awareness. Next, the issue might to take shape, and positions will be staked out. Special interest groups emerge and raise the alarm. They are beginning to explore the issue. The issue gathers momentum. The media will be involved and create widespread awareness of the risk. In the face of increased stridency, the public soon becomes anxious and requires stricter risk regulations.

By definition, issues management is the systematic identification of and action on public policy matters of concern to an organization. According to Heath (1988) „issues management is the management of organizational and community resources through the public policy process to advance organizational interests and rights by striking a mutual balance with those of stakeholders." The goal is to achieve harmony with key publics. The first task here is a stakeholder analysis, in order to get a clear idea about the stakeholders, their interests, power, and relationships to the other stakeholders.

A number of steps may facilitate this analysis:

- Create a stakeholder list
- Develop a power matrix
- Identify the most important stakeholders
- Explore access to these stakeholders.

The goal of these activities is to explore the opportunities for establishing a working relationship with these people. On the one hand, tactfulness and respect are an essential component of that exploration. On the other hand, it should be acknowledged that risk communication under these circumstances is above all a political issue. Thus, positioning one's own risk policy is a delicate task. It absolutely necessary to present an independent scientific view and to resist forming an alliance with any stakeholder. A second task is to analyse the conflict history in order to ascertain the issues about which the stakeholders disagree. In conflicts, the issues are not only related to the factual risk aspects. Above all social aspects, e.g. stakeholders' images, their motives, the alleged intentions and objectives as well as previous experience of each other, usually play a dominant role in the struggle.

One should also try to appraise what kind of discourse climate is to be expected. Is this going to be emotion-laden, maybe even hostile? Or are stakeholders willing to compromise? After clarifying one's own risk policy, the setting of realistic communication goals and the implementation of discourse rules are the next steps. On the assumption that there can be no zero risk and no zero conflicts over risks, the following goals can be specified for risk communication:

- The reduction of risks according to the ALARA principle,
- The turning of conflicts over risks into a rational discourse, and
- The containment/mitigation of societal conflicts over risks. This list shows clearly that risk communication cannot be viewed as dealing solely with information about and explanation of risk: far more essential is the establishment of a mutually accepted platform for a rational discourse.

In this context, two main issues have to be dealt with: coping with distrust, and being aware that risk management (and not risk assessment) tasks have first priority. It is worth noting, that both the social amplification and the issues management framework should not be viewed as theories. They cannot be expected to yield predictions regarding which issue is likely to be the subject of attenuation or amplification in the future. Nevertheless, they are useful in alerting managers and public officials to the dynamics of risk issues.

Reputation Management

Reputation management is the process of tracking an entity's actions and other entities' opinions about those actions; reporting on those actions and opinions; and reacting to that report creating a feedback loop. All entities involved are generally people, but that need not always be the case. Other examples of entities include animals, businesses, or even locations or materials. The tracking and reporting may range from word-of-mouth to statisical analysis of thousands data points.

Reputation management has come into wide use with the advent of widespread computing. Reputation management systems use various predefined criteria for processing complex data to report reputation. However, these systems only facilitate and automate some aspects the process of determing trustworthiness. This process is central to all kinds of human interaction, including interpersonal relationships, international diplomacy, stock markets, and sports.

Real-world Communities

Small Town

The classic example of reputation management is the small town. Population is small and interactions between members frequent; most interactions are face-to-face and positively identified — that is, there is no question who said or did what. Reputation accrues not only throughout one's lifetime, but is passed down to one's offspring; one's individual reputation depends both on one's own actions and one's inherited reputation.

There are generally few formal mechanisms to manage this implicit reputation. The town diner and barber shop serve as forums for exchange of gossip, in which community members' reputations are discussed, often in frank terms. Outstanding members may receive small, symbolic awards or titles, but these are mere confirmations of general knowledge.

There is exceedingly little deviation from community norms in a small town. This may be seen as either good or bad; there is little crime, but also little room for dissent or change. The small-town model scales poorly; it depends on each member having enough experience of a large number of other members, and this is only possible up to a point.

Big City

The large metropolitan area is at the other end of the spectrum from the small rural town. Community members come and go daily, and most members are only personally acquainted with a small fraction of the whole. Implicit reputation management continues to work within subcommunities, but for the city as a whole, it cannot.

Big cities have developed a large array of formal reputation management methods. Some apply only to subcommunities, such as, say, an association of local dentists. There are four methods (among others) which apply quite generally to the entire population: elections, appointments, the criminal justice system, and racial or ethnic prejudice.

- The city is governed in part by elected officials — persons who are given special powers by popular vote at regular intervals. Campaigns are often well-financed efforts to force a positive image of a candidate's reputation upon the electorate; television is often decisive. Elected officials are primarily concerned with preserving this good reputation, which concern dictates their every public action. Failure to preserve a good reputation, not to mention failure to avoid a bad one, is often cause for removal from office, sometimes prematurely. Candidates and officials frequently concentrate on damaging the reputations of their opponents.

- Appointed officials are not elected; they are granted special powers, usually by elected officials, without public deliberation. Persons wishing to be appointed to office also campaign to increase their perceived reputation, but the audience is much smaller. Effective actions and demonstrated merit are often important factors in gaining a positive reputation, but the definition of this merit is made by the elected, appointing officials, who tend to evaluate merit as it applies to them, personally. Thus persons who work hard to increase an elected official's reputation increase their own, at least in their patron's eyes. Some appointees have no other qualification beyond the fact that they may be depended on at all times to support their patrons.
- The stresses of big city life lead to much crime, which demands punishment, on several grounds. The severity of this punishment and of the efforts of the system to inflict it upon a community member depends in no small part on that individual's prior experiences within the system. Elaborate records are kept of every infraction, even of the suspicion of infractions, and these records are consulted before any decision is made, no matter how trivial. Great effort is expended to positively identify members — driver's licenses and fingerprints, for example — and any use of an alias is carefully recorded. Some small punishments are meted out informally, but most punishments, especially severe ones, are given only after a long, detailed, and formal process: a trial, which must result in a conviction, or finding of guilt, before a punishment is ordered.

Although it is sometimes said that serving one's punishment is sufficient penalty for the commission of a crime, in truth the damage to one's reputation may be the greater penalty — damage both within the system itself and within other systems of urban reputation management, such as that of elections to office. Between the explicit punishment and the damage to one's reputation, the total effect of a conviction in the criminal justice system so damages a person's ability to lead a normal life that the process, at least ostensibly, is meticulous in determining guilt or lack thereof. In case of "reasonable" doubt, a suspected malefactor is freed — though the mere fact of the trial is recorded, and affects his future reputation.

- The ordinary citizen, meeting a stranger, another citizen unknown to the first, is rarely concerned that the second may be an official, elected or otherwise; even so, he may be aware of the relative failure of reputation management in this regard. He does not have easy access to the database of the criminal justice system, and portions are not publicly available at all. Lacking other means, he often turns to the mock-system of racial or ethnic prejudice. This attempts to extend the small-town model to large communities by grouping individuals who look alike, dress alike, or talk alike. One reputation serves for all. Each individual is free to compose his personal measure of a group's reputation, and actions of strangers raise or lower that reputation for all group members.

The high incidence of crime, the proverbial incompetence of officials, and constant wars between rival, self-identified groups speaks poorly of all systems of urban reputation management. Together, they do not function as well as that of the small town, with no formal system at all.

Chapter 2

The Need for Strategic Public Relations Management

Strategic public relations planning and research techniques have evolved into the most powerful tools available to public relations practitioners. Today's competitive business environment increasingly puts pressure on communication managers to demonstrate in a measurable way how the results from public relations Programmes benefit the organizations they serve. Practitioners well prepared to use the tools available to them can enjoy bigger budgets, more autonomy in decision making, and greater support from management. Managers relying on an intuitive model of public relations practice based on their knowledge of media markets and a well-developed network of contacts, however, tend to have less credibility, enjoy less autonomy, receive lower priority, and suffer greater risk of cost cutting that threatens job security.

SURVIVING AMID FIERCE COMPETITION

The increasingly competitive business and social environment makes it critical for public relations managers to understand how to apply public relations planning, research, and Programme-evaluation practices that help ensure success and accountability. Research-based public relations practices enable managers to solve complex problems, set and achieve or exceed goals and objectives, track the opinions and beliefs of key publics, and employ Programme strategies with confidence they will have the intended results. Although the use of research in public relations management cannot guarantee Programme success, it allows practitioners to maximize their abilities and move beyond creative reactions to scientific management. A more strategic management style can help control the ways a situation will develop and the outcomes practitioners achieve in those situations.

Consider the following scenarios in which communication professionals can use research-based planning to develop effective strategies for solving a problem and demonstrate Programme success:

Community Relations

You are the public affairs director for the largest employer in a community. The local media have been running stories about problems at the company, claiming management has lost sight of its unique role in the community. The board of directors wants a clear understanding of public perceptions of the company. It also wants to develop new Programmes that will better serve the community and improve community relations. You are not convinced the company needs to establish new Programmes as much as it needs to support its existing Programmes. How do you determine the opinions and attitudes of community members toward the company? How do you measure community perceptions of existing Programmes, as well as community interest in new Programmes?

Special Events Planning and Promotion

You are the manager of a performing arts coliseum. The coliseum has lost money on several events over the past 2 years and now is threatened by competition from a new community theater scheduled for construction in 2 years. Coliseum management and its board of directors sense they are out of touch with the community and are unsure how to address the situation. How can management determine community programming interests and begin to reorient itself to the needs and desires of community members without wasting valuable resources?

Political Campaign

You are the campaign manager for a state senatorial candidate. The mostly rural district has 75,000 registered voters, many of whom work as farmers or in farming-related businesses and industries. The election is 3 months away, and the candidates are engaged in a close contest. How do you track changes in voters' perceptions of your candidate as the election nears?

Nonprofit

You are a public relations practitioner at a small, nonprofit organization. Your new assignment is to rescue a local special event with a troubled history. The event, sponsored by the local chamber of commerce, is supposed to raise money for your organization while attracting visitors to your community who patronize local businesses. Last year's event was a disaster, however, despite a strong media relations effort. Because of low attendance, the organization barely broke even on the event, and local businesses have lost interest in participating next year as sponsors. How do you find out what went wrong and make next year's event a success?

Development

You are a senior development officer at a major university. Development has become increasingly important as state budgets have dwindled. The university is making preparations for the largest development campaign in its history. Unfortunately, students let their partying get out of hand after a big football win over cross-state rivals, and the fracas attracts national media attention. You are concerned the negative media attention will significantly hinder university development efforts. You need to understand the opinions and attitudes of key publics to develop a quick plan that win allow you to respond in an effective manner. How do you determine the responses of donors and nondonors to news of the altercation? Public relations practitioners face problems like these on a regular basis.

DECISION MAKING

Research helps practitioners get accurate information quickly at a relatively low cost to aid them in sophisticated planning and problem solving such as this every day. When practitioners respond to organizational problems and challenges by engaging in media relations campaigns, they typically respond tactically instead of strategically. Tactical decision making can allow public relations Programmes and campaigns to drift aimlessly, lacking direction or purpose. Practitioners often use media clips as the basis for Programme accountability in this instance, but the benefits of clip-based evaluation are limited. It is impossible, for example, for practitioners to determine message effects on targeted audiences' opinions, attitudes, or behaviour using clips.

Practitioners find their ability to solve organizations' problems through such a response also severely limited because no basis exists for determining the extent of a problem or evaluating the results of their Programmes. Finally, organizations can become frustrated in their attempts to adapt to changing internal and external environments because practitioners have no basis for understanding and accomplishing the steps necessary to successfully address or accommodate stakeholders' opinions. The result is that practitioners' success may be limited. They typically end up in a defensive position with external and internal audiences, having no basis for effectively communicating the benefits of their campaigns and Programmes to organizational management.

When practitioners respond to problems and challenges strategically instead of tactically, they have a much greater likelihood of helping organizations meet their challenges, solve or avoid protracted problems, and adjust to the expectations of key stakeholders in mutually beneficial ways. Research and planning are not simple remedies for every organizational problem. No amount of research or planning, for example, can rescue an organization from the consequences of its own poor performance. Nevertheless, practitioners' use of research, planning, and evaluation contribute to an informed organizational decision-making process with a greater likelihood of success.

When practitioners use these tools, their Programmes and campaigns can have clear goals that direct Programme implementation. Practitioners can use formative research to find initial benchmarks for goals and objectives, and to determine campaign strategy. Practitioners using tactics purposefully and selectively can communicate the benefits of public relations campaigns and Programmes to organizational management more easily. Ultimately, practitioners have the opportunity to enjoy greater success at placing their organizations in stable, mutually beneficial relationships with key stakehoders.

As Cutlip, Center, and Broom (2000) noted, public relations is a management function that identifies, establishes, and maintains mutually beneficial relationships between an organization and the publics on whom its success or failure depends. This definition and many others like it, although simple on their face, actually suggest a complex set of processes. For public relations practitioners to operate as managers, for example, they cannot simply input the decisions made by others in an organization.

They need to assert themselves as members of what is commonly called the dominant coalition, those with the authority to make decisions and set policy. In other words, they need to lead organizations and not just act as "service providers." Dozier, Grunig, and Grunig (1995) stated, "Just as communication flows one way, so too does influence". What Dozier et al. meant by this is that service providers implement decisions made by others instead of influencing organizational decision making. As a result, practitioners operating as service providers commonly are limited to advocating organizational viewpoints. This prevents them from helping the organization build and maintain long-term relationships that ensure long-term organizational success, which requires some adjustment to public perceptions and needs.

Misunderstood Role of Public Relations

Public relations practices encompass a broad range of activities that can lead to confusion about how it differs from marketing and advertising. The goals of each differ in important ways. Advertising focuses on selling products to consumers through controlled placement of paid media messages, a narrow and specific role. Marketing, including integrated marketing communications, often uses public relations techniques to sell products and services. The marketing role is broader than that of advertising but still focuses on consumers rather than on all the key publics of an organization.

Public relations, on the other hand, strives to help organizations develop and preserve the variety of relationships that ensure long-term success, which is broader than those of advertising or marketing. These stakeholders can include consumers but also includes government regulators, community members, shareholders, members of the media, and employees. Therefore, although public relations techniques often are employed in marketing and advertising, it is more appropriate for organizational management to treat public relations as the umbrella under which other activities including marketing and advertising occur.

Many practitioners struggle with the fact that this is difficult to put into practice, and they often find their role misunderstood. A survey of New York chapter members of the Public Relations Society of America (PRSA), for example, found that 92% believed that most people do not understand what public relations is. Public relations also suffers from low credibility. In the New York survey, 93% of the professionals enjoyed their work, and 68% were proud of their field, but 67% believed the field did not have a good image, and 65% believed they were not as respected as members of other professions. This image problem was supported by a recent credibility study undertaken by PRSA, which found the public relations specialist ranked almost at the bottom of a list of approximately 50 professions.

It could seem that public relations' image problem stems from its reputation as being a "velvet ghetto", rather than from unsatisfactory practitioner performance. Women dominate the public relations field, and even though they perform more tasks at the managerial level than men do, they tend to earn less than men in the field. In addition, more women still perform tasks at a tactical level while operating as managers, which could contribute to the devaluation of women and of public relations. We believe, however, that managers—whether male or female—can enhance their status and perhaps also their salaries by adopting a more research-based, strategic management style.

To improve their stature within organizations and among a broad range of publics, public relations professionals must take a planned, strategic approach to their Programmes and problem solving. When operating as subordinates instead of organizational leaders, practitioners implement decisions made by others instead of contributing to organizational decision making. In short, they work at a tactical level. As leading experts continue to emphasize, communication specialists who operate as technicians cannot effectively build public consensus or position an organization on issues of strategic importance.

USING RESEARCH TO ENHANCE THE CREDIBILITY OF PUBLIC RELATIONS

One reason communication specialists experience frustration and insufficient credibility appears to lie in how they conduct and apply research. A national survey of 300 professionals in 1996 assessing their research practices found managers in a double bind. Professionals reported clients and CEOs as enthusiastic about research, but reluctant about providing the budget to pay for it. Meanwhile, the more the managers performed a specific type of research, the less they valued it, and the more they valued a particular research method, the less they employed it.

Use and Value of Research Measures Among Public Relations Practitioners

	Mean for Use (Rank)	Mean for Perceived Value (Rank)
Advertising equivalency	3.71(9)	3.37(9)
Volume of media pickups	5.43(2)	4.57(8)
Favorable media treatment	5.35(3)	4.96(7)
Media coverage	5.47(1)	5.19(5)
Changes in awareness	4.95(4)	5.64(4)
Changes in knowledge	4.85(5)	5.90(2)
Changes in attitudes	4.74(6)	5.77(3)
Changes in sales	4.07(8)	5.08(6)
Changes in behaviour	4.64(7)	6.02(1)

Note. All measures on 7-point scales, with I indicating less use or value and 7 indicating more use orvalue.

As shown in Table practitioners relied most on measures of volume of media pickups and tracking of media coverage, which they found the least beneficial. On the other hand, practitioners relied least on measures of changes in awareness, knowledge, attitudes, sales, and behaviour, which they found the most valuable. The results also showed that the professionals almost uniformly embraced research as vital for proving that public relations Programmes are effective, but less than half agreed that research is accepted as an important part of public relations.

A 1995 PRSA survey also found that 92% believed research was talked about more than used (Public Relations Society of America, 1995). Finally, although 68% of practitioners attending a seminar on PR measurement said they do evaluations, only 23% said their research was providing useful results. This pattern of results suggests that constraints prevent communication professionals from doing enough research, or at least enough of the type of research that clients and senior executives find compelling. In response, PR Reporter proclaimed measurement and evaluation as the field's top issue for the year 2000.

Moving from a tactical approach to a strategic management style requires skillful use of research and planning techniques. Recent discussions among senior public relations practitioners at professional meetings and in the trade press have consistently emphasized the need for managers to demonstrate forward thinking by anticipating instead of reacting to problems and opportunities. In an increasingly crowded and complex media and social environment, practitioners need to design innovative Programmes they can prove will work.

Gaining autonomy and the support and confidence of clients and upper management for their ideas requires several things. These include the ability to provide evidence supporting the need for communication Programmes, reasons why proposed strategies will work, and evidence at the end of a Programme that the Programme has indeed worked. In short, strategic public relations management demands a set of abilities that require competence in planning principles, research methods, communication theory, and effective communication presentation skills.

Experts in public relations seem to agree that public relations practitioners have the most success when they operate from a research-based, strategic management style. As a result, this book provides professionals and advanced public relations students with the information they need to engage in strategic public relations management. Communication specialists who apply these skills should secure a place for public relations at the leadership level in organizational decision making.

Chapter 3

Taking Stock

For public relations practitioners trained more as writers rather than as social scientists, the new bottom-line-oriented environment presents a major challenge. Organizations want cost-effective results. Many public relations practitioners argue that the cultivation of relationships is a fuzzy business, difficult to document with numbers. The result: Public relations positions become vulnerable to corporate restructuring."

The best insurance against cost cutters, and the best way to gain credibility and mobility in hotel management, is to adopt what Broom and Dozier called the scientific management approach. This approach does not discount the importance of creativity and communication skills, but it does put them into an effects-oriented context. Say a hotel wants to open a new wing in the hope that it will increase business. For a hotel, this is a touchy subject: It doesn't want to appear greedy to take advantage of people's bad news and emergencies. Moreover, the promotion budget is probably limited because many hotels are struggling to keep up with increasing service costs and decreasing reimbursements. Hotels also do not want to appear wasteful, particularly if financed publicly. How can the hotel increase business without causing offense, and without spending too much or appearing unseemly?

In what Nager and Allen called traditional public relations, the communication manager would come up with creative ideas for communication vehicles such as brochures and advertisements according to the budget and staffing available. Should we use two-colour or four-colour? Glossy or matte? The manager's decision making would focus on what looks best, sounds best, and works within the budget.

The scientific manager, on the other hand, would begin with a different set of questions: Why do we need this new wing? To whom are we targeting this campaign? How much increased traffic do we need, and how much is realistic to expect? What will motivate people to take advantage of this new service? The bottom line: What goal should we set for this campaign?

The effects emphasis is goal oriented, lending itself to the bottom-line perspective of most organizations. Once you know what you must accomplish, you can focus your efforts more efficiently and to greater effect. The two major components of the scientific management approach are planning and research.

MANAGEMENT BY OBJECTIVES

The most common planning tool used by communication managers is known as management by objectives (MBO). MBO is an effects-oriented process for developing what are essentially campaign "recipes." If you write an easy-to-follow recipe, and you have skilled personnel in your kitchen, you can have confidence that you will cook up a successful campaign. Just like writing a recipe, however, MBO requires that you make strategic decisions about what you want to serve (a meal or just a dessert), how many you want to serve (your definition of bottom-line success), whom you expect for dinner (your publics), and when they will arrive (your deadline).

You can adjust the ingredients according to your budget. Not every recipe for chocolate cake needs Belgian chocolate, and not every campaign will need glossy, four-colour brochures. But just as you would not leave flour out of a bread recipe, the MBO approach can help you identify which campaign ingredients cannot be compromised. Moreover, the MBO approach can provide the hard evidence and persuasive reasoning you will need to convince your key decision makers that the campaign ingredients you identify as essential really are essential. In short, the MBO approach gives the communication manager credibility, flexibility, and control.

The MBO approach sounds easy but frequently confuses managers because practitioners often have an incomplete understanding of the elements that go into MBO recipe building. If you've ever wondered what the difference is between a goal and an objective, you have a lot of company. Definitions of goals and objectives are rarely provided, even in public relations textbooks.

The Accountable Manager

Let's begin by comparing the communication manager's role in traditional and scientific management approaches. As discussed by Nager and Allen, the bottom line of communication Programmes differs fundamentally. Traditional practitioners do lots of communication activities, but they may have a piecemeal perspective. For example, they may produce newsletters, brochures, news releases, and an occasional special event without much thought to how each news story or communication piece serves a specific and an overall purpose.

MBO practitioners, on the other hand, have lots of goals they plan to accomplish. Their perspective is more holistic. As a result, everything MBO managers do has a clear, effects-oriented purpose. Because they organize their activities according to a results perspective, they can show the need and the effectiveness of each effort more readily than traditional practitioners can. Each newsletter, brochure, news release, and special event serves a clear purpose that is part of a larger framework.

The MBO manager, or scientific manager, focuses on six activities. As summarized by Ehling, these include:

1. *Conceptualization:* A leader must hold the big picture and be able to identify and organize the smaller elements to fit that larger picture. The goal is to

identify specific tasks and responsibilities that need to be fulfilled to maintain mutually beneficial relationships between an organization and the publics on which its success depends, such as budgeting, goal setting, strategic planning, organizing, administering, and evaluating (notice these elements constitute Tasks 2-6).

2. *Monitoring:* Monitoring is, in other words, research. The scientific manager will do much issue tracking to stay ahead of emerging trends and on top of potential crises. The goal is to anticipate and evaluate opportunities and challenges that arise out of the organization's interactions and relationships with other organizations and society.
3. *Planning:* The manager must be able to build the recipes that will guide the organization through the opportunities and challenges identified in the monitoring process. The goal is to ensure the achievement of measurable results that fulfill needs identified in the monitoring process.
4. *Organization and Coordination:* The manager must make effective use of available resources. These include budget and person nel within the organization as well as opportunities for cooperative partnerships with other organizations that can help them achieve mutually beneficial results. The goal is the effective and efficient implementation of strategies for the communication Programmes developed in the planning process.
5. *Administration:* The manager must fulfill the promises made in the planning process. The manager will supervise the Programmes to activate and adjust communication Programmes. Nothing ever goes exactly according to plan, because resources and the environment continue to change, so the manager must maintain motivating, creative leadership throughout the implementation of each Programme.

The goal is the fulfillment of communication Programme goals on budget and on deadline.

6. *Evaluation:* The scientific manager remains accountable. Every communication activity must have a clear purpose and an anticipated result. The manager must show results and an ability to use Programme successes and failures as part of the monitoring process, to develop even more effective future Programmes. The goal is the accountability, credibility, and guidance to make future communication Programmes even more successful.

The MBO recipe-building process, then, parallels the four-step public relations process familiar to many practitioners. The first step is defining the public relations problem. The definitional process helps the manager identify the effects campaigns need to accomplish. This encompasses Roles 1 and 2. The second step is planning and programming. At this point the manager develops the campaign recipe in detail. This encompasses Roles 3 and 4. The third step is taking action and communicating, or implementing the Programme which encompasses Role 5. In the fourth step, evaluating the Programme, the manager identifies Programme successes and failures for accountability and future use. This encompasses Role 6.

With the manager's roles and planning process identified, we turn to the products the manager will use and produce at each stage. These are the key elements of the recipe the manager must develop. The elements include (a) a mission statement, (b) a problem statement, (c) situation analysis, (d) goals, (e) objectives, (f) strategies, and (g) tactics.

The Mission Statement

We can think of these elements as a pyramid, for which the mission statement forms the base. Everything we do must show clear relevance to the organization's mission. A mission statement is the statement of philosophy and purpose for an organization. Every organization should have one, so your first step as a manager is to get a copy, and, if one does not exist, to develop one. Mission statements can take a lot of time and effort to develop and can stretch for pages.

The communication manager needs some sort of summary, however, to guide the daily activities of everyone connected with your organization. Everyone should have a clear idea of why your organization exists, beyond "to make money"—something along the lines of an abstract or point summary. The Robert Mondavi Winery, for example, has developed a one-line "vision statement" that appears in every voice-mail message from the CEO, in all statements to analysts, in most official statements, and at the beginning of most formal presentations to employees.

The statement, "We will be the preeminent fine wine producer in the world," drives all strategic planning. Development of the deceptively simple statement required input from all employees to make sure they would buy into it. The senior management drafted a statement and met with 6 to 10 groups of 15 to 20 employees to discuss and evaluate the statement. A second draft based on their comments was tested the same way, resulting in the final version.

Displaying the mission statement prominently on internal and external communication pieces ensures that everyone with whom the organization has a relationship will have a clear understanding of what the company has on its list of priorities. Unfortunately, many companies fail to do this. Because the mission statement provides the organization's justification for existence, communication managers can effectively justify their existence as a department and as individual staff members by showing how communication Programmes enhance the organization's mission. Using the mission statement, you can show how the public relations department's activities are central to the organization's success. No longer is public relations marginalized, and the result is that public relations departments become much less vulnerable to the budget axe.

The mission statement should identify the products the organization produces, the services it provides, and the types of relationships it strives to cultivate. A regional charter airline such as Champion Air in the Minneapolis area focuses on "surpassing the expectations of our customers," reflecting its specialist status, whereas a discount passenger airline such as Southwest Airlines focuses on "low fares, lots of flights, and the friendliest service in the sky." Northwest Airlines, with a global focus, aims to make the travel experience "the most convenient, most enjoyable, and safest possible," with attention to establishing new routes and implementing electronic services. Airborne Express, meanwhile, delivers packages not people, and so its mission is "to provide businesses customized distribution solutions at lower cost than the competition."

Because public relations is the construction and maintenance of mutually beneficial relationships, the mission statement provides the guidelines for all planning and monitoring. In particular, it enables the manager to produce the problem statement. To do so, the manager must address two key questions: How do you know a problem when you see one, and what is a problem statement?

A problem occurs when the organization encounters something in its environment or in its relationships with key publics that threatens its ability to fulfill its mission. The hospital, for example, may have encountered new insurance rules on maternity hospitalization that cut in half the number of days patients may stay following a healthy birth free of complications. The average stay in 1996 was down to about 1 day, after shrinking from 2 weeks to 1 week to 3 days to 2 days.

Clearly, this trend threatens the hospital's ability to maintain a healthy bottom fine. This does not give the communication manager anything substantive to guide planning, however. "We need to make more money" provides no clues to identify which ways of making money are appropriate for the hospital, nor does it provide any reason why key publics inside and outside the organization should feel motivated to care whether the hospital makes its money. The manager needs to know the philosophy and purpose of the organization—its mission—to guide planning and to build mutually beneficial relationships.

So, what is the mission of a hospital and how does the reduction in insurance coverage for maternity care threaten this mission? The mission may be to provide high-quality care for the community. Some hospitals also will have a research-related mission or a teaching-related mission. These statements help the communication manager identify publics and activities that are appropriate.

The Problem Statement

If the mission statement represents the organization's foundational guiding document for all of its operations, the problem statement becomes the communication manager's foundational document to guide a communication campaign. The problem statement summarizes the key elements of the issue or opportunity and how it relates to the organization's ability to fulfill its mission. The problem statement is concise and specific, much like the lead of a news story. According to Kendall, it should be 18 to 25 words, phrased in a simple subject-verb-object construction. Kendall noted that, in some cases, the problem statement may be more appropriately considered an "opportunity" statement. Armed with no information other than the problem statement, a manager still should be able to at least rough out some ideas for a successful campaign.

The Situation Analysis

Frequently the communication manager receives a request to develop a campaign based on an initial issue statement that contains few of the elements necessary for a complete problem definition. To develop a complete problem statement usually requires formative research to flesh out the details. These details are known as the situation analysis.

The situation analysis is a detailed explanation of the opportunities and challenges (sometimes called opportunities and "threats") that exist within the organization and in its environment. Sometimes the analysis of opportunities and challenges is called SWOT analysis, for strengths, weaknesses, opportunities, and threats. The terminology may differ, but it means the same thing: The manager needs to find out as much as possible about the problem, the relevant publics, and the environment.

A situation analysis usually begins with the problem statement, followed by a discussion of the history of the problem and how it conflicts with the organization's mission. The situation analysis then includes a discussion of the relevant publics, as well as a discussion of opportunities that should help solve the problem and challenges that could pose barriers. Assumptions should be made clear, and all assertions should be backed up with evidence—data, theory, management and communication principles, expert sources, and so on. The situation analysis represents everything you have been able to find out about the problem. It shows your familiarity with the organization, its publics, the environment, and the problem. It also helps you identify what additional information you may need to design a successful campaign.

The situation analysis makes it possible for the communication team to develop hypotheses, or hunches, about possible causes and solutions for your problem. You may conclude from your analysis that a problem initially presented as poor communication is an informed lack of public support for a company's vision. On the other hand, research might reveal that an apparent lack of support stems from the noisy complaints of a small minority, with the majority unaware of the issue but ready to mobilize on the organization's behalf. These discoveries will affect the type of communication Programme an organization designs.

Sources of Information

The development of a situation analysis requires a thorough understanding of the issue or problem, the client organization, the environment, and the relevant publics. Original research often is necessary, such as surveys and focus groups, but library research and an examination of organizational records also can provide important information. The communication manager's ability to solve a problem depends on available resources (such as time and funding), available expertise, political realities, and the reasons for the problem.

The manager's challenge, therefore, is to gather as much background information as possible, as quickly as possible, to determine the scope of the problem as well as the challenges and opportunities that will affect problem solving. Forces for or against change exist both within an organization and outside in the political and social environment. Along with the internal and external factors, the practitioner may find Hubbell's Helpful Questions useful, developed from the lessons of Ned Hubbell, director (retired), Project Outreach, Michigan Education Association, as a set of questions to ask before beginning to plan.

Internal Factors

Often an organization attributes its problems to outside forces (the media are a favorite target for blame), but the communication manager should begin to understand the problem by developing an understanding of the organization itself. Important types of information include the organization's mission, its decision-making and operating structure, its evolution and history, and its culture. Sources of information include the following:

- Written documents such as mission statements, charters, and bylaws;
- Biographical statements of key members of the organization;
- Descriptions of products and services;
- Records regarding budgets, expenditures, staffing levels;
- Records regarding business policies and procedures;

- Published documents such as annual reports and newsletters;
- Specific records related to the problem, such as memos;
- Records regarding organizational calendars of events;
- Decision makers and other staff knowledgeable about the issue;
- Existing surveys or other research of internal publics;
- Web sites and records related to web use.

External Factors

Sources of information outside the organization can provide an understanding of opportunities and challenges that the organization needs to anticipate or that it has encountered in the past. Important types of information include publics who come in contact with the organization, information networks linking individuals inside and outside the organization, portrayals of the organization by key individuals and the media, and information about political, social, economic, and environmental issues that can affect the organization's ability to control an issue. Sources of information include:

- Consumer and trade publications in which the organization or the issue is mentioned;
- Publications in which competing organizations or issue positions are mentioned;
- Records of broadcast news coverage of the organization or the issue;
- Records of internet sites relevant to the organization or issue;
- Individuals and organizations that favor or criticize the organization or its stance on the issue (sometimes an organization has lists of key contacts, friends, or critics);
- individuals at key media outlets who cover the organization or the issue;

- Calendars of events for the community and other relevant regions;
- Existing surveys of relevant publics from national, regional, or specialized sources;
- Lists of relevant government agencies and key contacts that deal with the organization and relevant issues;
- Records of relevant government regulations that are pending, current, and repealed.

Once existing background information has been reviewed, the communication manager can assess the situation more effectively. The exercise of drafting the problem statement can reveal information gaps that require further investigation. Only when all of the elements of a problem statement can be written with specifics can the manager determine appropriate strategy.

A significant part of Programme planning, as a result, depends on research. The manager's confidence in the effectiveness of a Programme plan, and the manager's ability to demonstrate accountability to a client, increases with each bit of relevant information obtained. Public relations Programmes exist in an environment filled with uncertainty and variables that managers simply cannot control. The better the manager's understanding of all elements of the situation, the more control—or at least predictability—the manager will have over the result of a communication Programme.

Chapter 4

Elements of the Campaign Recipe

Once public relations managers have performed precampaign research they can revise the problem statement and situation analysis and go on to design the campaign. Keep in mind that change is constant, so all planning documents must respond to changes in resources, context, and available information. The manager will revise a problem statement if research demonstrates the initial problem diagnosis overstates, understates, or misstates the problem. Similarly, managers can revise the situation analysis as the situation changes. It follows that the campaign plan, too, may require adjustment occasionally. If, however, you have done thorough precampaign research, the campaign plan rarely will need a major change.

GOALS

The campaign plan includes at least four levels of information, all presented in writing. The first is the goal. A goal is a conceptual statement of what you plan to achieve. The goal is essentially a set of statements that together negate the problem. For example, if the problem for an organization is a lack of awareness, the goal will focus on increasing awareness. If the problem is a lack of credibility, the goal will focus on increasing credibility. If the problem is a lack of volunteer involvement, a series of goals may focus on new volunteer recruitment, increasing involvement among existing volunteers, and increasing opportunities for volunteer activity. Managers can provide clients with long-term or short-term goals, depending on the context of a Programme or campaign.A goal statement includes the following elements:

1. The word "to." This signals the reader that an action statement will follow. It also demonstrates a results orientation. Both of these characteristics make goals easy for busy clients and CEOs to understand quickly.
2. An active verb. This demonstrates that a proposed communication plan will have specific effects. The verb should reflect an effect rather than an action. In other words, the goal should not promise to do something such as disseminate newsletters; instead, it should promise to accomplish something, such as improving customer loyalty. Appropriate verbs include increase, decrease, and maintain. Occasionally, others are appropriate, such as initiate or eliminate.
3. A conceptual, quantifiable statement of the desired outcome. This specifies what will be changed and by how much. The focus may be on outcomes such as knowledge, beliefs, opinions, behaviors, sales figures, membership figures, or donation levels. This signals the reader how the manager plans to measure success. As a result, this outcome must be quantifiable in some way. For example, levels of employee satisfaction may be quantified in terms of a combination of sick time, complaints, longevity, work quality, and self-reported opinions. Each proposed measure on its own may not adequately represent "employee satisfaction," but as a group they seem appropriate. Each proposed measure will become a stated objective of the campaign. Increasing levels of employee satisfaction, therefore, can be the focus of a goal statement. Each goal should focus on only one outcome. A Programme designed to change several outcomes should state each outcome as a separate goal.

4. Identification of relevant target publics. Not only should the client see at a glance what is to be changed, but the client also should know among whom it will change. A single communication campaign cannot promise to improve a company's reputation among every individual in the world, so the manager should offer some parameters. This will guide the development of strategy, which will tend to differ depending on the target public.

For example, Blockbuster and CIM, Inc., created a Silver Anvil Award-winning campaign to launch video sales of the Titanic movie. The Silver Anvil Award is awarded annually by the Public Relations Society of America to honor public relations Programmes that incorporate sound research, planning, execution, and evaluation. Goals for the Titanic campaign included, "to capitalize on consumers' fascination with the Titanic to attract customers to Blockbuster Video stores" and "to generate media coverage of Blockbuster's guaranteed availability of Titanic."

OBJECTIVES

Although these Blockbuster goals are not measurable, they are quantifiable. In other words, they cannot count "capitalizing on consumers' fascination with the Titanic," which is an idea, but they can count things that represent that idea, such as the number of people who come to Blockbuster as a result of a Titanic promotion. They cannot count "media coverage," per se, but they can count the number of articles, column inches, or minutes broadcast that mention the movie and Blockbuster together. Nager and Allen (1984) wrote that it helps to think of a goal as a directional statement, such as planning to "go north" You cannot ever "arrive" at "north," because north is an idea, a concept.

It is relative to where you are now, or where you used to be, or where you will be some other time. So you have to supply some context if you want to turn the direction into some sort of destination so that you will be able to say, "I have arrived!" You can go north from someplace, and you can go specific places located in a northerly direction, but to know you have done it right, you need to give yourself some checkpoints. You need to know where you are starting out—known in communication campaigns as the baseline—and you need to know where you want to end up—known as the objective.

If the goal has promised to "improve employee morale," the manager will have created a directional statement, but will not yet have any concrete destinations to guide campaign planning and provide accountability. You never will arrive at "improving morale." You can, however, find things to measure that will represent improvements in morale, just as you can find cities that represent north. These things that you measure—your destinations—will serve as your objectives.

In the Blockbuster example, the outcomes for the goals include connecting use of Blockbuster stores with the Titanic movie and connecting media coverage of the movie with its availability at Blockbuster. The manager cannot count either of these outcomes. To quantify these ideas, such as media coverage, you might count the number of news stories that contain references to both the movie and the video store. Or you might count the number of on-air promotions and contests connecting the movie and its availability at Blockbuster. To measure high visibility, you might count the number of news stories that make the front page of the entertainment section of the newspaper, or you might be satisfied with the number of stories that make it into the news at all.

All of these would be measurable outcomes, or destinations, for your image and visibility campaign.An objective, then, is a measurable destination that represents the achievement of a campaign goal. Much confusion exists regarding objectives, most likely because several types of objectives exist. Many communication managers, for example, write conceptual statements (goals) and call them objectives. A true objective, however, is specific and measurable, stating not what the campaign will do, but rather what a campaign will accomplish. Three types of objectives exist. Global objectives focus on general Programme outcomes.

They summarize the overall effect of a campaign. For example, a global objective might be to obtain the necessary legislative support to enable a company to proceed with a planned expansion. Although concrete—the expansion either proceeds or doesn't—the objective does not specify the details that have to be in place for the expansion to take place. For example, the company needs to have enough sympathetic legislators win election or re-election in the next election.

In addition, someone has to write and introduce the legislation. Advocacy groups with alternative views need to be persuaded or countered. These process-oriented or task-oriented outcomes are known as intermediate objectives. Finally, the campaign may state terminal objectives, which provide specific measurable or observable results to the campaign, measured by behaviors or actions, such as at least 51 senators voting for the passage of a particular bill.An objective must include the following elements:

1. The word "to." Again, this signals that a promise of accountability follows.
2. An active verb. As before, this indicates that something specific will happen as a result of the public relations Programme.
3. The "criterion outcome" or measurable destination. This puts the focus on a concrete "operationalization" of the idea presented in a goal. This outcome must be measurable or reliably observable. Each objective should focus on a single criterion outcome, which means that several objectives may correspond to quantify a single goal statement. The wording of the criterion outcome should make clear what measurement technique is required for accountability. For example, an objective promising "to increase self-reported confidence in the institution" by a certain amount requires a survey; an objective pledging "to increase the number of

participants in professional development seminars by 20%" requires an attendance record.

4. The relevant target public. Some objectives, such as those focused on raising awareness, may not be relevant to all target publics in a campaign. Therefore, to avoid overpromising, specify which objectives relate to which publics.
5. The amount of change expected. This critical piece of information distinguishes the objective from the goal by providing concrete verification of goal attainment. This can take the form of a number or a percentage. The amount of designated change should be ambitious enough to require real improvement, but realistically attainable.

   Stating too high a level can impress a client in a pitch meeting but can make a competent campaign look like a failure. Understating the level can lead a client to think the campaign will be a sham and not worth the investment. As a result, objectives are difficult to write. However effective the campaign strategies may be, the objectives ultimately determine whether a campaign is a success or a failure.

How much change is necessary or realistic can be determined only through research and still may require the best judgment of the communication manager. In addition, objectives sometimes require negotiation, particularly when they are chosen on the basis of political judgments or intuition instead of on the basis of research. Sometimes clients impose minimum levels of change, and sometimes these levels may not be realistic.

The Washington State Legislature, for example, determined in 1997 that all state universities had to improve student retention and graduation rates by specified amounts. The universities knew they would not be able to achieve the amounts. Ironically, the ability to achieve some of the stated objectives, such as cutting time to graduation, would be compromised by increases in enrollment and retention, which were the focus of other objectives.

The university administrators knew that many students drop out or change institutions because they are struggling, and so keeping them from leaving would probably hurt overall time-to-graduation rates. The universities' challenge, as a result, was to make their best effort to achieve the stated objectives while acquiring evidence to convince the legislators that alternative objectives would be more appropriate. Although the universities had to sacrifice some state funding because they failed to meet the original objectives, they were successful in guiding the legislature to more reasonable objectives during the next legislative session.

6. A target date or deadline. This seals the promise of accountability and is an essential element of the objective.

Note how concrete and specific the objective is. Many managers find objectives discomfiting because they represent a clear promise. They state in no uncertain terms what will be accomplished and by when. The obvious danger is promising too much. The manager, however, has only two viable alternatives: make promises that can be kept or make no promises. Because promises provide accountability, they make or break your reputation. To make no promises in a bottom-line oriented environment potentially keeps public relations marginalized and powerless.

As a result, the only choice for the successful communication manager is to make promises that can be kept. The only way to do this—to determine realistic objectives—is through research. Blockbuster was able to set objectives and develop strategy based on continuing market research of theater attendance and video sales, customers' video rental and purchase habits, the usefulness of incentives, and the attraction of "being among the first" to buy the movie. It also used the movie attendance research to determine the target audience, which was dominated by young females.

Objectives Drive Evaluation

Every objective, if written properly, necessitates some form of evaluation and dictates the form the evaluation should take. In the case of Blockbuster's Titanic promotional campaign, some of the objectives included the following:

- To develop a promotion/special event that attracts at least 500,000 customers to Blockbuster throughout the United States and encourages them to purchase or rent Titanic at Blockbuster sooner than at other video stores;
- To obtain at least $2 million in free media exposure for Blockbuster during the launch;
- To determine how many customers came to Blockbuster stores as a result of the Titanic promotion. (Blockbuster was able to count the number of people who attended the special midnight launch of Titanic video sales, including the number who lined up around the block ahead of time. Blockbuster counted the average transaction amount during the sale, which increased 321% over that of a normal business day. It also did research, which established that nearly 50% of consumers who purchased the movie during the event would not have done so if the store hours had not been extended. To determine how much media coverage was worth, Blockbuster applied a formula to the print and video coverage of the event, which it estimated at $9 million.)

The Importance of Coordinating Objectives With Evaluation

As an example of coordinating objectives with evaluation, the American Medical Women's Association (AMWA) and Fleishman Hillard, Inc., teamed up to increase awareness, diagnosis, and treatment of thyroid disease. The campaign took place in response to figures indicating that more than half of the estimated 13 million Americans with thyroid disease, most of whom are women, remain undiagnosed. Untreated, thyroid disease can cause cholesterol problems, osteoporosis, and infertility. Meanwhile, a simple blood test can detect the disease, and treatment is straightforward. As a result, the AMWA and Fleishman Hillard's stated objective was to increase the number of women being tested for thyroid disease by at least 10% in the first 15 months of the campaign.

This objective dictated that campaign success would depend on tracking figures of women tested for thyroid disease. The campaign documented an increase of more than 40% in the number of women tested. The campaign included other measures of success as well, such as the number of total prescriptions of thyroid treatment medication, which increased by 10%, and indicated that more women were being treated for thyroid disease.

The campaign had several associated results as well. More than 6,600 individuals were screened during local market screening events, at a rate of over 300 people per hour. The AMWA and Fleishman Hillard achieved exposure to over 100 million people with media coverage that included national coverage on television shows such as Good Morning America, CNN, FOX, and MSNBC; national coverage in print venues such as the Associated Press, USA Today, The Washington Post, and several magazines; and local print and broadcast coverage in various markets.

A television public service announcement was broadcast 3,800 times, reaching an estimated 128 million viewers. A radio public service announcement reached an estimated 40 million listeners. The campaign also brought the issue to the attention of Congress through invited testimony and visits to four key Congress members' home districts. These achievements, however striking, would not in themselves demonstrate campaign success as promised. If the stated objective promises behaviour change in the form of increased blood tests, success must be measured in those terms.

It may seem unfair that a campaign might achieve results but still seem like a failure if the ultimate objective is not met. This makes it especially useful to include intermediate and terminal objectives along with global objectives for a campaign. In the case of the thyroid disorder campaign, an appropriate global objective would be to track treatment of thyroid disease and the incidences of related osteoporosis, cholesterol problems, and birth defects, which the campaign managers documented. An appropriate terminal objective would be to increase testing, which the campaign planners documented.

Appropriate intermediate objectives would include media impressions, congressional hearings, and local screening successes, which they also documented. Even if the ultimate campaign objectives had not been met, the campaign managers would be able to show that progress had been made and that future efforts might have more striking results. Indeed, the success of the thyroid campaign led to a campaign expansion that attracted the collaboration of additional health organizations.

STRATEGIES

Apparent success depends on how objectives are stated. Actual success depends on the competent use of appropriate strategy. If the goal represents the direction we plan to go, and the objective represents destinations at which we plan to arrive, then strategies represent how we plan to get there. A strategy is a statement of the communication themes or vehicles that will be used to accomplish a specific objective. It represents an overall plan of action that will tie together each action taken to implement the campaign. The communication manager constructs strategies based on the following elements:

1. Available data. This includes the situation analysis and all the research that has gone into creating it. It also includes the manager's knowledge from previous experience with an organization and with communication campaigns. In the case of the thyroid campaign, available data included research by Fleishman Hillard with consumers, healthcare professionals, media, managed care organizers, professional societies, and consumer groups. It found that only 30% of women had been tested for thyroid disease in 1996, that nearly 90% of people did not know that thyroid problems could do things such as elevate cholesterol levels, and that although half of all women experienced three or more symptoms associated with a thyroid disorder 75% of them did not discuss the symptoms with a doctor.

2. Communication and public relations principles. This includes knowledge of the public relations function and its parameters. Fleishman Hillard knew it could help by boosting public awareness, bringing the issue to the attention of Congress, and promoting testing among individuals at risk (women). It had expertise in all of these areas of promotion.
3. Communication and persuasion theories. The body of knowledge in the social sciences can provide you with the ability to make hypotheses, or likely informed guesses, about the types of strategies that will accomplish the stated objective and be relevant to a situation. Social science theories are essentially explanations of how and why things happen the way they do. In short, theories can tell you how people are likely to react to your campaign and why.

In the case of the thyroid campaign, Fleishman Hillard realized that the problem was a lack of awareness instead of active resistance to testing. People demonstrated they did not know much about the importance of the thyroid gland, its effects, or how easy it was to diagnose and treat thyroid problems.

As a result, Fleishman Hillard knew it needed to build knowledge. It also knew from persuasion theories that people are more likely to take action if they understand the relevance of an issue and if they can see that taking action is both easy and effective. As a result, Fleishman Hillard developed three related strategies:

1. Build consumer knowledge, particularly among women, about the thyroid gland's function and effect on the body.
2. Humanize thyroid disease by demonstrating its effect on quality of life and risks to long-term health.
3. Demonstrate the ease and simplicity of a sensitive thyroid stimulating hormone (TSH) test to detect thyroid dysfunction.

TACTICS

These strategies, of course, are ideas for guidance instead of a list of actions to implement. They are, in fact, counterparts to goals, which are ideas about campaign results. The communication campaign, therefore, also must include an action counterpart to the objective. These are called tactics and are the tasks that must be accomplished to achieve a stated objective. The tactics are the specifics of your recipe. They are, essentially, job assignments. Tactics include the following:

- The task;
- The responsible parties for completing the task;
- Deadline for completion of the task.

Tactics include the development of specific communication vehicles, such as public service announcements, logos, brochures, training materials, and special events. For Fleishman Hillard, the tactics included the development of an engaging theme, the identification of a celebrity spokesperson (Gail Devers, the Olympic Gold Medalist who had previously suffered with undiagnosed thyroid problems for 3 years), the development of high-profile events that attract both national and local media coverage, the implementation of special events such as a VIP breakfast to bring the spokesperson and physicians together with key members of Congress, a free TSH testing event on Capitol Hill, and more. Each stated tactic related to a specific strategy, which was designed to achieve a stated objective, which demonstrated the accomplishment of a stated goal.

THE STRATEGIC PLANNING LADDER

As the thyroid campaign illustrates, the campaign plan becomes a tightly organized set of specific tasks that put carefully selected strategies into action to accomplish stated objectives that represent organization goals that enable an organization to achieve its mission. To make sure all elements of the campaign plan are necessary and appropriate, it helps to think of the progression of specificity as a ladder. When going up the ladder, such as considering the appropriateness of a tactic, ask "why are we doing this?" In other words, does every action have a stated purpose?

The answer to the why question for a tactic should be a strategy. The answer for a strategy should be an objective. The answer for an objective should be a goal, and the answer for a goal should be the problem, to which the answer is the mission. Why do we need to produce a brochure? Because we need to provide information to potential applicants to spark their interest and gain their confidence. Why do we need an informational campaign? Because we need to increase applications from this target public by 30%. Why do we need to increase applications? Because we want to increase representation from this target public in our Programme. Why do we want to increase their representation? Because our organization strives to serve the entire community, and they have not been represented in the same proportion in which they exist in the community.

In reverse, going down the ladder, the manager should ask "how will we accomplish this?" To solve a problem requires a goal statement. To achieve the goal requires objectives. To meet the objectives requires a strategy, and each strategy requires tactics to put it into action. How can we increase representation of the target public in our Programme? We can increase the number of applications by the next deadline date.

How can we increase the applications? We can develop an information campaign targeting interested community members from the target group. How can we implement the campaign? Among other things, we can develop brochures.

INITIATING THE PLANNING PROCESS

The public relations Programme plan represents the culmination of much research, analysis, and expertise. Sometimes it can be difficult to determine where to begin the planning process. Client representatives may have nonspecific or conflicting ideas, and public relations personnel may have varying interests in and interpretations of the issue as well.

As a result, it can be useful to begin the planning process with an old-fashioned brainstorming session. Several brainstorming techniques exist. One especially effective strategy is called story boarding. Story boarding, originally developed by the Walt Disney Corp. to design Steamboat Willie, is a highly visible, highly interactive way of gathering and sorting ideas. Story boarding refers to the process of creating the story that will guide strategic planning. In effect, it is a way to approach the process of analyzing the situation and identifying the strengths and opportunities that will inform decision making.

Besides helping participants work through a problem, the technique provides a mechanism for tracking the decision-making process so others can see how collaborators arrived at a final decision. This gives confidence to participants who can be reminded of the factors that produced a decision, and it adds credibility to the decisions made because they are based on evidence clearly presented.Managers can use story boards for four purposes:

1. Planning is used to outline the steps required to reach a specific result, such as preparing for a special event.
2. Idea is used to develop a concept or a theme for a specific purpose.
3. Communication is used to determine who needs to know something, what they need to know, and how best to interact with them.
4. Organization is used to determine who will take responsibility for designated tasks, and how to work together as departments, individuals, or organizations to accomplish a plan.

Story boarding uses a "creative thinking" process to guide brainstorming. The process includes three stages of idea generation, critical review, and consensus building to create a shared vision of a plan. It is a little like a focus group, requiring a facilitator to guide discussion and encourage freedom of thought. During the idea-generation stage, participants offer ideas for issues such as the who, what, where, when, why, and how of a problem; the identification of important target publics, opportunities, and constraints for a campaign; and the creation of campaign themes.

Each idea is noted on an index card, which gets pinned or taped onto walls or tackable surfaces. During critical review, the group sifts through ideas to organize, refine, and prioritize them. Finally, during consensus building, the participants try to arrive at an agreement for the plan, idea, communication strategy, or organization. The rules for the creative thinking process include the following:

- The more ideas, the better;
- No criticism;
- Hitchhiking is good (triggering ideas from others' ideas);
- Spelling does not count;
- Handwriting does not count;
- One idea per "card";
- "Yell out" each idea during brainstorming.

This technique helped the state of Washington develop a campaign focused on alcohol abuse prevention that required the cooperation of a wide spectrum of individuals from organizations with various agendas and perspectives. Representatives from the Department of Alcohol and Substance Abuse (DASA), the Governor's budgeting office, the state liquor control board, the public schools, higher education, and other organizations all gathered to determine how to focus the campaign and how to assign responsibilities.

Beginning from the DASA's stated goal, to "teach that alcohol is a drug," participants shared their personal experience, knowledge of research, and awareness of practical constraints such as how to ensure the cooperation of important stakeholders. The discussion gradually identified an agreed-upon target group: parents of children younger than the usual age of first experimentation. From there, the group developed an action plan for developing benchmark and formative research, which led to development of campaign materials.

The research for the campaign included a statewide survey of parents with children between the ages of 3 and 10 that would serve as a benchmark for later evaluation and would provide useful information for media relations activities. It also included a series of focus groups used to test the proposed message strategies.

The goal of the campaign was to educate parents of young children about talking to their kids about alcohol at an early age. A process goal was to equip parents with the knowledge and awareness that they can be the most significant source of help in influencing their children's attitudes and behaviour toward responsible drinking habits. Objectives included distributing 100,000 informational brochures to parents over a 2-year period, increasing awareness of the "alcohol is a drug" message among Washington parents by 10% each year over a 2-year period, securing statewide media commitments to run $250,000 of pro bono advertising in support of the campaign each year, increasing by 10% the number of Washington parents who rank alcohol use by kids as a "serious problem," and increasing by 10% the awareness of "the harmful effects of alcohol use by children."

The strategy for the campaign included the development of a multiyear, multimedia statewide campaign focusing on increasing parents' knowledge that alcohol is a drug and that they can be the most powerful deterrent and source of help to their children regarding potential alcohol use. The strategy also included securing cooperative funding sources to sustain the campaign for two years; to maintain high visibility through the use of public relations and media relations activities throughout the campaign; and to coordinate all campaign activities at state, county, and local levels to ensure a successful launch.

The nine primary tactics for the campaign included implementing the statewide surveys; developing three distinctly different conceptual treatments of the "alcohol is a drug" theme; obtaining commitments from magazines, newspapers, newsletters, television stations, and radio stations; developing a poster and a parent guide; and securing co-op partners.

The campaign achieved its objectives, distributing 103,265 informational brochures to parents over a 2-year period, increasing awareness from 53% to 62% (an increase of 17%), and securing over $250,000 of pro bono advertising in support of the campaign. The campaign did not greatly increase the percentage of Washington parents who were "extremely concerned" about alcohol use by kids and considered it a "serious problem," which already was at 45% and averaged 5.8 on a 7-point scale.

The number of parents who mentioned alcohol as the "most used drug" by children increased by 13%, rising from 46% to 52% among parents who recalled the campaign. The postcampaign survey demonstrated that 72% of parents saw or heard one of the public service advertisements produced for the campaign.

The DASA campaign embodied all of the essential elements of scientific Programme planning, from the development of the situation analysis at the beginning of the campaign to the demonstration of accountability at the end of the campaign. The use of careful research and a clear plan ensured that every campaign tactic fulfilled a necessary strategy and that every strategy responded to a desired objective. Every objective realized a relevant goal, and the goals took aim at the problem of underage drinking.

The clarity of the MBO process makes it easy for an outside observer to understand the purpose of the campaign, the reasons for actions taken in pursuit of campaign goals, and the results achieved at campaign's end. The MBO technique cannot guarantee success for the practitioner, but the focus it provides will make success a more likely outcome. Because of its overt emphasis on accountability, the MBO technique also makes an achievement impossible to dismiss.

Chapter 5

Determining Research Needs: Developing the Research Plan

Now you know that you need to develop an effective public relations plan, and that to do this you need to develop strategies that will achieve stated objectives. To arrive at this plan, a public relations manager needs to apply what Lloyd Kirban, executive vice president and director of research for Burson-Marsteller in New York, called "informed creativity." The role of research is to focus brainstorming, confirm or disconfirm hunches, and help fine-tune your strategies.

THE ROLE OF RESEARCH

Because the strategic manager is goal oriented, the decision to do research depends on its relevance to Programme goals and an organization's mission. In other words, research should be goal oriented, like the Programme plan itself. "Doing research" may seem intimidating to those without a social science background, but research spans a range of activities, many of which managers do instinctively. What does it mean to do research, and what are the goals of research? Research is systematic listening used in an attempt to reduce uncertainty. The goal of research is to gain maximum control of the things that can be controlled, and maximum understanding of the things that cannot be controlled.

Examine a simple model of the communication process and consider what elements we can control and what elements we cannot control. This varies with the context in which a manager works, but communication research has demonstrated that, overall, managers have the most control over the source, and the least control over the receiver. With the use of paid advertising, the manager can control the source, the message, and the channel. Public relations messages, however, often must go through "gatekeepers," or people between the original source and the ultimate message recipient. These include editors, reporters, and opinion leaders, among others. As a result, you may have control over who your initial source will be, such as the CEO of a corporation, and you can agree with your source on a message, but you can lose control quickly as the message goes through gatekeepers and evolves. Your best hope for control, therefore, is to gain a thorough understanding of everything that might affect the dissemination, evolution, and interpretation of your key messages.

THE BENEFITS OF RESEARCH

Research offers benefits that can help the strategic manager develop the understanding necessary to design and maintain successful public relations Programmes. First, research can help managers make sense of the increasing fragmentation of audiences in global, multimedia communication environments. Research can probe attitudes, identify opinion leaders, and help determine appropriate timing for actions and messages.

Second, research can help keep top-level management from losing touch with important stakeholders from which they may become insulated. According to the "homophily" principle, people tend to exchange ideas most frequently among those who share similar characteristics, such as beliefs, values, education, and social status. Without extra effort, therefore, management can lose touch with nonmanagement employees, as well as with other stakeholders.

Homophily refers to the degree to which pairs of individuals who interact share similarities, which tend to help them understand each other and value each other's perspectives. Because effective public relations focuses on relationship building, it is important for stakeholders who depend on each other to understand and respect each other; two-way communication is essential to effective public relations. One survey found that 24% of unionized companies that used attitude surveys to gather information from employees suffered strikes, while 48% of those who had not done opinion research suffered strikes. Among all companies surveyed, 64% of those that suffered strikes had not performed survey research in the past year.

Monsanto, for example, discovered through a benchmarking survey of employees that the employees were suffering from information overload. In response, the company consolidated 22 newsletters into one, and made more use of E-mail, less use of video and audio media, and more use of face-to-face communication. The company also adopted an open communication policy that fostered trust on the premise that trust increases productivity. Following the changes, a new survey showed that 80% of employees felt they were getting good information, exceeding their objective of at least 50%.

Third, research can help confirm whether complaints about an organization are widespread beliefs or whether they represent the impressions of a vocal minority that holds little credibility with key stakeholders. It also can prevent organizations from wasting effort on nonexistent issues. For example, the American Dairy Association (ADA) knows from recent research that it does not need to do a multimillion dollar campaign to dissuade Americans from thinking cheese is an unsuitable lunch food because of its fat content.

A recent survey of 1,002 respondents demonstrated that cheese already was the most common food chosen for lunch, that the top reason for choosing it was its taste, and that eating nutritiously was the second highest priority (after taking a break) at lunchtime (American Dairy Association, 1999). Because "low in fat" was one of the top two factors cited by respondents as making a meal nutritious, the ADA could safely conclude that fat in cheese was not preventing people from putting it into their lunch boxes. In fact, because no cheese-fat-lunch connection seemed to exist in public opinion, implementing a campaign acknowledging the connection could create a problem where none had existed before.

Fourth, research can guide strategy so that funds and efforts are spent wisely. Research can reduce the cost of a campaign and, as a result, can enhance the credibility of the public relations professionals with top management. An organization may find that a mass mailing, besides being expensive, is less effective than a few targeted, customized contacts. Editors commonly grouse that they receive, many shotgun style news releases that go straight into the garbage because the releases do not show immediate relevance to their readers or viewers.

Fifth, research can help prevent unintended effects. A firm called Successful Marketing Strategies found out the hard way, when a "tease and deliver" promotional strategy for a high-tech product backfired. The promotion for the product, which was designed to save data from accidental destruction on diskettes, included a mailing to trade publication editors, in a plain brown envelope, which featured a note that read, "Who's been shooting.

A second mailing, 2 days later, was stamped Case File 7734 and had a card that read, "Who's been shooting readers in the foot?" The answer, inside the fold-out card, was that they were shooting themselves in the foot by not having the product to protect their data. Had the firm done advance research on the target public, it would have learned that several editors had received bonafide threats in the past, which made them sensitive to this sort of mailing. Had the firm done pretesting, it might have caught the typo on the first mailing (leaving out "in the foot") that increased the perception of real threat. It also might have discovered that editors receiving the anonymous mailing might call in the FBI or the Postal Service to investigate, which happened. Fortunately, the company managed to assuage the nerves of most editors through individual follow-up contacts and ended up with a lot of attention for the product. The firm learned, however, that public relations professionals need to consider the perspective of the people who will receive their messages to make sure messages will be received as intended. As Settles (1989) wrote, "Success in public relations comes from the ability to incorporate the lessons learned from past mistakes into bold future steps". To the extent the manager can catch mistakes in the pretesting stage, fewer lessons will have to be learned the hard way.

Sixth, research can provide facts on which objectives for accountability can be based. Baseline data on consumer attitudes or behaviour, for example, are necessary to demonstrate change after a campaign is finished. NewsEdge Corp. demonstrated that a campaign to address high employee turnover following a merger of three competing companies reduced turnover from 40% to 6%, earning the company a Platinum PR Honorable Mention from PR News.

SPECIFIC RESEARCH FUNCTIONS

As a manager, you will consider three types of research in planning: formative research, Programme research, and summative (or evaluation) research. Formative research provides data and perspective to guide campaign creation. Programme research guides the implementation of the Programme to ensure that strategies have the intended effects instead of unintended, counter-productive effects. Summative research provides data to evaluate the success of a public relations Programme based on the achievement of stated objectives. More specifically, research can help strategic planning in six key areas:

1. Problem identification. First, research can show whether a problem suspected to exist truly does exist. It also can help identify where the problem is, when the problem occurs, or when it developed.
2. Problem effects or Implications. Research can demonstrate how big a problem is, as well as for whom it poses difficulties.

3. Strategic direction. Research can suggest ways to communicate effectively about a problem and actions to solve the problem.
4. Strategy testing. Research methods as diverse as focus groups and surveys can be used to test creative strategies to make sure they work as anticipated. Some companies now monitor their reputation through the use of chat rooms, mail fists, and news groups.
5. Evaluation of results. Research can provide accountability to help public relations practitioners prove Programme impact by demonstrating Programme results that confirm success.

ELEMENTS OF A RESEARCH PLAN

Research plans, like public relations plans, are vital to the success of public relations Programmes. Because they too are goal oriented, they help keep strategic planning on track, on time, and within budget. A research plan includes an explanation of research needs; research goals; research objectives; hypotheses or hunches; and research questions to guide data collection and analysis, help propose research strategies, and prompt a discussion of how the results will be used.

RESEARCH NEEDS

To develop a research plan, you must determine your research needs. Your initial situation analysis can help you do this. What do you know about the problem, the situation, your opportunities, and your constraints? What do you need to know? For everything you think you know, test whether you have evidence to confirm that your information is correct. You use many types of evidence, ranging from experts' observations to survey or sales data. The more scientific your data, the more convincing it will be, and the more it can be trusted. More specifically, you can consider the following as evidence:

1. Public relations principles, laws and professional guidelines can provide guidance for procedural and ethical issues.

2. Communication and persuasion theories are scientifically tested ideas about how and why things happen the way they do. Theories do not provide hard and fast rules about how things work. The way social science works, a theory cannot be proven right; it only can be proven wrong.
3. Expert observations can provide some validation, particularly at the brainstorming stage, but they are not as unimpeachable as hard data from surveys, sales, spreadsheets, or experiments. Quotes from individuals with high credibility and relevance to the situation are most useful.
4. Quantitative data can include survey data, sales figures, content analysis, results of experiments, budget histories, formal tracking data from web sites, customer service calls, and so on.
5. Qualitative data can include focus groups, interviews, field observations, informal tracking of communication among stakeholders, and so on. These tend to be most useful at the brainstorming stage.

You may find that some of your ideas about the problem are based on assumptions instead of on hard evidence. If possible, test the veracity of these assumptions. For example, service organizations frequently assume that poor attendance, low subscriptions, or low registrations reflect a poor reputation that requires improvement. Upon further research, however, organizations may find that their problems stem from low awareness instead of from negative attitudes, requiring a public relations Programme different from what a reputation management Programme would entail. The reverse also is true.

TARGET PUBLICS

You want to know as much as possible about target publics. First you need to identify and, perhaps, prioritize them. This process is called segmentation. Then you need to understand more deeply their interests, their needs, their concerns, their beliefs, and their behaviors.Your target publics are subcategories of your stakeholders. Stakeholders are those who should care and be involved, or those who can be affected by or who can affect your Programme. Since public relations focuses on the development and maintenance of mutually beneficial relationships, ask yourself who benefits from your organization's activities, directly and indirectly, and on whom does your organization depend to achieve stated goals, both in the short term and in the long term. Who belongs in your problem statement? You can segment publics by various characteristics. These include the following:

1. *Demographics:* These include common census-type categories, such as age, gender, race or ethnicity, education level, occupation, family size, marital status, income, geographic location, political party, and religion.
2. *Psychographics:* These include personality and attitudinal characteristics, including values, beliefs, and lifestyle. These characteristics can help you identify who holds hopes, fears and interests that most help or hinder your public relations and organizational goals.
3. *Sociographics:* A wide variety of categories can be called sociographics, but they tend to focus on behaviors and characteristics common to an easily identified group of people. Broom and Dozier (1990) summarized several sociographic categories of value to public relations professionals, including the following:
   - *Covert power:* This represents an attempt to discover who holds indirect power over persons who may more directly affect your Programme's success. For example, an administrative assistant holds a great deal of covert power over a busy executive who relies on the assistant to screen calls and help prioritize schedules. Family members also hold covert power over many

business decisions, and certainly over purchasing decisions. Marketers refer to the power of children in sales as the "nag factor."

- *Position:* This represents an attempt to identify occupations or leadership positions that make individuals important stakeholders and depends greatly on the context in which you work. For example, lobbyists, journalists, legislators, union representatives, PTA officers, and teachers all can act as opinion leaders with wide-ranging effects in certain situations.
- *Reputation:* Sometimes people who influence others' opinions and behaviors cannot be categorized neatly into occupations or positions but can be identified by other stakeholders. For example, particular older peers may influence the extent to which younger schoolchildren embrace a recycling or health-promotion campaign. People in a community may identify individuals who have credibility over a zoning issue by virtue of their social ties or community activism.
- *Organizational membership:* A special interest group will care who is a member and who is not. It is important to identify who is a member of competing or complementary organizations that can be of assistance to your Programme directly or indirectly. When the Seattle Sheraton wanted to gain the business of corporate executives, for example, it determined on which organizations the executives served as board members. Targeting its community service activities to these organizations helped the Sheraton cement ties with these important decision makers.
- *Role in decision process:* Decisions often are made in incremental steps by a combination of individuals and committees. Gaining support at each step can require different strategies.

4. *Behaviours:* Purchasing patterns and attendance histories can provide useful information about who is using your organization's services, who might use them, who has rejected them, and so on.
5. *Communication behaviors:* These include latent (inactive but relevant) and active publics. You need to determine levels of awareness and the extent to which individuals care or don't care about your organization and its activities. These characteristics are likely to affect how they react to information about your organization. Grunig and Hunt (1984) suggested three measures to determine activity:
   - *Problem recognition:* This represents the extent to which publics sense that a problem exists. If they see no problem, they will not be "active" or interested in the issue. Their level of recognition will affect the extent to which they seek to process information related to the issue.
   - *Constraint recognition:* This represents the degree to which individuals believe they have the ability to affect an issue or situation. They may see constraints, or impediments, that limit their ability to change a situation or participate in an activity. If they do not feel they can participate or make a difference, they will be less likely to make an effort to think extensively about the issue.
   - *Level of involvement:* This represents the degree to which individuals feel a connection between a situation or issue and themselves. The more they believe an issue can affect them, the more likely they are to take an active interest. Less involved individuals take a more passive approach.

Grunig proposed four types of publics: (a) those active on all relevant issues, (b) those apathetic on all relevant issues, (c) those active on issues only if they involve most people in a relevant population, and (d) those active only on a single issue. More recently (" Grunig Paradigm," 1998), Grunig suggested that stakeholders can be divided into three segments, depending on their level of "excitement" or interest in an issue. The groups include:

- Long haul types, deeply interested in a topic and its ramifications;
- Special Interest types, concerned only about certain elements of a topic, such as how a newly proposed school building will affect their property taxes;
- Hot button types, interested only by elements that spark emotional debate, such as gun control.

DETERMINING PROGRAMME OUTCOMES

You need to identify what your Programme outcomes will be, as well as whether you need to evaluate Intermediate outcomes along with ultimate outcomes. Motivating some sort of behavioral outcome helps public relations demonstrate bottom-line value. Often, however, a number of intermediate steps are required before you can achieve that final outcome. For example, a campaign to promote donations for the hungry could find it difficult to gain people's attention, particularly if the campaign takes place at a time other than the Christmas season, when donation activity tends to be high.

Holding an event attractive to a public potentially interested in the issue could encourage them to bring a donation (even a single can of food). Once present at the event, they can be encouraged to make additional donations or to become a member of the sponsoring organization. Attendance would be an intermediate behaviour, can donations would be a second intermediate behaviour, and memberships would be the ultimate behaviour.

TESTING COMMUNICATION CHANNELS

You need to know as much as possible about the potential channels of communication available for your public relations Programme. Some channels will be more expensive, or more time consuming, or more efficient, or will reach different audiences. People who are more interested will go to more trouble to get information about an issue, but an organization frequently must assume that target publics are not interested or at best are easily distracted by competing messages and priorities. This may vary depending on your market and the publics with whom you wish to communicate. The National Cancer Institute has developed a helpful chart of mass media channel characteristics that can serve as a general guide. To choose effective communication vehicles, you need to assess the following:

1. *Credibility:* This refers to the extent to which the target publics trust the source of your messages, believe the source is unbiased, and believe the source is competent or expert in the topic under discussion.
2. *Reach and exposure frequency:* Is it easy for the target publics to gain access to information via this channel? How much exposure can you achieve?
3. *Efficiency:* You need to consider relative cost (in advertising called "cost per thousand") against relative benefits. Costs include production and distribution costs in terms of monetary investments, and time and staff requirements. To what extent can you reach target audiences versus other audiences less critical to your Programme?
4. *Control:* You need to determine to what extent the content and distribution of the message can be managed, and to what extent control is important for the public relations Programme. In crisis situations, companies often buy advertising to get their messages out without any filters. In other cases, a lack of control is preferred because of the increased credibility for a message that appears as editorial copy instead of as a purchased advertisement.
5. *Flexibility:* This refers to the extent to which the target publics can gain access to the message in a way convenient to them. The Internet, for example,

provides users with the flexibility to review as much information as they wish whenever they wish, as opposed to having to wait to learn about a topic until the 11:00 news.

6. *Context:* This refers to the environment in which a message is presented, such as in the middle of a sports or entertainment Programme, during the news, or on the ceiling of a subway train.

You want to be able to predict how a message will be received by those you wish to receive it. To do this you need to know how your target public feels about your organization, and possible information sources, and how their attitudes relate to specific message strategies you might employ. Keep in mind that you need to be able to anticipate the extent to which unintended recipients may have access to your message and how their reactions may affect your Programme goals.

You don't want to have to remove your product from the shelves, as one company did in at least one region, because of serious unintended effects. In the case of the cereal company, the promotion on the cereal box invited children to get the prize (a cookie shaped like a person and named Wendell Cookie) out of the box in several silly ways. These included, "Tell a good elephant joke. When you hear Wendell laughing, you'll know where he is," but also included, "Call the fire department. Tell them to rescue a guy from your cereal box." Unfortunately, some children took the admonition to call the fire department seriously, resulting in costly calls to 911 that required authorities to respond.

You also don't want to pull costly advertising, as did the Ad Council and Connect for Kids, a child advocacy initiative of the Benton Foundation, when humor in their ad campaign disparaged other child advocates. The copy in the ad called school board members "boogerheads," attracting nationwide protest from school boards and superintendents for being disrespectful in a campaign that was intended to promote respect.

TESTING MESSAGES

The Center for Substance Abuse Prevention has developed a helpful guide for avoiding problems in message development. They recommend checking to make sure messages are clear, accurate, and relevant. Clarity means checking whether the target public might interpret a message in a way other than, especially opposite to, what was intended. Mixed messages may appear to include contradictions. Pretesting can help the message designer avoid confusion.

Accuracy means making sure factual statements are correct and based on solid, verifiable evidence. Taking information out of context can change its meaning so that it no longer can be considered accurate. Unfortunately, many "facts" spread over the Internet without the benefit of fact checkers and editors, and they sometimes end up in print in credible media. Be careful to verify information independently such that the original source can be traced and checked. Second-hand information should not be considered real information. According to Kogan Page, Ltd., creators of a Corporate Communication Handbook, the lack of accurate information is one of the three most important characteristics of a crisis. Supplying accurate information, therefore, can be one of the most effective tools for defusing a crisis.

Relevance means making sure the intended receivers win pay attention to the message. Messages must appeal to their values and interests, and communicate in a language they use and understand. Porter Novelli, for example, found that calling obesity a "disease" instead of a "condition" made overweight individuals more receptive to messages about an antiobesity drug. Attempts to use current slang and dialects can backfire and require careful pretesting.

TESTING INFORMATION SOURCES

When testing a message, it is imperative to test the credibility of the source. Research can guide you as you consider who should serve as information sources for your public relations Programme messages. Sources must be credible, expert and relevant, and—you hope—interesting. To the social scientist, credibility includes various elements, but in general it simply means that people will find the source trustworthy. Public relations issues often boil down to a lack of trust. Expertise means the person seems knowledgeable about the topic. Relevant means that the target public will relate well to the person. Teenagers, for example, often would rather hear from another teenager than from an authority figure. In a crisis, even if the public relations officer is knowledgeable about company policies and plans, and even if the officer has a credible reputation among journalists, the most relevant source still is the CEO, because the CEO is the person in charge.

One way of testing credibility is to have the moderator of a focus group, a semistructured group interview, ask what participants would think of a message if the sponsor were a commercial advertiser, or a religious organization of some type, or the government, or a local chamber of commerce. A clear, accurate, and relevant message from a source perceived as untruthful, biased, or incompetent can backfire.

RESEARCH STRATEGIES

A myriad of approaches are available for tackling a problem and developing a complete situation analysis. Each approach explained here offers a slightly different emphasis; so, depending on the context, one or a combination of these techniques may be most appropriate.

It has been said that asking "why is this happening?" five times in a series reveal the cause of a problem, which may initially be obscured. This technique, called the Five WHYS, is especially useful when a problem is difficult to understand or particularly unusual. For example, when a large piece of the Jefferson Monument in Washington, DC, fell off, threatening the safety of visitors and creating a public relations worry, the Five WHYs traced the problem as follows. The observation was that acid rain appeared to be eroding the monument, causing it to crumble. This suggested that a shelter might need to be built to protect it, which would be an expensive and potentially unattractive solution. But why was the erosion also evident on the inside of the monument, where rain would not be a factor?

WHY #1: This erosion was traced to the strong soap used to clean the monument daily, combined with jet fumes from the nearby National Airport. Why was it necessary to do so much more cleaning than at other monuments in the area?

WHY #2: It was pigeon droppings that required the extra cleaning. Why were pigeon droppings such a problem at this location?

WHY #3: An infestation of spiders that pigeons find especially tasty had occurred. Why was there an infestation of spiders?

WHY #4: Spiders were finding a bounty of midge eggs to eat, which they loved. Why were there midge eggs?

WHY #5: Midges live in the reeds in the backwaters of the Potomac River, which runs near the monument. At sunset, they swim and mate and lay their eggs, but they can get distracted by bright lights, which they love.

The solution was to turn on the lights by the monument one hour later. It was inexpensive, effective, and not unattractive (Geistfeld, 1995)!Whatever strategy you use while researching an issue, this example nicely illustrates a tactic useful for delving into the heart of a problem. Some specific types of research strategies include the following:

1. Communications audit. According to Kendall (1996), an audit examines, describes, and evaluates the status of a designated Programme. A communications audit examines the vehicles through which messages are sent and received from stakeholders. The audit requires:
   - Identifying the relevant internal and external publics;
   - Collecting data from designated publics, using methods such as interviews, focus groups, and

surveys to determine their use of communication vehicles, as well as their impression of the vehicles and of the organization;

- Analyzing current Programmes, personnel, and materials used for communication;
- Examining trends, opportunities, and challenges relevant to the organization.

2. The audit, which can focus on the public relations department or on the organization as whole, culminates in recommendations for action. Just as financial audits occur regularly, communication audits also should take place on a regular basis. Because audits are broad based, they can help address specific problems but audits also can help guide more global, long-term planning.
3. Social responsibility audit. This is a more specific form of the communications audit. Kendall (1996) recommended a social responsibility audit as an examination of an organization's performance related to corporate citizenship. As described by Kendall, the social responsibility audit focuses on factors that affect the organization, rather than on publics and communication activities. The social responsibility audit involves:
   - Identifing issues that have social or civic implications;
   - Ranking the issues based on when the issue will affect the organization, the extent to which its effects will be direct or indirect, and the significance of the issue to the organization;
   - Examining which departments can affect or will be affected by the issues;
   - Developing possible responses.
4. Reputation audit. Reputation is so important that it may be helpful to quantify. A reputation audit can provide a situation analysis focused on reputation. The audit involves:

- An identity analysis, which is essentially a communications audit;
- An image analysis, to determine how the organization is perceived by key constituencies via surveys;
- A coherence analysis, to compare the desired identity with the perceived identity.

5. GAP research. The gap method uses a series of four questions to ask target publics to perform their own diagnosis of an organization's strengths and weaknesses. The questions include the following:
   - On a scale (such as 1-9), how would you rate us on?
   - Why did you give that rating? (This could evolve into the five WHYS.)
   - Knowing the organization as you do, how good could we get if we really tried (on the same scale as used for question 1)?
   - What would we have to do to get there?

The gap method is a way to perform focused brainstorming with a variety of stakeholders. Sometimes a more sophisticated analysis is unnecessary.

6. Co-orientation research. This is a perspective especially appropriate to public relations problems because of its focus on relationships. According to co-orientation theory, successful communication depends on accurate perceptions from all parties involved, with ultimate success defined as consensus. In the case of a controversy, an organization can ask the following questions:
   - What does the organization think about X?
   - What does the organization think the public thinks about X?
   - What does the public think the organization thinks about X?
   - What does the public think about X?

By asking these four questions, the public relations manager can determine the extent to which the problem is one of true disagreement or one of perceived agreement or disagreement. Co-orientation, as a result, is a good way to diagnose the potential for miscommunication that can hurt attempts at building consensus and damage an organization's reputation. According to Broom and Dozier (1990), the most common public relations audit involves establishing an organization's view on an issue, determining the target public's view on the issue, and determining the distance between the two views.

This type of audit, however, does not account for the extent to which these views may be based on misperceptions of the other paryt's views or intentions. The co-orientation model accounts for both actual disagreement and perceived disagreement, which makes it a more powerful strategic planning tool. Co-orientation analysis determines actual agreement, perceived agreement, and accuracy. True consensus cannot occur until both parties agree and know they agree.

REALISTIC RESEARCH PROPOSALS

It may appear that an organization can perform unlimited types of research endlessly. Clearly, organizations cannot afford the time and expense involved. As a result, the development of a research plan also requires an examination of constraints and priorities that can guide the type and extent of research pursued. The manager needs to prioritize research needs and appropriate research methods, because the ideal research will never take place. Some mysteries will remain unsolved, and good research often raises additional, new questions (recall the five WHYS). The manager can rely on four issues to develop realistic parameters for the research plan:

1. *Time:* When are the results needed to develop the final public relations plan by the required deadline? If the organization faces an immediate crisis, lengthy research cannot occur. If the organization's focus turns to long-term planning, more time can be devoted to research.

2 *Budget:* How much money and staff time can be devoted to research? Some types of research, such as face-to-face surveys, are expensive. You don't want to spend too much of your Programme budget on research and have too little left for implementation of the campaign itself. As a result, Broom and Dozier (1990) and Ketchum ("Bottom-line," 1999) both have offered a rule of thumb to guide research spending, suggesting that 8% to 10% of a total Programme budget should be used for research. Recent data collected from interviews with 110 American companies by PAG/Best Practices ("corporate communication," 1998) suggested that in reality only about 5% of communication budgets go toward research. Most of that research focuses on media exposure and corporate reputation, rather than on more sophisticated, outcome-oriented research.

3. *Levels of expertise available:* Consider who will collect the data and how knowledgeable they are about data collection and analysis procedures. If data collection cannot be farmed out to an independent research firm, make sure the project does not require specialized expertise.

4. *Need for precision and depth (how research will be used):* Sometimes sophisticated research is overkill, but other times more refined information is required. For example, an election on a controversial issue can hinge on the details. Be ready to explain how research will be applied to strategic development and why the level of research proposed is necessary for Programme success. Public relations managers surveyed in 1996 commonly reported that clients wanted research but did not want to pay for it. The Programme manager needs to provide convincing reasons for performing desired research. This is where it is helpful to include hypotheses, or hunches, regarding what results you expect to find. The ability to explain how the results will direct strategy and

how they will affect the likely outcome of the Programme can help convince the recalcitrant client.

A carefully conceived research plan will lay a strong foundation for Programme planning. Clear research goals and well-considered research strategies that correspond to the needs and constraints of the situation at hand give the manager the best chance of success in the later stages of Programme planning. Managers can refer to these as they consider how to make choices that will not cost too much or take too long to implement, but that will guide the effective selection of target publics, Programme outcomes, communication channels, and message strategies.

Chapter 6

Research Decisions and Data Collection

Traditionally, public relations practitioners have relied on strong media relations skills and key media placements to succeed in public relations. Practitioners, executives, and clients generally bought into the myth that public relations works with nuances of public opinion and other intangibles that simply cannot be measured. Public relations campaigns were based on practitioner hunches, knowledge of the market, and simple common sense. Practitioners used savvy media relations skills and well-honed campaign tactics to generate media attention for publicity-seeking organizations. Thick, clip-filled binders were used to demonstrate the value of public relations to promote a company or cause.

Although some practitioners continue to successfully operate this way, several organizational and environmental changes have made this model of public relations nearly obsolete. Fewer financial resources, increasingly competitive markets, and increasing costs, in particular, have resulted in greater organizational attention to public relations Programmes. The result is that practitioners who enjoyed past success based solely on their practical understanding of local media markets, a well-developed network of contacts, and strong media relations skills increasingly find themselves struggling to gain organizational resources and maintain organizational support in an era of greater Programme accountability.

Even though practitioners' reliance on research has increased, not every successful campaign requires original research. Research can require a substantial investment of resources, and many organizations prefer to plan and evaluate campaigns based on their existing understanding of markets and their assessments of key audience responses. Some situations may require only the tracking of public responses to media placements, for example, or votes on political initiatives.

In addition, some public relations efforts are so limited in scope that they simply do not require or receive the resources necessary to conduct even small-scale research. In these situations, both practitioners and the organizations with which they are working may be satisfied with subjective interpretations and the obvious outcomes resulting from public relations Programmes. Unfortunately, practitioners who lack research are limited to arguing that, perhaps based on their years in the business, they know a situation and can recommend a solution. With no concrete evidence to support these claims, there is little basis for organizational support of such recommendations, and others with different backgrounds or similar levels of experience commonly recommend different options.

Research reveals the perceptions, interests, and opinions of targeted audiences; produces evidence used to select from among competing solutions; and provides a benchmark from which to evaluate campaign success. Research also allows campaign planning and evaluation based on facts rather than on intuition, rule of thumb, or past practices. Practitioners find research particularly useful as the costs and importance of a campaign increase, or as the certainty concerning an issue or public decreases. In practice, each research setting is unique and research decisions often are affected by several constraints, the greatest of which are time and budgetary limitations. The result is that no single "best" research method exists. Instead, the best research method is the one that most completely meets your information needs within the constraints of a given project.

Given the often confusing decisions that practitioners must make regarding research projects, discuss the practical issues that should be considered before final decisions are made concerning a research project. These issues include questions you should ask and answer before you begin a research project; various constraints that affect research method choices; an overview of formal and informal research techniques; the steps taken in a typical research-planning process; and some issues to consider when dealing with research firms, in-house departments, or consultants.

Strategic managers use research throughout the Programme-planning, implementation, and evaluation process. The ways research applies, however, change as the Programme evolves. The uses of research also depend on the manager's communication needs. For example, precampaign, or formative, research is used before a campaign is launched to better understand, define, and help segment targeted audiences. Practitioners commonly make use of focus groups or surveys, to examine people's perceptions, opinions, and sources of information regarding a key issue.

Practitioners also can use these and other research methods to develop campaign strategies and test messages with target audience members as part of the precampaign or campaign-monitoring process. Practitioners use these research methods to provide benchmark measurements of the awareness, attitudes, and behaviors of targeted audiences. Once practitioners have conducted a campaign, they use benchmark measures to test the effectiveness of a campaign using postcampaign, or evaluative, research. In many cases, postcampaign research really is between-campaign research, because practitioners use it as a platform from which to begin another campaign. Public relations professionals' use of research normally results in fact-based evidence of a campaign's accomplishments (or failures) and may serve as the basis for requesting additional organizational resources or creating new campaign initiatives.

The use of research to measure campaign effectiveness at the end of a communication Programme helps achieve credibility with organizational management. Organizations are looking for a concrete return on what they perceive as an "investment" of limited resources in public relations. In today's highly competitive markets, practitioner intuition and past experience rarely provide an acceptable basis from which to plan a communications campaign. Practitioner voices are drowned out by competing voices in an organization when their experience and intuition are pitted against research data. Practitioners who have access to such data have a strong credibility advantage over their intuition-reliant peers when it comes to influencing organizational decision making, developing communication strategies, and receiving organizational resources.

Practitioners can use research to help management monitor changes in internal or external environments. It is too easy for organizational management to become insulated from key publics in the busy and often chaotic world of management. The hectic pace and rigorous demands often leave decision makers unaware of the critically important attitudes and opinions of consumers, community members, employees, and other key groups. In this case, public relations research can be used as what Peter Drucker called an organizational "hearing aid" to keep management in touch with the attitudes and opinions of those on which organizational success or failure depends.

Practitioners can use research to keep in touch with the competition. The current international marketplace is extremely competitive, as is the struggle for access to limited media space and the contest for the limited attention of target audiences. Savvy public relations practitioners and their clients make it a priority to understand the strategies and tactics of their competition, to increase their own chances for success. Research can provide insight into various interest areas, such as an analysis of the features and appeals in competitors' messages and of audience responses to those message strategies.

Finally, practitioners can use research to generate publicity for organizations and clients. In most cases, organizations produce legitimate research with newsworthy results that benefit the sponsor of a project. In other cases, however, organizations manipulate participants' responses and purposefully misinterpret research results to attract as much media attention as possible. The result is that the media, and ultimately the public, may be mislead by unscrupulous research firms or practitioners who engage in unethical practices in an attempt to make a media splash. Serious research scientists and public relations practitioners should be careful when using research for publicity purposes. There is a strong potential for organizations to misuse research findings, and the media are increasingly skeptical about projects sponsored by organizations with a vested interest in the results. Ultimately, the potential uses of research in public relations are nearly endless; research results can be used to inform nearly every aspect of the public relations process.

BEFORE STARTING THE RESEARCH PROCESS

Before starting a research project there are some basic issues to consider that often are critical to its successful completion. You should start by determining what you want to know from the project with as much specificity as possible. Even exploratory projects should have a clear purpose. Although this may appear obvious, few research projects start with well-defined objectives. Instead, many research projects start with a vague sense of purpose that is so general it is nearly useless. Organizations that want to use research to "better understand the market" or "see what people think of us" probably are wasting their time and money. Keep in mind that research projects are an expensive investment that should provide an anticipated return. The company that engages in a poorly conceived research project and receives a relatively small benefit as a result will pay just as much for its research as the company that uses a well-designed project with specific objectives and benefits accordingly. Although determining informational needs and project objectives can be time consuming and even difficult, it is the first important step in the successful completion of a research project and helps provide the best return on a research investment.

Several questions should be asked when considering a new research project. The first is, "What do we already know about the subject of our research?" Answering this question should help to narrow the scope and focus of a project. Once a project is started, several potential topics and questions typically compete for limited project resources. Unfortunately, specific questions and even whole topics typically must be thrown out of research projects as time and budgetary realities force unrealistic expectations into real-world constraints. When tough decisions must be made about what to keep and what to discard in a research project, an understanding of your current knowledge base is essential.

The next question is, "What are the gaps in our information base?" Although it seems obvious, the answer to this question provides concrete direction to an organization as research topics and potential methods are considered. Avoid approaching a research project as a single study. Think of a project, instead, as part of an ongoing Programme of research consisting of all the information an organization has collected or is likely to collect concerning a given public or issue. In reality, no single project can answer all the questions an organization has concerning a topic, particularly given the increasingly complex and competitive environment in which many organizations exist. In fact, research studies may raise more questions than they answer. When single studies are viewed as part of a larger, ongoing Programme of organizational research, their scope and function take on greater focus.

The result is a valuable contribution to an organization's base of knowledge concerning key audiences and issues.

The third question that should be asked is, "What other research currently exists that might be useful?" An organization typically has an array of research available that it can use to inform its decision-making processes. Various syndicated research exists, for example, that provides useful information about target audiences' product and service usage, lifestyle, media usage, and other important characteristics.

Similarly, Census Bureau data are available from a university library, and this high-quality, detailed information may be useful for organizations addressing a variety of issues. Professional associations often support research projects that benefit association members. This research, while fairly broad in scope, can provide useful background information from which to begin a new project. Databases may provide useful information concerning a surprisingly diverse array of topics. Finally, trade publications often report research results concerning topics of interest to readers in the field they serve.

Researchers also may be able to reuse previously collected data as part of a new research project. This practice, called secondary data analysis, is essentially recycling data. It occurs when researchers use a set of data for a purpose different from its original use. Once researchers collect and analyze data, they often catalog it and set it aside. In other instances, educational institutions, foundations, and other organizations conduct large multipurpose surveys and release the results to the public.

In either case, practitioners may reanalyze these data for their own purposes if the data are available for use. If an organization is interested in interpreting changes in public opinion during an election year, for example, it may get access to candidate polling data after the election. In this case, the organization is bound by the methods and questions used in the original study; however, the data still may be useful, and they may cost little or nothing to access. Any of these resources, and various additional ones, may provide information that has a significant bearing on a research project currently in the planning stages.

The fourth question that should be asked is, "What will we do with the results?" Practitioners often initiate research projects as part of a problem-solving process. Research is most useful in this process when organizations know how they will use the results to begin the problem-solving process. Unfortunately, it is not uncommon for organizations to complete major studies and, after a short time, set the results aside and never look at them again. In reality, conducting a study does nothing for an organization. Research findings are only useful when they are put to work by skillful managers who understand how the results will be used as part of the planning and problem-solving process.

The fifth question that should be asked is, "What special constraints do we need to consider for this project?" Project decisions will depend on the time available to perform the research, budgetary limitations, the expertise available for performance and interpretation of the research, and the extent to which precision and depth are required from the research. In addition, some special situations can arise that may make it advisable to consult a research specialist.

First, practitioners may have trouble collecting information about certain issues and may also have trouble collecting information from hard-to-reach audiences. In some instances, for example, people may be unwilling to discuss their private behaviour with intrusive researchers. In other cases, practitioners may find it difficult to locate sample members. How do you find a random sample of pregnant women, for example? What if you want to survey urban residents, 25 to 34 years old who use public transportation? In each of these cases, research methods and sample selection strategies can be customized to provide information concerning specific issues and hard-to-reach populations.

A second special issue that may discourage data collection is a lack of appropriate research facilities. In this case, specialized help is the answer. Research firms, research consultants, statistical analysts or other specialists can provide the facilities to help solve difficult research problems. Practitioners spend their money wisely when they use knowledgeable professionals who have access to appropriate facilities to help them solve difficult data collection issues.

By answering these questions, practitioners will gain a better understanding of the purpose of a research project and the conditions that must be met to make it a success. They also will be able to use research results to give a project the direction necessary to make it a worthwhile investment with an anticipated and valuable return.

APPROACHES TO PUBLIC RELATIONS RESEARCH

At its most basic level, research simply is collecting information, and any number of methods can be used to gather information, each with its own strengths and weaknesses. The most basic designation researchers typically make concerning research methods is formal versus informal or casual approaches to data collection. Rather than fitting research methods neatly into one of these categories, however, research methods range from nonscientific, casual research methods to fully formal, scientific research methods. Just because a research method is casual does not mean it has no benefit or practical application. Instead, casual research methods simply fail to meet the standards demanded by formal, scientific research.

A quick look at some casual research methods should make it obvious why researchers consider them nonscientific. One of the most common forms of public relations research, for example, involves using clip files to monitor newspaper and magazine coverage of an organization or issue (similar services can monitor broadcast or web coverage). A practitioner using a clip file can examine the messages targeted audiences receive, gain some understanding of public opinion concerning an organization or issue, and even determine the need for potential responses to media coverage, if necessary.

Using a network of personal contacts is another common form of casual research. When practitioners want to know how members of a targeted audience might respond to an issue or event, for example, they may simply call several acquaintances who generally fit the audience description and ask them for their advice and opinions. Practitioners can use such information as the basis for organizational decision making, even though it is not scientific. Other types of casual research include analyses of letters organizations receive or an analysis of field reports from organizational sources such as agents, representatives, or recruiters. In each instance, information collected by these methods provides an organization with a potentially useful basis from which to make decisions about key issues, events, and targeted audiences.

What is it about this information that makes it casual and nonscientific? For one thing the information may be gathered from a sample that is not representative. When researchers collect data, they usually collect information from a subset, or sample, of the targeted population. When a sample is representative, it has the same distribution of characteristics as the population from which it is drawn. Because of this, the opinions collected from a representative sample should accurately represent the opinions that exist in a population. Although researchers never draw a perfectly representative sample, some samples—based on probability sampling methods—have a greater likelihood of being representative than other samples. When practitioners contact a few people to ask their opinions, the opinions expressed cannot possibly represent the range of opinions that exist in a target audience consisting of perhaps millions of people. When practitioners use informal research methods, they typically collect information from a sample that is not representative.

A second characteristic of casual research methods is that practitioners use an informal process when collecting and recording information. When they contact different people, for example, researchers are unlikely to use a standard set of questions with predetermined response categories for each person. Such a questionnaire would defeat the purpose of the research by not allowing practitioners to take advantage of the different areas of expertise and experience of each of their contacts. As with other casual research methods, contacting selected friends or experts does not follow a formal process or set of procedures that practitioners can use to collect information in a precise, reliable manner.

As an additional note, practitioners cannot accurately know or understand public opinion based solely on media portrayals. This practice fails the test of formal research because it is not based on a scientific test of the nature of the relationships among media coverage and the attitudes and opinions of target audience members. There are times, for example, when information and portrayals in the media have an obvious and direct effect on public attitudes or behaviour. Tickle-me Elmo, for example, was launched as a 1996 Christmas-season sellout because the toy appeared on the Rosie O'Donnell and Today shows, arranged by a public relations agency for the toy's manufacturer, Tyco.

In this instance, Tyco actually canceled advertising for the toy as stores ran out of the product and skirmishes broke out between parents tying to get their hands on this must-have toy. In other instances, however, media portrayals have little or no effect on attitudes or behaviour. In fact, the media are full of persuasive messages warning people not to do some things and encouraging them to do other things. Whereas some people heed these messages, many others simply ignore them. Even when formal research is used, determining causation requires careful attention and planning. Practitioners' observations and assumptions about public opinion based on media placements are risky and necessarily fall into the casual-research category.

In the middle of the casual-formal research continuum are various methods that typically require a more formal process than purely casual methods, but still do not fulfill the requirements of formal, scientific research. The most commonly used research method in this category is focus grouping. Basically, a focus group is a directed group discussion typically consisting of 8 to 12 people. Participants usually are similar with respect to key characteristics such as age, gender, product brand usage, political party affiliation, or any other characteristics deemed important by the project sponsor. The discussion is led by a moderator who asks questions and probes participants' responses. The process is recorded and transcribed, and research professionals and their clients attempt to gain key insights and draw meaning out of the results.

Even after all this effort, researchers still understand that focus group research is only quasiformal because of the size of the sample and the lack of formal research procedures. A study must have an appropriate sample size to qualify as formal research. Even the largest focus group normally is too small to meet sample size requirements. In addition, under the best circumstances, scientific research follows a formal set of procedures that researchers apply equally to everyone in a study. When researchers conduct focus groups, the procedures they use generally are not equally applied to everyone. In some cases, for example, a moderator may wish to ask certain participants additional questions based on their unusual opinions. Other participants may be reluctant to speak up or may hesitate to express their true opinions. In these situations, focus groups do not follow a standard procedure closely enough to qualify as formal, scientific research.

Other commonly used quasiformal research methods include surveys that suffer from flaws in the data-collection process, including the use of nonrandom sampling methods. When mall intercept surveys are conducted, for example, members of an interview team typically position themselves at key locations throughout a mall and interview willing shoppers. The shoppers who participate in the survey make up what is called a convenience or incidental sample because they are selected on the basis of accessibility. Researchers use the information collected this way to gain quantitative information concerning the insights, opinions, attitudes, and behaviors of shoppers considered generally representative of a target audience.

Convenience sampling, however, is a nonprobability, nonrandom sampling method. Even though standing in a mall and talking to shoppers as they happen by appears to rely on a random-selection process, this sampling procedure falls short of the requirements of probability sampling. When truly random sampling methods are used, every person in a population has an equal chance of being included in the sample. In this case, even when a carefully constructed questionnaire is used that contains specific response categories, the use of a convenience sample still makes the project's findings unrepresentative and leaves the project short of the standards necessary to qualify as formal, scientific research.

INFORMAL RESEARCH CONCERNS

When researchers label a method casual or quasiformal, it does not mean it is without merit. In reality, casual research methods are when conducted properly, scientific research methods are more likely to result in accurate observations by following a formal process and well-conceived research design to its logical conclusion. As Nachmias and Nachmias (1981) noted, scientific research methods differ from other methods of acquiring knowledge based on their assumptions. At a philosophical level, the assumptions of science include, for example, that nature is orderly and regular, that it is possible to know nature, that nothing is self-evident, and that knowledge is derived from experience.

At an applied level, scientific research methods are built on a system of explicit rules and procedures that, when correctly applied, have a high likelihood of producing accurate, reliable results. These research methods are by no means complete and infallible. In fact, social scientists have worked to develop new methods and approaches to observation, inference, and generalization that are consistent with the scientific research approach. The result is that formal research methodology has slowly grown and evolved, as scientists exchange ideas and information. Social scientists have developed standard rules and procedures from this process, resulting in formal research methods and techniques.

These rules and procedures are applied in public relations research to produce valid and reliable information. Various formal scientific research methods are available, including experiments, media content analyses, and surveys. In addition, several commercial databases and syndicated research resources are available that rely on scientific research methods. Survey research is the most commonly used scientific research method in public relations. When researchers use probability sampling procedures and an appropriate formula to determine sample size, they can generalize or project survey results from a sample to a population with a high level of confidence and a known range of error.

Newcomers to research methods should not be intimidated by the lofty goals and sometimes confusing terminology used in scientific research. Just as math expertise is not required to use a calculator, a scientific background is not required to understand formal research methods. Instead, practitioners should learn the strengths, weaknesses, and assumptions of each research method so they clearly understand the advantages and limitations of the information they are using for strategic planning and evaluation. Research methods that may be appropriate for some projects may be inappropriate for other projects. Substantial risks are associated with the misuse of research methods that provide unreliable or misleading information, which results in negative consequences for organizations.

RESEARCH ISSUES TO CONSIDER

Any time researchers collect information, they must consider several issues that affect the quality of the information collected. In some cases, research results should not be trusted as the basis for major decisions because they contain liabilities that may not be well understood. In other cases, researchers understand study limitations and can control them though the use of selected research and sampling methods. Ideally, practitioners' trust in research results should be appropriate to the level of accuracy, precision, reliability, and validity of a research method and the results it produces.

The first of these areas, accuracy, concerns whether a research method produces error-free data. Although researchers establish a minimum degree of accuracy for every research method, they do not always require highly accurate research results in applied research settings. In some cases, a general understanding of the attitudes, opinions, and behaviors of targeted audiences is enough, and a research method that provides that kind of information, such as a focus group, is appropriate.

When researchers demand a high degree of accuracy, however, they use scientific research methods and probability sampling methods to provide relatively error-free results. In fact, when researchers use probability sampling procedures in survey research, they can calculate the range of error for participants' responses. Although no study is without some degree of error, when research managers use scientific research methods, rely on an appropriate formula to calculate sample size, and use probability-based sampling methods, they are able to evaluate the accuracy of research results with relative confidence.

Research managers also must consider the precision of research findings that result from the use of different research methods. When research findings are precise, they are exact. Consider the difference between asking a friend what the weather is like outside and using a thermometer to determine the temperature. In the first instance, our friend may say it looks "warm" or is "hot" outside. In the second instance, a thermometer may indicate it is 98° Fahrenheit. Both answers are informative and useful; however, one answer is more precise than the other.

Although researchers generally desire precise research findings over imprecise research findings, not all research methods produce results with the same degree of precision, and at times precision may be less important. Some research methods produce results that generally lack precision. Because focus groups are essentially a group discussion, for example, it is nearly impossible to measure results exactly within the context of the discussion. A focus group may provide impressions, ideas, or general group agreement or disagreement, but these results will be broad and interpretive to an extent. When researchers require precision, they will more likely turn to a survey questionnaire that contains specific questions and numerical response categories to record the attitudes and opinions of respondents.

This is not to suggest, however, that practitioners find focus groups or other less precise research methods less useful.

To the contrary, a high degree of precision often is not necessary in applied research and may even be undesirable. When researchers are exploring people's attitudes and opinions, for example, a highly precise questionnaire is likely to hurt their ability to gather useful information. At this point in the research process, practitioners want to explore people's attitudes and opinions rather than measure them precisely. As an additional note, do not confuse precision with accuracy. It may be more precise to learn it is 98° outside rather than it is "hot," but both answers are inaccurate if snow is on the ground.

Research methods that produce accurate and precise results also should produce reliable results. Strictly speaking, reliability is essentially "repeatability." If researchers make repeated measurements of sample members' attitudes, opinions, or behaviors, the results should be similar each time. When researchers use informal research methods, a lack of reliability often is a concern. If call some of my friends to get their advice on an issue, the results are likely to vary considerably depending on whom contact.

This research method is not reliable. The same reliability concerns are true of quasiformal research methods including mall intercepts and focus groups. When research managers use scientific research methods to collect data, the results generally are highly reliable. As an additional note, research methods that are reliable are not necessarily accurate. As Babbie (1999) noted, a scale that consistently weighs people five pounds lighter than their actual weight (we should all have such a scale) is high in reliability but not accuracy.

Finally, the validity of results produced using various research methods should be considered. At a basic level, valid research results are legitimate or genuine. An IQ test is valid measure of intelligence, for example, if it genuinely measures the intelligence of the individual taking the test. Social scientists have divided validity into numerous components in an attempt to reflect all of the nuances of the term and their implications for data collection. Although it is important for research professionals to understand validity concerns in all of their manifestations, we purposefully simplify our discussion and selectively consider applied aspects of validity in keeping with the purposes of this text and the patience of our readers. Kerlinger (1973) suggested two broad categories of validity: external and internal.

External validity refers to the representativeness, or generalizability, of research results. When researchers conduct a study, they draw a sample, or subset, of people from a population as potential participants. When they draw a sample, researchers must be certain it accurately represents the population. In many instances, only a few hundred people will actually complete a survey, and research professionals will use their responses to make inferences about the entire population which may consist of millions of people.

When research results are representative, researchers can accurately take sample responses and project them to the entire population. Researchers use probability sampling methods, which require random-selection procedures, to ensure that everyone in a population has an equal chance of being included in a sample. If the sample accurately reflects the population and researchers use a scientific research method, the results of a study will be high in external validity and researchers will be able to generalize study results from a sample to the population with confidence.

In terms of practical implications, informal and quasiformal research methods generally lack external validity. When researchers use focus groups, for example, they do not use probability sampling methods or choose a large enough sample size to make the focus group results high in external validity. In fact, a lack of generalizability is one of the reasons researchers consider these methods informal. Researchers must use fully formal, scientific research methods, including probability-based sampling, to achieve a high degree of external validity.

Kerlinger illustrated internal validity with the simple question, "Are we measuring what we think we're measuring?" If, for example, we want to measure people's voting habits but instead ask for their opinions about how important it is to vote, we have not measured behaviour and the measure lacks internal validity. Many methods exist for identifying internal validity.

One of the simplest methods of determining validity is called face validity. When researchers check for face validity, they examine a research measure to determine whether it appears to assess, in an obvious way, what it should measure. This form of validity relies on researchers' judgments and generally is nonscientific. This does not mean, however, that face validity is unimportant. For years, market researchers measured brand awareness, for example, when they ultimately wanted to evaluate the effect of an advertising campaign on consumer purchase behaviour. It seems obvious that an increased awareness of a brand name should indicate that an advertising campaign has had some effect.

Measuring top-of-the-mind awareness and using it as an indicator of consumer behaviour, however, raises issues regarding the face validity of the measures.Content validity refers to the comprehensive nature of research measures. A set of questions high in content validity most fully represents the idea it is supposed to measure. When examining consumers' media-use habits, for example, a questionnaire that asks only about newspaper reading and television viewing lacks content validity. In this case, consumers use a variety of media that are not even part of the questionnaire. A lack of content validity makes a project seriously flawed by compromising its relevance.

A final type of validity, predictive or criterion validity, concerns the soundness of a research measure when tested against an external standard. In applied research, predictive validity most commonly concerns the ability of a research measure to predict actual performance. Predictive validity is critical when organizations use research to understand and predict the behaviour of targeted audiences based on research results.

When a driving test has predictive validity, for example, it should be able to predict driving performance. People who perform well on a driving test should actually be able to drive a car safely. If they drive poorly despite performing well on the test, the test may lack predictive, or criterion, validity. In public relations campaigns, awareness and knowledge often are measured with the assumption that they lead to behaviour. These measures often lack predictive validity, however, making the research findings an incomplete or incorrect basis from which to develop campaign strategy and predict campaign outcomes.

STEPS TO RESEARCH PROJECT DESIGN

Once managers consider accuracy, precision, reliability, and validity as they relate to the research project at hand, they can turn to the actual design of the project. Despite the uniqueness of every research project, it helps to follow a series of steps in a more-or-less sequential order to guide the design and implementation of a project. The research plan discussed corresponds to the steps followed to implement the project itself. The research-design process briefly discussed here contributes to a logical, orderly decision-making process that maximizes the benefits of a study and the information outcomes it provides. It also minimizes study costs and the risks associated with poor quality data.

1. Identify or clearly define the research problem. When research projects lack a well-defined purpose, they produce results that, though interesting, have little usefulness. Clients often approach research firms with a relatively vague understanding of what they need to learn. Their expectation is that the focus of the project will emerge and they will know what they want when they see it. Even exploratory research projects should have clear direction.
2. *Review the literature:* This refers to checking existing sources of knowledge for useful information. At one time, it was difficult to get accurate, reliable market research. As organizations have increased in

sophistication, their reliance on research has grown and the supply of existing research available to any organization has greatly increased. Various syndicated market research, databases, and similar forms of archival research resources can prove useful in developing a project. These resources can help define targeted audiences; provide insight into audience opinions, attitudes, and behaviour; answer secondary questions related to the research project; and identify trends that may affect the project.

3. *Develop research questions or hypotheses:* After examining existing sources of research information, managers can develop hypotheses or research questions. In academic research, hypotheses (and research questions to a lesser extent) typically drive the research process and provide expectations about variable relationships and other important research findings. In applied research settings, researchers commonly use research questions instead of hypotheses. Both hypotheses and research questions can be used in applied research settings, however, to help determine the project purpose and to help inform the research-design process. Essentially, hypotheses and research questions concerning key variables help researchers understand their study and the outcomes it is supposed to produce. In this way, they become part of the problem-identification process and give researchers specific outcomes to look for as they engage in a research project.
4. *Determine the appropriate research method and design the project:* Several methods exist for collecting information, and in this book we address the most common methods. Whether practitioners do a research project on their own, or, more likely, deal with an in-house research department or outside research firm, they must understand the strengths and weaknesses of different research methods to make informed decisions and get useful and affordable

information. Practitioners who stick to research methods because of familiarity, or who blindly follow the advice of others without understanding the strengths and limitations of different research methods, risk disappointment and can get stuck with inaccurate or useless study outcomes.

5. *Collect data:* Implementation of the study follows research-method selection and study design. Informal research designs require less specific procedures than formal research methods.
6. *Analyze and interpret data:* Analysis and interpretation vary depending on the research method used and the nature of the data. Qualitative data, such as comments provided by focus groups, require broad, more subjective interpretation. Quantitative data, such as answers to surveys, require statistical analysis and more objective interpretation. Meaningful data analysis and interpretation are the natural outcomes of a well-designed, properly conducted research project.
7. *Determine implications:* Managers should not conduct a meaningful research project and simply set the results on the shelf. Instead, they should examine the results for their practical implications. What do these results suggest in terms of strategy or tactics? How should an issue be positioned in the mind of a critical audience? What public affairs Programmes are likely to have the greatest audience impact according to study results? What media do these audiences regularly consume and whom in the media do they trust? How do these results help improve understanding or, more important, motivate behavioral change? It is a waste of time and money to conduct a study and simply put the results on a shelf and leave them there.
8. *Replicate studies:* It can take some time for resistant clients to believe the results of research when the

results provide bad or surprising news. This makes it critical for managers to make studies replicable, meaning reproducable, so that important findings do not get dismissed..

Public relations Programmes increasingly rely on research-based planning and evaluation. The benefits of research—to illuminate the perceptions, interests, and opinions of targeted audiences; to produce evidence used to select from among competing solutions; and to provide a benchmark from which to evaluate campaign success—often far outweigh the costs of research. Some managers have the luxury of hiring out research projects to specialists, while others need to implement research projects on their own. Either way, a personal investment in learning about these sometimes-complex topics can lead to increased credibility and autonomy for the communication manager.

Chapter 7

Informal Research Methods

In a sense, research simply is listening and fact finding, and practitioners most commonly rely on informal methods when engaged in simple fact finding. Such research often is critical to hotel organizations as they monitor their internal and external environments, track public opinion concerning emerging issues, and address potential areas of conflict with target audience members before they become a problem. Informal research methods often provide organizations with quick, inexpensive, and useful ways to listen to critical publics. These include employees, community members, consumer groups, and government regulators. Despite these potential benefits, practitioners take a sizeable risk when they use informal research methods as the sole basis for public relations planning and problem solving. Because these methods lack the rigors of scientific research, they have a much greater likelihood of producing inaccurate results.

Recall that one of the reasons researchers consider a method casual or informal is that it lacks a systematic process. In scientific research, a formal process ensures that every participant is treated in the same way. In a survey this means, for example, asking participants the same questions in the same order and giving them the same response options except when open-ended questions are being asked. Informal research methods typically do not try to use the same question wording to collect information from every person. This moves the research to the informal side of the continuum, but the depth and flexibility gained sometimes can provide advantages over formal fact finding. Sometimes researchers do not, or cannot, use formal research methods. In these cases, the research methods used automatically fall into the informal research category.

The second characteristic that distinguishes informal from formal research has to do with the samples used. As previously noted, researchers rarely conduct a census because of cost and time factors. Instead, they commonly draw a sample from the population and study sample members with the expectation that the responses of the sample accurately represent the opinions, attitudes, and behaviors of all members of that population. When researchers conduct formal research, sample responses generally are representative of the population from which they were drawn, and research staff can calculate the percentage of error that exists in sample responses.

When researchers conduct informal research, however, the sample may not represent the population from which it was drawn. In this case, the sample may be too small or may not reflect the views of everyone in the population, and researchers cannot make meaningful error calculations. When a company analyzes the mail it receives from its consumers, for example, the opinions expressed in this small group of letters are not likely to accurately represent the range of opinions among all members of its targeted audience. This does not mean that informal research methods such as a mail analysis are not useful. It is important, however, to understand the limitations of the information collected. Informal research methods generally are useful for exploring problems and for pretesting ideas and strategies. It is not advisable, however, to use them as the sole basis for Programme planning and evaluation.

PERSONAL CONTACTS

The most obvious and common form of casual research involves talking to people. Practitioners can learn a surprising amount simply by asking people—ideally those who are members of a target audience or other important group—for their opinions and ideas. When political candidates or elected officials want to know what voters care about, for example, they may simply get out of their offices and ask people. Personal contacts also might include personal experience in some cases.

When practitioners experience the problems and benefits associated with a situation on a first-hand basis, it gives them valuable insights that cannot be gained by sitting in an office reading a report. Practitioners may find personal contacts especially useful when combined with scientific research methods. Contacts may help practitioners gain insight before a formal survey is conducted, for example, or help them understand survey findings that are surprising or counterintuitive. Although talking with people has serious limitations—a few people cannot represent the range of opinions and behaviors that exist in large targeted audiences—practitioners often gain valuable insights and ideas from their personal contacts.

PROFESSIONAL CONTACTS, EXPERTS, AND OPINION LEADERS

Practitioners keep in regular contact with their public relations peers, friends in related fields, superiors, and others who typically possess a wealth of useful experience and knowledge. These contacts may be especially valuable, for example, for practitioners planning or implementing a new Programme for an organization. If an organization interested in holding a special event never has conducted one, it makes sense to talk to contacts who specialize in events planning and promotion to take advantage of their knowledge and experience. Veteran practitioners are likely to have a wealth of practical advice and their own set of contacts that can benefit the novice. In some cases, it may be advisable to hire consultants or firms who specialize in certain areas of public relations, either for a single project or on a continuing basis.

Public relations professionals also may benefit from talking to key informants or groups, those who are experts in their fields or recognized opinion leaders. This group may include, for example, members of state or local government, editors and reporters, special-interest group leaders, teachers and educational leaders, or union leaders or trade association managers. Normally the procedures used to collect information take the form of an open-ended interview. Practitioners use the discussion to glean information and insights from a select group that is uniquely informed about a topic. The fact that these leaders are experts and opinion leaders, however, raises an important point to consider when using this type of research. These people, because of their position and knowledge, do not reflect the majority of citizens likely to make up a targeted public. In this case, experts' opinions and insights are not necessarily reflective of the broader audiences practitioners normally try to reach.

In addition, their opinions may be shaped by the organizations for which they work. In fact, some organizations such as unions, trade associations, and activist groups typically conduct research that they make available for little or no cost. In many instances, such research provides valuable information and insights to practitioners and their organizations. In other cases, however, organizations may conduct research, not to impartially learn the attitudes and opinions of the public, but to gather support for existing organizational positions and official viewpoints.

It is easy to create a research project that looks formal and scientific, but contains untrustworthy results because leading questions or a purposefully selected sample were used. When you use research that has been gathered by a different organization, it is important to learn as much as possible about the research method, including sample-selection procedures and the actual questionnaire or other research instruments used to collect data. This win ensure that you are aware of the potential limitations of the information you are using. Even with its limitations, such information may provide you with unique insights only possible through meeting with experts or opinion leaders, or by examining the information they have at their disposal.

ADVISORY COMMITTEES OR BOARDS

Advisory boards, standing committees, specially appointed panels, and similar bodies provide organizations with specific direction, help them plan and evaluate their Programmes and events, and help them identify and respond to feedback from the publics they serve. The nature and qualities of such groups differ widely according to their purposes. Public relations professionals may serve on the advisory board of a local nonprofit organization, for example, to help plan and direct its media relations and special events projects. Many local governmental bodies are advised by citizens committees as they address community issues such as urban planning, public transportation, or local safety issues. Other advisory groups may consist of employees, consumers, or students. In fact, any group an organization is serving or anyone who may benefit an organization through expertise or ability generally is qualified to serve in an advisory capacity.

Through their knowledge, experience, and insight, those who serve in an advisory capacity provide organizations with information critical for their successful operation. It is important for organizations to listen to advisory panel members and, when appropriate, work to incorporate their advice into their plans and actions. Members of advisory groups are quick to recognize when they are being used for appearances and their advice has no effect on organizational behaviour because it is not given earnest consideration. In these cases, group members are likely to become a source of derision and potential conflict rather than a useful source of information and advice.

In addition, the blind usage of advice and information from an advisory group has liabilities. The accuracy and validity of the advice received from such groups provides a limited reference for public opinion and, therefore, cannot represent the range of attitudes and opinions held by all members of a target audience. With this in mind, information gleaned from such groups should be used only as counsel and should not serve as a substitute for scientific approaches to determining the opinions, attitudes, and behaviours of target audience members.

FIELD REPORTS

Many organizations have field representatives including, for example, district agents, regional directors, or sales and service people. These people may have more direct contact with important target audience members than anyone else in an organization as they work their way through a district. The activity reports routinely filed by some field representatives may be a useful source of information to an organization, especially if it contains appropriate questions and has room for additional feedback. Perhaps more important, these people should be encouraged to ask questions, follow up on complaints, and undertake other activities that help them to informally monitor and evaluate an organization and its standing among target audience members.

An organization's desire to learn the truth is one of the most critical aspects of any research, especially with this form of investigation. Field reports—in fact, any formal or informal research method—will not be useful to an organization seeking to justify its actions rather than to learn the truth. The information provided by those in the field only is useful when organizations are willing to hear the truth from their representatives. Having said this, keep in mind that the information provided by field representatives has limitations. These people do not talk to a random sample of targeted audience members and so their observations and suggestions are based on selective information. Input from the field, therefore, should be given appropriate weight, and formal research methods should be used to confirm or disconfirm this information when appropriate.

COMMUNITY FORUMS/GROUP MEETINGS

Public relations practitioners may attend community forums or other formal or informal group meetings to better understand issues of concern to community citizens and to get a sense of community members who are vocal, active, and involved in an issue or topic of importance to an organization. Organizational presence at such meetings should not be concealed, but in most cases also should not be vocal.

Organizational members who attend meetings to learn the views of others run the risk of gaining a wrong sense of opinion if they involve themselves in the process because they may temporarily influence or alienate those who might otherwise share their opinions. Instead, those who attend these meetings should report useful information back to an organization so the need for additional, perhaps formal, research can be considered, and a planned and strategic response can be developed to emerging issues or other situations. When conducted properly, this type of informal research helps an organization monitor its internal or external environments, keep abreast of issues and opinions as they develop, and position itself as both positive and negative future developments occur.

TELEPHONE CALLS, MAIL, AND ELECTRONIC MAIL

It is in organizations' best interest to listen carefully when individuals, whether local community members, consumers, members of activists groups, or others, go out of their way to communicate with them. Many people who have questions, concerns, or other grievances never make the effort to communicate with an organization. They may simply sever their ties with the organization, or, depending on their options, complain to their friends and colleagues as they maintain a frustrated relationship with an organization they increasingly dislike. In an era of greater consumer sophistication and public activism, groups are increasingly likely to express their anger in ways that attract public and media attention. Depending on the situation and organizations involved, such expressions may include, for example, public protests, meetings with legislators or government regulators, demonstrations at shareholders' meetings, letter writing campaigns, or other efforts designed to pressure an organization to respond to issues and change its behaviour.

Organizations can track phone calls, mail, and e-mail to learn about issues, gauge the level of individual concern, and help determine how to avoid these situations. Toll-free telephone numbers, in particular, are a relatively quick source of information for organizations and can be used to help track the concerns and issues expressed by important publics. Proctor & Gamble, for example, was the target of vicious rumors that it was a proponent of Satanism. At the height of the crisis, the company handled more than 39,000 calls during a 3-month period.

The calls not only were a valuable source of information for Proctor & Gamble, they gave the company the opportunity to respond individually to consumers' concerns. Similarly, the American Red Cross analyzed more than 1,700 telephone calls in response to concerns about AIDS and the existence of the virus that causes AIDS in the blood supply provided through the Red Cross. Not only were individual questions answered, but the Red Cross determined the informational needs of targeted publics by analyzing a brief form that was completed for each call. This simple analysis provided the organization with invaluable information, even helping it determine specific words to avoid when addressing questions concerning the transmission and prevention of the disease.

Organizations routinely use toll-free phone numbers to establish, maintain, and strengthen relationships with consumers. Butterball Turkey, for example, established a Turkey Talk Line in 1982 to answer consumers' questions about all aspects of turkey preparation, ranging from thawing to cooking to carving. Staffed by professionally trained home economists and nutritionists, the line runs 24 hours a day in November and December, and receives 8,000 calls on Thanksgiving Day alone. Butterball also established a web site in conjunction with the Talk Line that received more than 4.4 million hits in 1996. The Talk Line and web site serve as an important reminder to consumers about Butterball's expertise in turkey preparation and provide the company with important information about consumers' questions and interests.

The mail received by an organization, including e-mail for many companies, can be tracked in a manner similar to telephone calls and is a potential source of important information. Once again, tracking mail may be a way for organizations to discover issues of consequence to important audiences and to help them assess the need for formal organizational action concerning an issue or event. Most of the time, those who write or call an organization have problems or complaints.

As with many informal methods of research, the sample is not representative of the range of opinions and attitudes that exist among all members of a target public because it is self-selected. At the same time, however, organizations that dismiss negative comments, questions, and criticism as the off-base complaints of a few disgruntled people likely make a serious error in judgment. It is best to take all potential issues seriously, recognizing that the few who speak may represent the opinions and attitudes of a much larger but silent group. In some cases, early warning signs produced through this type of informal research indicate a clear need for formal research to further investigate an issue.

LIBRARY AND INTERNET RESEARCH

Accessing information over the Internet or at the library may constitute formal or informal research depending on the kind of information being sought and, when applicable, the methods used to generate a sample and collect data. Neither the library nor the Internet is a research method, but each provides access to resources that practitioners are likely to find valuable. In fact, Marlow (1996) noted the Internet is transforming the role of the media and libraries because these organizations have large collections of content—or databases—continually open to access from almost anywhere in the world. The resources available over the Internet now include organizational sales, service, and promotional material; informal chat rooms and bulletin boards; media and library systems; and other highly useful databases. In addition to books and other publications, many libraries contain comprehensive media collections that include, for example, years of national, state, and local newspapers and magazines.

University libraries also are likely to contain Census Bureau data, an overwhelming array of government documents, and the results of privately and publicly funded studies.

In many cases, practitioners use this information for what is called secondary data analysis, which is the use of data collected by a previous researcher or another research organization for a purpose other than was originally intended. When practitioners use Census Bureau research to learn the demographic characteristics of residents in a specific region, for example, they are engaging in secondary research. In other cases, the reference materials, special collections, online databases, and even some forms of original research conducted over the Internet may be of value to practitioners.

The Internet, which began as a computer network to share information among multiple locations in the 1960s, has proven itself as an irreplaceable tool in the collection and distribution of public relations information. The Internet has become an almost instantaneous source of information for its users, and it allows organizations to communicate directly to potentially interested individuals with no media gate keeper and few conventional geographic, political, or legal boundaries. As an informal research tool, the Internet allows organizations to conduct competitor research. Organizations increasingly place key documents online to promote themselves, build customer relationships, and sell products and services. Every business with a web site is a potential publisher and may provide a range of promotional literature, product and service manuals, annual reports, position papers, speech texts, and other documents. Communication professionals can easily access these documents to learn about their competition and other organizations.

Organizations also may actively solicit information over the Internet by posting questionnaires or by using bulletin board systems and chat groups that allow people to "talk" online. In fact, this form of communication potentially broadens the range of those who may be contacted for advice or other important information by practitioners. Keep in mind, however, not everyone engaged in online communication is listening or participating in an attempt to be helpful to an organization. In the same way, the advice or other information received from a bulletin board may be from an experienced professional or from a college freshman. In addition, the opinions expressed in a self-selected, or volunteer, sample do not represent all of the opinions and attitudes among members of a target audience. These limitations aside, online communication vehicles provide potentially important sources of communication to practitioners.

More than 5,000 online databases available to practitioners provide access to a previously unimagined amount of information ranging, as one text puts it, from anatomy to zoology, and in business, from advertising to wholesaling. Various directories help practitioners find online database resources, including the Directory of On-Line Information Resources published by CSG Press in Rockville, Maryland, and Database Catalog published by Dialog in Palo Alto, California. One of the most important and quickly growing uses of the Internet for public relations practitioners is to engage in issue tracking and other forms of information retrieval using online subscription databases such as Nexis, Dun and Bradstreet, Dow Jones News/Retrieval, Data Times, and Burrelle's Broadcast Database.

Practitioners access these databases to seek information in news and business publications, financial reports, consumer and market research, government records, broadcast transcripts and other useful resources. Online database searches typically provide comprehensive results with speed and accuracy. Although such services can be costly, their use often is relatively cost-effective given the benefits of the information they provide. In addition, the results of research conducted by governments, foundations, and educational organizations may be available online at little or no cost. Such research may provide important information about trends and major developments in fields as diverse as agriculture, education, and labour. In each of these cases, online technology has made it possible for practitioners to cost effectively gather a wealth of information with amazing speed.

Libraries also contain a wealth of information that practitioners are likely to find useful. Almost any public library contains resources of use to practitioners, including Internet access. University libraries, and some state libraries if there is a state capital nearby, contain an almost overwhelming amount of material practitioners will find useful including reference material, special collections, archives, government documents, and similar resources. In fact, large universities typically have one primary library and several smaller, specialty libraries such as a business library or science library. In addition, many metropolitan areas contain special libraries or collections that are privately maintained by a business or association. These libraries contain a depth of material unavailable from other sources on specific topics such as advertising or broadcast history, some of which may be accessible online.

Practitioners looking for specific information or resources but not sure where to begin may find it useful to start with a reference librarian. These experts can locate a surprising number of directories, statistical facts and figures, studies, and other information. If you are looking for specific information, the chances are excellent there is a directory, abstract, book, or other resource that a reference librarian can locate, often in a short amount of time. Although the list of available reference materials would fill volumes, basic indexes include the Reader's Guide to Periodical Literature, which contains a listing of articles in 200 major magazines and journals categorized by topic; the Business Periodicals Index, which indexes articles in 400 business publications, and the New York Times Index, which provides abstracts of news stories chronologically by subject.

Other useful resources vary based on need, but may include the Statistical Abstract of the United States, which contains more than 1,000 pages of tables and data about aspects of the United States and provides an overview of the range of additional information that is available; The Corporate Directory, which provides information on more than 10,000 firms in the United States including names of their officers, directors and subsidiary firms; The National Directory of State Agencies, which, for each state, indicates state agencies by function and provides an alphabetical telephone listing for more than 23,000 state representatives, state government officials, and staff members; the Thomas Register of American Manufacturers, which provides information on more than 100,000 product manufacturers including product classifications by city within state; and Simmon's Market Research Bureau data, a series of syndicated market research publications that provide invaluable information including consumers' product and service usage, media consumption, and related information. It is beyond the scope of this text to list and explain the wealth of reference material available at many university libraries; however, this brief discussion should provide some idea of the potential resources available.

One additional library resource that merits special attention because of its potential benefit to public relations practitioners and ease of access is the Census Bureau data contained at many university libraries. The work of the Census Bureau results in one of the most abundant and beneficial set of data available to practitioners, and it is free. The Census Bureau uses different length forms when it conducts the census. Most citizens respond to a basic, short questionnaire that provides a small amount of information. A sizeable portion of citizens, however, fill out in-depth questionnaires that provide additional information of benefit to practitioners. The results indicate where people live and provide additional information, including demographic characteristics such as age, sex, ethnicity, size and disposition of their living unit, type of dwelling, and rental or value of their dwelling unit. This information is available to any individual or organization.

Campbell's Soup, for example, uses Census Bureau data to guide its development of products and refine its marketing strategies for existing products. In one case, marketers for the company surmised that Americans' eating patterns were changing and that breakfast was no longer a traditional group meal. The conclusion was based on data indicating that the number of two-income families was increasing, even though the number of members in a household were declining. The company launched Great Starts, a line of single-serving frozen breakfasts, following additional research to confirm their assumptions. The product line quickly gained a sizable share of a rapidly expanding market. In another instance, the company used Census Bureau data indicating that the population was aging, along with other market research concerning the health interests of older people, to estimate the demand for reduced-salt soups. The result was Special Request, a line of healthier soup products. In each of these cases, Census Bureau data were used in conjunction with other market research to inform the company in its attempt to meet consumer needs and increase company success.

Census Bureau research results and a vast array of reference works are just some of the many library materials available. Other useful resources include trade and professional publications, media archives, and other materials. Practitioners generally make the best use of these materials if they have as much information as possible when they begin an information search. When practitioners are seeking specific information, they are likely to find an existing resource that contains the desired information, and both the library and online resources are excellent places to start the research process.

CLIP FILES AND MEDIA TRACKING

Clip files are used by organizations to follow and understand media coverage, to help evaluate public relations campaign outcomes and to get a sense of public opinion based on reporters' stories. In fact, it is safe to say that any organization that is in the news on a regular basis has some way to track media coverage, the results of which typically are organized into some sort of useful file system and analyzed. Although clip files do not serve all purposes well— as the

Institute for Public Relations has noted, they measure "outputs" rather than "outcomes" such as gauging public opinion—they allow organizations to track and analyze media coverage. When greater accuracy, precision, and reliability are desirable, a formal content analysis should be conducted. Most organizational clip files and other forms of media tracking fall far short of the demands of a formal content analysis, but still serve useful purposes.

Clip Files

A clip file is a collection of media stories that specifically mention an organization, its competition, or other key words, and issues an organization wants to learn about. In terms of print media, for example, a clipping service is likely to clip from virtually all daily and weekly newspapers in any geographic region, including international regions. Other print media that may be covered include business and trade publications and consumer magazines. Once stories are located by a service, they are clipped and tagged with appropriate information typically including the name of the publication, its circulation, and the date and page number of the story. Clients or their agencies then can organize and analyze the clips in whatever format is most beneficial. Services are available to monitor all types of media outlets. Companies such as Burrelle's Press Clipping Service, Bacon's PR and Media Information Systems, Luce Press Clippings, or the Delahaye Group, for example, offer comprehensive services for national and international media. Specialized services can be hired as well, such as same-day clipping to help organizations monitor breaking news or crises, or broadcast monitoring to track video news release use.

Although there are differences among each of the services in terms of how they operate, a client generally provides a list of key words, terms, and topics that it wants its service to locate in specific media. The words and terms provided by an organization vary considerably but typically include its own name and the names of its products and services. Other information that may be tracked includes the names of competitors and their products and services, the names of senior management, or other important topics or individuals an organization wants to track. The client also may send its service information about its print or video news releases, public service announcement copy, or other collateral material it expects will generate news coverage,

Practitioners can analyze clip file contents using various techniques. In many cases, practitioners simply count the number of media clips a campaign produces and use their own judgment concerning the purpose of their campaign and the media's treatment of a topic. Such an analysis may be useful for informal campaign reviews and exploratory decision making, but it lacks the quantitative specificity and accuracy necessary to truly determine a campaign's effect on targeted audiences' opinions, attitudes, and behaviour.

Advertising Equivalency

In an attempt to quantify the value of media placement, many practitioners compare the results of their publicity efforts with equivalent advertising costs. It is relatively common, for example, to compare the column space and broadcast time generated by a campaign with the "equivalent" cost for advertising placement had the space been purchased. This method of clip evaluation allows practitioners to claim a dollar amount for the media coverage their campaign generates. In some cases, the value of publicity placements are increased or, more commonly, decreased using an agreed-upon formula. This is done because publicity placements are thought to lack some of the benefits of advertising: in particular, a specific message delivered to a specific audience and timed according to planned schedule. The result is that editorial placements typically are given less value than advertising placements because their contents and placement cannot be controlled.

This issue raises a point of contention concerning the benefits of advertising versus the benefits of publicity, and it reveals some of the serious problems associated with claiming dollar amounts for publicity media placements. In reality, it is nearly impossible to compare advertising and publicity placements in terms of their relative value. How do you compare, for example, the value of a full-page print ad that appears in the middle of a publication with a front-page publicity placement? In terms of different publicity placements, how do you determine the value of a story on the front page with a story placed in the middle of a section? Or, how do you compare the value of clips in different media—a narrowly targeted publication that reaches an identified target audience, for example—with general media placement that reaches the public broadly? Also, how do you compare the value of different editorial contexts: a story that is positive, for example, versus a story that is negative or mixed? Each of these issues, and more, presents practitioners with difficult obstacles when determining the relative value of advertising versus publicity, and when determining the value of different publicity clips.

COST PER THOUSAND

Another commonly used method of determining publicity-clip value is based on the cost of reaching audience members. Advertisers, for example, commonly determine the most beneficial combination of media, Programmes, and schedules by evaluating and comparing the costs of different media and different media vehicles, as well as by considering the percentage of an audience that is part of a specific target audience for a campaign. One of the simplest means of comparing media costs is to compare the cost per thousand or CPM (M is the Roman numeral for 1,000) of different media. This figure tells media planners the cost of reaching 1,000 people in an audience. If a daily newspaper has 500,000 subscribers and charges $7,000 for running a full-page ad, for example, the cost per thousand is $14 (7,000 ÷ 500,000 × 1,000).

Cost Efficiency

To determine the relative cost efficiency of different media, media planners use the same general formula, but reduce the total audience figures to include only those audience members that specifically are targeted as part of a campaign. Using the previous example, if the campaign primarily is directed at males 18 to 34 years old, and 30% of the newspaper's audience fits into that category, the circulation figure can be reduced to 30% of the total audience, or 150,000. The resulting cost efficiency figure is approximately $47 (7,000 ÷ 150,000 × 1,000).

Cost Per Impression

These same formulas can be used in public relations to measure the relative value of publicity clips. The results of publicity clips in public relations are sometimes referred to as publicity Impressions, so the cost per impression (CPI) of publicity clips can be calculated after a campaign has been conducted and compared with advertising campaign costs or other public relations campaign costs. In the same way, cost-efficiency measures of publicity impressions can be calculated. CPM-type measures are difficult to use to compare the value of advertising versus publicity clips, primarily because CPM calculations are performed in the early stages of an advertising campaign and used for planning and forecasting, whereas a campaign must be over before publicity impression costs can be calculated because clips depend on media placement.

More important, neither CPM nor CPI calculations measure message impact; they only measure message exposure. In fact, they are not even a true measure of message exposure, but instead are a measure of the greatest potential message exposure. The exposure numbers they produce are useful in a relative sense, but are "soft" and likely to overestimate audience size.

LIMITATIONS OF CLIP AND TRACKING RESEARCH

Although any of these methods can be used to quantitatively evaluate publicity-clip placements, they are relatively unsophisticated and should not be used as the basis for determining message impact or campaign success. In most cases, formal research methods are necessary to evaluate a range of campaign outcomes from changes in the opinions and attitudes of target audience members to changes in individual behaviour. This is not meant to suggest, however, that the use of clip files is not beneficial as a form of casual research.

In fact, there are various potential improvements on the standard clip file and several valuable ways such information can be used. McElreath (1997) described two uses of media tracking and the ways it can benefit an organization. In the first example, Porter Novelli (then known as Doremus Porter Novelli) conducted a substantial issue-tracking project for a pharmaceutical trade association in support of a national public education and lobbying campaign. The project was conducted by the agency as part of what it called its background review service.

After meeting with the client to determine and refine the list of topics and issues, the agency conducted computerized database searches to find past media coverage of the issues and topics in newspapers, trade publications, consumer magazines, and wire services; relevant opinion polls and market surveys; and other information including key demographic and economic trends. This information was used to develop a national campaign that included important information on drug liability intended to inform and persuade lobbyists and state legislators about the need for legal reform.

In a second example cited by McElreath (1997), a federal health organization wanted to determine why the airings of its public service announcements (PSAS) concerning the control of high blood pressure were decreasing in some markets. An agency was hired to help solve the problem. As part of its work, the agency brought in a company that specialized in monitoring broadcast media specifically to track electronic media placements. Because the campaign relied on free media placement by editors, reporters, and producers, the agency conducted what it called a gatekeeper audit. Using distribution lists and the results from the broadcast monitoring service, agency executives determined which stations were using the PSAs and their frequency of use. Next, telephone interviews were conducted with representatives from the high-play and low-play stations. Several PSA distribution, scheduling, and formatting changes were made based on the results of the research project. The broadcast monitoring service was used to track use of the improved

PSAS. The new results indicated PSA usage greatly increased among all stations, including the previous low-play stations. In both examples, media tracking provided highly beneficial information used to address specific goals and increase the chances for campaign success.

It is important to reiterate a key point in the use and interpretation of media tracking and clip files at this point. As a rule, this research reveals only the media's use of messages. Of course, it provides information concerning a targeted audience's potential exposure to messages, but clip files and tracking studies reveal nothing about message impact. Sometimes the results of media placements are obvious and no additional research is necessary. In fact, in many cases no formal campaign evaluation is conducted because an organization or client believes it easily can identify the impact of a particular campaign.

At other times, however, it is desirable to learn more about a message's impact on an audience's level of knowledge, opinions, attitudes, or less obvious behavioral outcomes. When this is the case, clip files and analyses of media-message placements tell practitioners nothing about these outcomes. In addition, public relations campaigns that claim success based on media placement as revealed by clipping services and tracking studies may be overstating the impact of their campaigns. Although clipping services and media tracking may be valuable and important, it is unwise to attempt to determine public opinion and similar information based on media-message placement.

IN-DEPTH INTERVIEWS

In-depth interviewing, sometimes called intensive interviewing or simply depth interviewing, is an open-ended interview technique in which respondents are encouraged to discuss an issue or problem, or answer a question, at length and in great detail. This research method is based on the belief that individuals are in the best position to observe and understand their own attitudes and behaviour. This interview process provides a wealth of detailed information and is particularly useful for exploring attitudes and behaviors in an engaged and extended format.

Initially, an interview participant is given a question or asked to discuss a problem or topic. The remainder of the interview generally is dictated by the participant's responses or statements. Participants typically are free to explore the issue or question in any manner they desire, though an interviewer may have additional questions or topics to address as the interview progresses.

Normally, the entire process allows an unstructured interview to unfold in which participants explore and elaborate about their attitudes and opinions, motivations, values, experiences, feelings, emotions, and related information. The researcher encourages this probing-interview process through active listening techniques, providing feedback as necessary or desired, and occasionally questioning participants regarding their responses to encourage deeper exploration. As rapport is established between an interviewer and a participant, the interview may produce deeper, more meaningful findings, even on topics that may be considered too sensitive to address through other research methods.

Most intensive interviews are customized for each participant. Although the level of structure varies based on the purpose of the project and, sometimes, the ability of a participant to direct the interview, it is critical that researchers not influence participants' thought processes. Interviewees must explore and elaborate on their thoughts and feelings as they naturally occur, rather than attempting to condition their responses to what they perceive the researcher wants to learn. As Broom and Dozier (1990) noted, the strength of this research technique is that participants, not the researcher, drive the interview process. When participants structure the interview, it increases the chances the interview will produce unanticipated responses, reveal latent issues, or other unusual, but potentially useful, information. Once collected, such information typically is confirmed or disconfirmed through the use of a research method possessing greater reliability and validity before it is used as the basis for a public relations campaign or Programme.

In-depth interviews typically last from about an hour up to several hours. A particularly long interview is likely to fatigue both the interviewer and the interviewee, and it may be necessary to schedule more than one session in some instances. Because of the time required to conduct an in-depth interview, it is particularly difficult to schedule interviews, especially with professionals. In addition, participants typically are paid a good sum for their work. Payments, which range from $50 to $1,000 or more, are normally higher than payments provided to focus group participants.

In-depth interviews offer several benefits as a research method. Perhaps the most important advantages are the wealth of detailed information they typically provide and the occasional surprise discovery of unanticipated but potentially beneficial information. Wimmer and Dominick suggested that intensive interviews provide more accurate information concerning sensitive issues than traditional survey techniques because of the rapport that develops between an interviewer and an interviewee.

In terms of disadvantages, sampling issues are a particular concern for researchers conducting in-depth interviews. The time and intensity required to conduct an interview commonly results in the use of small, nonprobability-based samples. The result is that it is difficult to generalize the findings of such interviews from a sample to a population with a high degree of confidence. For this reason, potentially important findings discovered in-depth interviews should be confirmed or disconfirmed using a research method and accompanying sample that provide high degrees of validity and reliability. Difficulty scheduling interviews also contributes to study length. Whereas telephone surveys may conclude data collection within a week, in-depth interviews may stretch over several weeks or even months. The usefulness of in-depth interviews is greatly limited by sample-selection issues.

In addition to sample concerns, the unstructured nature of in-depth interviews leads to nonstandard interview procedures and questions. This makes analysis and interpretation of study results challenging, and it raises additional concerns regarding the reliability and validity of study findings. Nonstandard interviews also may add to study length because of problems researchers encounter when attempting to analyze and interpret study results.

As a final note, the unstructured interview process and length of time it takes to complete an interview result in a high potential for interviewer bias to corrupt results. As rapport develops between an interviewer and an interviewee and a basic level of comfort is realized, the researcher may inadvertently communicate information that biases participants' responses. Interviewers require a great deal of training to avoid this problem, which also can contribute to study cost and length.

Despite these limitations, in-depth interviews can be successfully used to gather information not readily available using other research methods.

Q METHODOLOGY

Q methodology is a general term used by Stephenson to describe a research method and related ideas used to understand individuals' attitudes. This method of research combines an intensive, individual method of data collection with quantitative data analysis. Q methodology requires research participants to sort large numbers of opinion statements and to place them in groups along a continuum. The continuum contains anchors such as "most like me" to "most unlike me." Numerical values are then assigned to the statements based on their location within the continuum, and the results are statistically analyzed.

For the most part, Q-sorting is a sophisticated way of rank-ordering statements—although other objects also can be Q-sorted—and assigning numbers to the rankings for statistical analysis. In public relations, a Q-sort might work like this: A set of verbal statements concerning the image of an organization is printed on cards and given to research participants. Participants are asked to sort the cards into separate piles based on the extent of their agreement or disagreement with each statement.

The result is a rank order of piles of cards placed on a continuum from "most approve" to "least approve," with varying degrees of approval and disapproval between each extreme. Researchers assign the cards in each pile a number based on their location. The cards in the highest, "most approve" category, for example, might be assigned a 10. The cards in the next highest "most approve" category might be assigned a 9, and so on. The cards placed in the lowest, "least approve" category would receive a 0. The resulting Q-sort would contain a rank ordering of statements that reveal the participant's beliefs about the organization.

The number of cards used in a Q distribution ranges from less than 50 to 140. For statistical reliability, a good range for most projects is from 60 to 90 statements.

The sorting instructions provide a guide for sorting Q-sample statements or other items and are specified according to the purpose of the research. Researchers may ask participants to sort opinion or personality statements on a "most approve" to "least approve" continuum, or to describe the characteristics of an ideal political candidate or organization on a "most important" to "least important" continuum. Q-sort instructions also can concern fictional or hypothetical circumstances.

Finally, participants may sort statements according to their perceptions. In a political study, for example, participants may sort statements using "what you believe is most like a liberal" and "what you believe is most unlike a liberal" for continuum anchors. There are many additional anchors and instructions that can be used in Q-sorts, and the flexibility of the method in this regard provides a wealth of opportunities for researchers.

Sample-selection procedures are a particular challenge in Q-method research. It is difficult to draw a large, representative sample, particularly given the time requirements and intensive nature of the data-collection process. The result is that researchers typically draw small, convenience samples. The use of small, nonprobability-based samples makes it difficult to generalize study results from a sample to a population with confidence. Although some might suggest the use of nonrandom samples is a limitation of minor consequence, the reality is that both theoretical and descriptive research require testing on samples of sufficient size—ideally drawn using a probability-based procedure—to produce trustworthy results.

Q methodology is potentially useful, but also controversial. The research technique is flexible and may be particularly useful when researchers are exploring the opinions and attitudes of important target audience members. In fact, many participants seem to enjoy participating in Q studies. In addition, study results can be statistically analyzed, and Q methodology provides an objective way to identify and intensively study individuals' opinions and attitudes.

Nevertheless, the use of small, convenience samples greatly hinders the external validity of study results. There simply is no way to confidently generalize results from the sample of study participants to the population they supposedly represent. In addition, there may be complex statistical concerns about the assumptions of statistical tests applied to Q-sort results. In particular, Q-sorts may violate a key assumption concerning the independence of participant responses. When this assumption is violated, many forms of statistical analysis are no longer acceptable for use in analyzing study results.

These two limitations, in fact, are the primary reasons Q methodology is presented in this text as an informal research method. In addition to these concerns, some critics complain that the sheer magnitude of sorting 60 to 100 statements or more is beyond the ability of most participants and a high number of categories requires participants to make too fine distinctions among items. It is clear that, although Q-sorts provide a potentially rich and useful method of exploring the opinions and attitudes of key target audience members in great depth, they have limitations that should be considered carefully when interpreting study results. It is particularly important to consider the use of follow-up research, such as a survey that uses a large, probability-based sample, to understand the results of a Q-sort as they relate to a larger population.

It is important to keep in mind that informal research methods may suffer from several significant limitations that make them difficult to use with complete confidence. This, in fact, is the reason they are considered informal and casual. This does not mean informal research methods never should be used. Informal research methods generally are the most common research methods used by practitioners. But, practitioners should interpret the results of informal research carefully and understand the limitations of the methods they are using.

Considering the advice of selected members of a target audience, for example, makes sense in most situations and such input can be an invaluable help in the research and planning processes. At the same time, however, the prudent practitioner will consider this information for what it is—the opinions of a few people—instead of giving it the full weight of a scientifically conducted, formal opinion poll.

What does this mean for public relations practitioners? When possible, informal research methods should be used to supplement formal research methods rather than to replace them. This provides practitioners with information they can use as primary and secondary planning resources. Unfortunately, many practitioners engage primarily in informal research because of limited budgets, time, and other constraints. In these situations, it is wise to take every precaution in interpreting and using research results correctly. It is better to have no research than to base a campaign on incorrect research results. No research method is infallible, but special care should be used in interpreting research results produced through informal methods.

Chapter 8

Making Research Decisions: The Focus Group

The focus group long has been a mainstay of public relations and marketing research, but it remains a controversial method for research and message testing. Practitioners often tell horror stories about focus groups that provided misleading information for a campaign that later failed. Nevertheless, the method recently has begun to gain more respect as a valid research tool, rather than a "cheap and dirty" alternative to "real" research.

A recent proliferation of scholarly and how-to books and articles has made it possible for more practitioners to use the tool more effectively and wisely. Although focus groups still have limitations, careful application of the method can provide indispensable guidance available from no other tool. As John Palshaw of Palshaw Measurement Inc., cautioned (1990), focus groups are designed to generate ideas, not evaluate them.

CHARACTERISTICS OF FOCUS GROUPS

A focus group is a semistructured, group interview analyzed using qualitative methods. Focus groups explore the attitudes, opinions, behaviors, beliefs, and recommendations of carefully selected groups. Focused discussions, led by a moderator, usually include 6 to 12 participants and take place over 1 to 3 hours. Sessions attempt to define problems, gather reaction to proposed solutions to problems, and explore feelings and reasons behind differences that exist within the group or between the group and the organization. Organizations typically use focus groups to get feedback during product or service development, to test messages for product or service introductions, to guide decisions about packaging design and promotional messages, to determine appropriate types of outlets and target publics for products or messages, to gauge public reaction to issue positions, and to explore opinions concerning company performance and community citizenship. Message testing explores participants' perceptions of the accuracy, clarity, and relevance of a message, as well as the credibility of the source.

More specialized uses of focus groups also exist. Focus groups can be used to gain a better understanding of groups whose perspectives are poorly understood by an organization. This can help an organization respond more effectively to the group's concerns. Focus groups also can help an organization explore its strengths and weaknesses relative to other organizations. In addition, focus groups can be used for brainstorming purposes, to develop strategies for solving a problem instead of simply testing strategies already under development. Focus groups can help an organization gain insight into complex behaviors and conditional opinions, for which survey questionnaires could provide conflicting or seemingly definite information. As a result, focus groups often are used as a supplement to survey research.

Group dynamics in a focus group can be used to reach consensus on an idea, such as the most credible source for a message or the best location for an event. Finally, focus groups can be used to pretest and refine survey instruments, particularly when likely responses to a question are unknown, such as the biggest barriers to a customer's use of a proposed product or service.

Instead of questionnaires, focus groups use protocols to guide discussion. Protocols range from rough outlines to carefully constructed moderators' guides. Presession questionnaires can be used for screening. In addition, focus groups often use visual aids such as story boards, mockups, or other sample materials for pretesting. Whereas surveys try to take a dispassionate, outsider's perspective to obtain the most objective information about a targeted population from a representative group, focus groups try to work more from inside the target group, exploring individuals' perspectives in depth to gain a deeper understanding of their decision-making processes. Surveys, in other words, try to avoid bias; focus groups try to explore and understand it.

ADVANTAGES AND DISADVANTAGES

Focus groups should not be viewed as alternatives to survey research, as the two methods have different strengths and weaknesses. The focus group offers characteristics that give it a uniquely useful role in problem definition and message testing. Because focus groups are socially oriented, for example, they make it possible to uncover information about an issue that would not come out in individual interviews or in surveys. People initially may not recall using a product or service but may be reminded of a relevant situation as a result of another participant's observations during the focused discussion. In addition, the focused discussion makes it possible to probe positive or negative responses in depth. Because people can explain what they mean and moderators can probe for clarification, focus groups provide good face validity. In other words, managers can be confident they are interpreting what people said in ways consistent with what they meant. This can be more difficult in a survey, for which individuals must check a box even if the question seems vague or the possible response categories do not reflect their views perfectly.

Focus groups also provide quick, relatively inexpensive results to guide a Programme that requires fast implementation. Although overnight survey services are available, they can be expensive and make it difficult to develop a tailored survey instrument that maximizes the relevance of findings obtained. Political campaigns, meanwhile, can use focus groups to try out possible responses to a competitor's political advertisement in time to air a response within a day or two.

Another advantage of focus groups is their flexibility. Literacy, for example, is not needed for a focus group whereas it is required for a written questionnaire. People without telephones or with caller ID may never respond to a telephone survey but may participate in a focus group if recruited properly. In addition, focus groups can be held in different locations, even in a park. This makes it easier to recruit from populations that may be unable or unwilling to travel to a research facility.

Focus groups have drawbacks that limit their usefulness and increase the risk of obtaining misleading information that can compromise public relations Programme effectiveness. For example, although the group dynamics of a focus group make it possible for information to come out that might not be uncovered through individual interviews, group dynamics also make it more difficult to control the direction and tenor of discussions. A carefully trained moderator is essential to draw the full range of opinions out of focus group participants and to prevent individuals from dominating the group. Groups vary depending on the characteristics of the participants, the timing, and the environment, which makes their reliability questionable. They also can be difficult to assemble because individuals from targeted populations may be busy, resistant, or forgetful.

Because of these limitations, focus groups should never be used in confrontational situations, for statistical projections, if the unique dynamics of social interaction are unnecessary for information gathering, if confidentiality cannot be assured, or if procedures such as sampling or questioning are driven by client bias rather than by researcher design.

The usefulness of a focused discussion depends on the willingness of participants to share their perspectives freely and honestly. As a result, focus groups must take place in a comfortable, nonthreatening environment. The composition of an appropriate setting requires attention to the makeup of the group itself, as well as the surroundings in which the discussion takes place. A poorly constructed environment can hamper discussion or make it difficult to ascertain true opinions. A focus group of parents, for example, may mask differences in perspective between mothers and fathers. Misleading information obtained from a restricted discussion can doom a campaign.

SELECTING AND RECRUITING PARTICIPANTS

People tend to feel most comfortable when they are with others like themselves. As a result, focus group participants usually are selected to be "homogeneous," which means similar in certain characteristics. These characteristics depend on the issue explored by the group. For example, a discussion of a college's responsiveness to student financial aid issues could mix male and female students, because they are likely to share similar problems regarding funding their education. On the other hand, a discussion of date rape is less productive if the group includes both men and women. Because women often are the victims of date rape, this may make both the men and the women uncomfortable talking about it in front of each other. As a result, separate focus groups can take place to explore the beliefs and feelings of men and women about date rape. Similarly, a discussion of workplace issues may need to probe the views of managerial personnel and secretarial personnel separately because employees may not feel comfortable speaking freely in front of their supervisors.

The most productive focus groups recruit participants who are similar but who do not already know each other. If they know each other, interpersonal dynamics such as power roles already have been established and can make open discussion and discovery more difficult. This becomes important in focused discussions that must mix participants with different perspectives, such as employees and supervisors, to explore the dynamics between them. This type of situation can work only if the participants feel they can be open with one another and only if the discussion can take place in a constructive, civil way. In other words, if participants need to include employees and supervisors, they should not include employees and their own supervisors.

Focus group participants often are recruited with respect to homogeneity in demographic characteristics such as age, income, educational level, product usage patterns, or group membership. Screening tests ascertain these characteristics to ensure that participants qualify for inclusion in the study. Such tests can be performed via telephone during recruitment or in the outer lobby on arrival. Several separate focus groups may be required to obtain reactions from different target publics.

Because the focus group method is qualitative not quantitative, it is not necessary to hold a certain number of focus groups to ensure a corresponding degree of reliability. Whereas a survey uses probability sampling to provide reliable results within a 95% level of confidence, focus groups are inherently biased by design. As a result, organizations typically rely on a combination of intuition, budgetary restrictions, and time constraints to determine the number of focus groups that will be held. If time and budget allow, focus groups should continue until all vital target publics have been represented or until the information obtained seems redundant; that is, little new information emerges from additional focus groups. In reality, however, organizations rarely have the time or budget to hold more than two to four focus groups.

Cost varies widely for focus groups. Hiring a professional firm to run a focus group can require $3,000 to $5,000, but organizations can run their own focus groups if they prepare carefully. The cost using existing staff and volunteer participants can be as low as the cost of popcorn or pizza and soft drinks. According to Morgan and Krueger (1998), fees for professional moderators range from about $75 to $300 per hour, or $750 to $1,500 and upward on a per them or per group basis.

Focus group participants usually get paid for their time. The going rate depends on the type of sample recruited. Focus groups of children may provide prizes or free products as compensation. Focus groups of adults usually pay around

$35 to $50 apiece. Recruitment of expert participants such as executives, physicians or other professionals may require significantly greater payment, perhaps $300 apiece.

It is necessary to recruit more participants than are actually needed for the group. In fact, researchers usually recruit twice the number needed to allow for no-shows and individuals who for some reason become ineligible. When recruiting from special populations, in particular, unforseen circumstances can prevent attendance. People also tend to forget, so preparation requires a multistep process of recruitment, acknowledgment, and mail and telephone reminders.

When time is tight, recruitment of focus group participants can take place in a shopping mall that has a market-research facility on the premises. Usually, however, focus group recruitment takes place I to 2 weeks before the session. Respondents can be recruited using different methods, but often are contacted by telephone. Following the initial contact, recruits should receive a written confirmation of the invitation to participate that also serves as a reminder. Reminder phone calls the day or two before the session also helps to boost attendance. Attendees should provide contact numbers upon recruitment so they can be reached at home or at work.

The location of focus group facilities can help or hurt recruitment. The facility should be easy to find, such as in a shopping mall, relatively close to participants' home or work places, and should have plenty of safe parking available. When recruiting parents, it also may be necessary to provide child care. Proper facilities and staffing must be provided to gain the confidence of parents.

Timing can make a difference for focus group success. Most focus groups take place in the evening and avoid weekends or holidays. Other times, such as the lunch hour, may be appropriate for special cases. If two groups are planned for a single evening, the first typically begins at 6 p.m. and the second at 8:15 p.m.

FOCUS GROUP SETTINGS

Participants tend to speak more freely in an informal setting. Conference rooms are better than classrooms; circular seating is better than lecture-style seating; coffee tables are better than conference tables; comfortable chairs or sofas are better than office or classroom chairs. Some organizations rent hotel suites for focus group discussions, whereas others use rooms specifically built for focus group research. Focus group facilities typically include a two-way mirror, behind which clients can sit to observe the discussion as it unfolds, without disturbing the participants. They also include a buffet table or another area for refreshments, because snacks and beverages tend to promote informality. Snacks need to be simple, however, so that the participants pay more attention to the discussion than to their food. They can range from a complete meal such as sandwiches to a small snack such as popcorn.

To aid analysis and for later review by the client, discussions should be recorded unobtrusively on audiotape or videotape, or on both. Participants should be advised of all data-collection and observation procedures. Taping and observation should never be done in secret or without the participants' consent. They also must be informed if their anonymity may not be assured, such as by their appearance on videotape. Often, for the discussion, participants wear name tags but provide only their first names. Sometimes they go by pseudonyms for additional privacy protection. At no time should participants be identified by name in focus group transcripts or reports.

Staffing

Focus groups generally require a team effort. Besides staff for the planning and recruitment phases of the focus group, the interview itself usually requires several staff members. Besides the moderator, who leads the discussion, the event requires at least one other staff member to serve as coordinator. The coordinators (or coordinator) welcome and screen participants; handle honoraria; guide them to the refreshments and make sure refreshments are available; check and run equipment; bring extra batteries, duct tape, and other supplies; and interact with the client. In addition, the coordinator or another staff member takes prolific notes during the session. This is necessary because: (a) transcription equipment can and does break down, or someone pushes "play" instead of "record" on the tape recorder; (b) some people may speak too softly for their comments to register on an audiotape; (c) it may be difficult to identify the source of a comment, particularly if several participants speak at once; and (d) the note taker can provide an initial real-time analysis of themes emerging from the discussion. The note taker may develop the final report in collaboration with the moderator.

Characteristics of the Moderator

The focus group moderator is the key to an effective discussion. The moderator must be able to lead discussion, providing both structure and flexibility to keep discussion on track but allowing participants to pursue issues in depth. Because the moderator must be skilled in group dynamics, some people specialize in focus group leadership and can command an expert's salary to do so.

The moderator must display an air of authority while establishing an atmosphere of warmth and trust so that participants feel free to speak their minds. The moderator strives to keep the structure of the questioning strategy from becoming too obvious, because that could detract from the informality that increases the likelihood of open discussion. In addition, the moderator must treat all participants with equal respect, staying neutral while encouraging all points of view. Moderators never offer their own personal opinions. Moderators also avoid using phrases such as "excellent," "great," "wonderful," or "right," which signal approval or a particular point of view. The moderator also must be able to prevent any member of the group from dominating and must be able to draw out hesitant members.

Effective moderators memorize their topic outlines or protocols so they can pay full attention to the unfolding dynamics of the group. An abbreviated checklist can help them keep on track. The best focus groups direct the discussion themselves to a great extent, instead of having their discussion directed by a highly structured questionnaire. As a result, moderators must be ready to make adjustments, including the sudden addition or deletion of questions by the client, who can get messages to the moderator during the focus group by way of an ear microphone or notes. The moderator may need to modify a questioning strategy that fails with a particular group, or pursue an unexpected discovery that, while unplanned, can provide useful information. Morgan and Krueger recommended the use of 5-second pause and probe strategies to elicit more information from respondents. The 5-second pause can prompt others to add their comments to one just made. The probe responds to an information-poor comment such as "I agree" with a rejoinder such as "would you explain further" or "can you give an example of what you mean?"

Moderators have a sharp but subtle awareness of their own body language so they can provide nonverbal encouragement without biasing responses. For example, leaning forward toward a participant can encourage the individual to go more deeply into a point, but too much head nodding gives the appearance of endorsement that can make another participant hesitant to express disagreement. Similarly, eye contact can provide encouragement to a member who seems withdrawn, whereas a lack of eye contact can help prevent another individual from dominating discussion by denying that individual the attention desired. Eye contact can seem aggressive to individuals who are shy or who come from cultural backgrounds that consider direct eye contact confrontational, so the moderator needs to understand and act sensitively toward cultural differences.

Even the moderator's dress can make a difference. Although a blue suit, white shirt, and tie can provide an air of authority, for example, it also can give the impression of formality and leadership that some may find offensive or threatening. The moderator needs to both lead the group and fit in with group. As a result, there may be times when the ethnic background, gender, and age of the moderator emerge as important characteristics. Participants often assume the moderator is an employee of the organization under discussion, which can hinder or bias responses. The moderator needs to do everything possible to communicate neutrality.

Dealing with Difficult Group Members

Moderators must anticipate the possibility of losing control of a group. Usually, dominant or disruptive participants can be managed using body language and occasional comments. For example, a moderator can hold up a hand as a stop sign to one participant and signal to another, "let's hear from you now." A moderator also can suggest that participants answer a question one by one, going around the room, rather than allowing the most assertive respondents to speak out first every time. Seating charts, along with place cards on the table, can help moderators refer to people by name. If a group becomes too wild or conflictual, or individuals too antagonistic or disrespectful, a 5-minute break can help calm everyone down. In extreme cases, a particularly disruptive individual can be asked to leave during the break. The individual is thanked for participating and told that he or she was needed for the first part of the discussion but that the second part of the discussion will be different and not everyone will be needed. It is important to be firm but polite.

PROTOCOL DESIGN

The focus group protocol, or outline, is designed to provide a subtle structure to the discussion. Unlike surveys, which rely primarily on closed-ended questions, focus group questions should be open ended. They include a combination of uncued questions and more specific, cued questions (probes) that can help spark responses if discussion lags. Uncued questions are ideal ("What impressions do you have of the XYZ organization currently?") because they give participants the most freedom to introduce new ideas. Cued questions provide more context or probe for more depth ("What about the news coverage of the incident bothered you the most?"). The protocol provides just enough structure to help the moderator stay on track. It also progresses from general questions to more focused questions, so that participants have a chance to get comfortable before confronting the most difficult issues.

Closed-ended questions also can be useful if the focus group is being used to explore reasons for answers that might appear on a survey. Analysts, however, should be careful not to extrapolate from focus group participants' answers to closed-ended questions. Clients often appreciate both types of information but can be tempted to make more out of focus group "surveys" than is appropriate.

The subtleties of question construction can have a great effect on the type of discussion that takes place and the value of the information shared. Question phrasings should avoid using "why" because that term can seem confrontational and can stifle open responses. Instead, questions should rely on "how" and "what" phrasing. For example, instead of asking respondents, "Why do you dislike this poster?" ask, "What did you dislike about this poster?" Questions also should avoid dichotomous phrasing ("Did you enjoy the event?") because participants may answer the question literally or ambiguously without providing any context ("What do you remember about the event?"). Sometimes, however, a yes/no question can prod a reticent group into a simple answer that can be explored in depth through follow-up probes. Krueger (1994) also recommended opening with more positive questions and saving negative questions for later so that the overall tone of the group remains constructive, acknowledging both sides of an issue.

Two especially useful question strategies recommended by Krueger include sentence completion and conceptual mapping. Sentence completion questions can be introduced verbally by the moderator or handed out in writing. Participants are asked to complete sentences that request information on their motivations or feelings, often in writing using notepads and pencils provided for the purpose. This enables the moderator to obtain the initial views of every member even if they change their minds during discussion or feel hesitant to speak out. Conceptual mapping asks participants to consider how an organization or product relates to other, similar organizations or products. For example, participants could be asked to "map" political candidates such that the most similar are closest together. The discussion then focuses on what characteristics each participants used to establish similarity, such as trustworthiness, conservatism, or experience. Conceptual mapping requires that participants have some prior impressions or knowledge on which to base their judgments.

According to Krueger, the focus group protocol has five general sections of main questions, to which cued probes can be added to ensure discussion flows smoothly.

1. *The opening question:* This question functions as a warm-up or ice breaker and is intended to demonstrate to participants that they have characteristics in common with one another. It should be answered quickly by the participants, requiring only 10 to 20 seconds from each. Krueger advised that these questions should be factual ("How any children do you have, and how old are they?") rather than attitude- or opinion-based ("What is your favorite flavor of ice cream?"). Questions should avoid requiring disclosures of occupational status because that can create power differentials that hinder group dynamics.
2. *Introduction questions:* These questions set the agenda for the discussion by addressing the topic of interest in a general way ("What was your first impression of" or "What comes to mind when you think about"). These questions are designed to get participants talking about their experiences relevant to the issue but are not intended to provide much information for later analysis.

During this period, participants should begin to feel comfortable talking about the topic with each other.

3. *Transition questions:* These questions begin to take participants into the topic more deeply so they become aware of how others view the topic ("What events have you attended at the Coliseum this year?"). They provide a link between the introductory questions and the key questions that follow.
4. *Key questions:* These two to five questions form the heart of the focus group inquiry and directly address the issues of concern to the client. They can focus on message testing, conceptual mapping, idea generation, or whatever information is of interest to the client. These questions usually are written first, with the remaining questions built around them.
5. *Ending questions:* These questions bring closure to the discussion to make sure all viewpoints have been represented and to confirm the moderator's interpretation of overall themes expressed. These can take the form of suggestions or recommendations for the client. Respondents are asked to reflect on the comments made throughout the session. These questions take the form of a final reaction ("All things considered"), which often is asked of each member one by one; a summary confirmation, in which the moderator gives a 2 to 3 minute overview of the discussion followed by a request for verification ("Is this an adequate summary?"); and a final, standardized question ending the discussion following another overview of the study ("Have we missed anything?"). Krueger recommended leaving 10 minutes for responses to this question, especially if the focus group is early in a series. The answers to this question can give direction to future focused discussions.

MESSAGE AND IDEA TESTING

When using focus groups to try out campaign strategies, it is important to investigate a full range of possibilities and not just the one or two favorites of the client or agency. The manager does not want to limit the ability of the focus group to produce surprises or disconfirm assumptions. Given the crowded marketplace of ideas that exists in the media and everyday environment, breaking through the morass presents public relations Programmes with a challenging task. This challenge can tempt message producers to "push the envelope," going for the most shocking message or the most colorful message or the funniest message.

Extremes may or may not be necessary to break through the clutter, and extremes may help or may backfire once people begin to pay attention to the message. As a result, it is useful to test strategies ranging from the tame to the outrageous. The messages tested for the Talk to Your Kids campaign, provide such a range.

Managers should keep in mind that the target publics for messages may include gatekeepers as well as the ultimate audience. The Washington State Department of Alcohol and Substance Abuse, for example, wanted to run a media campaign exhorting parents of children between 3 and 10 years of age to talk with their children about alcohol. Because funds for paid placements were limited, they needed the cooperation of the Washington State Association of Broadcasters. As a result, they tested messages with parents and with broadcasters, who had different concerns. Because many broadcasters accept advertising for beer, they shied away from messages that seemed especially strident. They were supportive of the campaign, however, and ended up providing nearly $100,000 of free exposure for the final announcements during prime viewing hours.

RUNNING THE GROUP

The moderator begins by welcoming the participants, introducing the topic of discussion and purpose of the meeting very generally, and laying out the ground rules for discussion. The explanation of the study should be truthful but vague, to avoid leading participants. The strategy of the focus group method, after all, is to let the group steer discussion to the extent possible. Ground rules usually cover the following points:

1. Participants should speak up so everyone can hear what they have to say.
2. Only one person should speak at a time to make sure comments are not missed.
3. Each person should say what they think, and not what they think others want to hear. Honest responses are important, and respondents have been asked to participate because their true opinions are valued.
4. Negative comments are at least as useful as positive ones. ("If we thought we were doing a perfect job already, we wouldn't be holding this focus group. We need to know how we can do things better.")
5. No right or wrong answers exist to the questions asked.

Moderators sometimes find it helpful to have participants jot down their answers to questions before opening a discussion. Participants also can be asked to deposit note cards into labeled boxes on the table, so that the raw responses can be analyzed later and compared with opinions shared only during the discussion. This technique effectively reveals minority opinions.

ANALYZING RESULTS

Analysis of qualitative data can range from an intuitive overview to rigorous scrutiny using methods accepted by scholars. Computer Programmes for content analysis of qualitative data exist, such as VBPro. Time pressure usually prevents the most detailed analysis, but some scientific principles apply even to the most succinct report of results. Krueger and others recommended the following principles:

1. *Be systematic:* Establish a procedure ahead of time that makes it possible to disconfirm assumptions and hypotheses. The procedure can be as simple as searching for themes and using at least two direct quotes to illustrate each point. Every interpretation should consider whether alternative explanations might provide an equally valid analysis.
2. *Be verifiable:* Another person should arrive at similar conclusions using similar methods. Keep in mind that focus groups can provide information that a client will find threatening or disheartening. To convince a determined or defensive client that a change in policy or strategy is necessary, the evidence must be compelling.
3. *Be focused:* Keep in mind the original reasons for holding the focus group and look for information that relates to those points. Focus groups that go on for three hours can produce transcripts well over 50 pages. Researchers must have a strategy ready to reduce the voluminous mass of data into meaningful chunks of information.
4. *Be practical:* Perform only the level of analysis that makes sense for the client and the situation. A complete transcript, for example, may not be necessary if the issues explored were fairly simple, and it may take time away from other planning activities during a tight implementation deadline.
5. *Be immediate:* During delays, the focus group observers' impressions may fade, compromising their ability to analyze the data. All observers should make notes during the focus group and immediately afterward to identify themes and direct quotes that seem important. These observations can be confirmed, fleshed out, and supplemented during later analysis but often provide the most valid and vivid conclusions.

The focus group is probably the method most often employed by public relations professionals. It also is probably the method most often misused, which likely contributes to client and managerial skepticism of its value. The focus group offers tremendous benefits to the practitioner aiming to pretest strategies or understand communication processes in some depth. As long as the communication manager respects the limitations of the focus group, it can be an indispensable tool for responsive and effective communication Programme planning.

Chapter 9

Making Research Decisions: Formal Research Methods

Public relations practitioners need more sophisticated research methods as their informational needs evolve from simple fact finding and casual analysis to a more sophisticated understanding of the opinions, attitudes, and motivations of target audience members. In a perfect world, researchers follow a formal, scientific process; use a representative sample of participants that produces results that can be generalized from the sample to population with confidence; and produce objective results instead of subjective results that reflect the opinions or desires of the researcher or other interested parties. Rarely is the world of scientific research perfect, but carefully planned and conducted projects have a greater likelihood than informal research of serving as a reliable basis for campaign planning or evaluation.

Formal research in public relations examines the attitudes, opinions, behaviors, and other important characteristics of target audience members; measures and describes important media characteristics; learns about and explains audience motivations and behaviors; and explains and evaluates media messages and campaign effects. Ultimately, the results of such research help public relations practitioners and their organizations or clients successfully understand target audience opinions, attitudes, and behaviors; predict and measure Programme outcomes; and increase the likelihood of Programme success.

Even though all formal research methods could apply to some aspect of public relations, practitioners do not use all scientific research methods regularly. In addition, communication managers more commonly use informal research methods than formal research methods, despite the increase in sophistication, generalizability, known accuracy, and reliability that formal research methods can provide. For this reason, this chapter introduces readers to a range of formal research methods including surveys, experiments, and in content analyses. Detailed discussions of survey research methods and related topics, because surveys are the most commonly used formal research method in public relations.

CHRACTERISTICS OF FORMAL RESEARCH METHODS

Understanding research methods increases our knowledge of how to learn about the social world, including the world of our target audiences. The ways we learn about the world of our targeted audiences have benefits and limitations.

Understanding these benefits and limitations in methods used to learn about the world affects how much we can trust the data we use to inform our decision making as we plan, execute, and evaluate public relations campaigns. Data-collection methods greatly influence the degree of trust we can place in different kinds of information.

Although public relations research can greatly increase the likelihood of Programme success, poorly conducted research that misinforms campaign planners can have a strong, negative effect on Programme performance. In the same way, research conducted properly but misapplied to a public relations problem or campaign can have a negative effect on campaign effectiveness. This might be the case, for example, when a focus group (informal research) is used to gauge audience attitudes and opinions in the design phase of a campaign. If the results of the focus group are inaccurate, the campaign will fail to inform and motivate its target audience members. Most practitioners do not need to be formal research experts, but they must know and understand basic research issues to use research effectively.

In general, formal, scientific research is empirical in nature (derived from the Greek word for "experience"), or concerned with the world that can be experienced and measured in a precise manner. One way to learn about people, for example, is to read their horoscope. This may provide interesting information, but is such information trustworthy? Although some would argue it is accurate, others would prefer to use a more dependable research method to gather information, a method with proven reliability. This is where formal and informal research methods can differ significantly.

Research collected using informal methods may be interesting but not completely trustworthy because we are not sure about the accuracy of the results. Although the information produced by informal research methods may be highly accurate, researchers have no way to gauge its accuracy because there is no way to evaluate it scientifically. With formal research methods, however, researchers use several procedures to ensure that the information collected is trustworthy beyond a reasonable doubt, or at least that they understand the potential limitations and liabilities of such information. Because of this, researchers carefully monitor the level of trust they can place in data collected using formal research methods.

Sometimes informal research methods produce the same information as formal research methods, but often they do not. When practitioners talk to a small group of close friends who live in a specific school district, for example, they may discover the same general attitudes and opinions that would be expressed if they conducted a survey of randomly selected persons who live in the same district. Due to selection biases, however, the results practitioners obtain through informal conversations are likely to differ greatly from the results they would obtain through a formal survey. Formal research methods allow us to understand more about the limitations and risks associated with the information we collect. This is why it is unwise to engage in campaign planning or risk a large public relations budget on information collected solely through informal research methods.

No single feature makes a research project formal and scientific, but several study attributes contribute to a high degree of accuracy and scientific reliability when combined. We examine some of the most important features of formal research in this book, recognizing that not all formal research methods are the same, and each method has its own strengths and weaknesses.

First, research that is formal and scientific produces results that are objective. This means the research results do not unduly reflect the biases of researchers or the attitudes and opinions of a few selected individuals, but instead reflect events, facts, and behaviors as they exist or naturally occur in a population or group studied. When researchers conduct focus group research, for example, the results of the research depend on the participants in the group. With different focus group participants, the results will probably differ. The opinions of one or two domineering members of a focus group may sway group opinions despite the attempts of the moderator to counterbalance such influences. In addition, researchers must interpret the results of the discussion without a definitive method of objective evaluation. Focus group findings, as a result, are subjective interpretations by the researcher and client.

A formal survey, however, provides objective results. Even if different samples from the same population are selected for surveys, the results are demonstrably similar most of the time (normally 95%) when similar questions are asked, and appropriate probability sampling methods are used. This occurs because scientific methods help ensure the attitudes and behaviors measured in the survey are represented in approximately the same proportion as they naturally occur in a population. In fact, the use of probability sampling methods ensures researchers can calculate the range of error—the degree of skepticism we need to apply to the results—for descriptive results. This makes it easy to understand how trustworthy the data are. In addition, numerical results require little or no subjective interpretation. The result is that, although both research methods may produce useful information, the information produced by a focus group is less trustworthy than the information produced by a survey.

Second, scientific research follows a systematic set of procedures to provide for the uniform collection of data. This process helps ensure that each participant in a study gets treated the same way and that all participant responses get measured the same way. When focus groups are conducted, responses to questions are recorded verbatim and interpreted within the larger context of the group discussion. There is no formal, systematic method for measuring participant responses.

In fact, this is a strength of focus groups in that it allows each participant to express individual opinions, lets participants respond to each other, and allows the moderator to ask follow-up questions. It also is a weakness of focus groups, however, because measurement of participant responses is inexact and subjective. When a formal survey is conducted, systematic measurement methods typically include the use of numerical, or numerically based, scales. The use of such scales ensures that, to the extent possible, each participant's responses get measured and recorded in the same way. As a result, the use of systematic measures and an established process or set of procedures helps make a research method formal or scientific.

Third, scientific research results use a representative sample to the greatest extent possible, and the limitations of samples that are not completely representative are well understood. Researchers draw a sample and project research results to a population because it is uncommon (and usually impractical and unnecessary) for researchers to collect information from every member of a population. Instead, information typically is gathered from a selected subset, or sample, of population members. Statisticians have shown that a census is not necessary to gather accurate, reliable data in most instances. When probability-based sampling methods and a sample of appropriate size are used, they help ensure that the behaviors and attitudes of sample members reliably depict the range of behaviors and attitudes found in a population. The result is a sample that is representative, or has the same distribution of characteristics as the population from which it was drawn. In reality, no sample is perfectly representative; however, samples collected using probability methods have more trustworthiness than other samples.

This type of trustworthiness is called external validity or projectability. That is, survey results can be projected from a sample to a population with a certain level of confidence (which we can calculate mathematically). In practical terms, focus group results generally lack external validity, or projectability, because participants normally are selected using a nonprobability sampling method and the number of participants is small—too small to represent all members of a target audience with any degree of reliability. Scientific research, however, uses a probability-based sampling method and has a sample size sufficient to represent the target audience members from which it is drawn.

Fourth, researchers should be able to reproduce the results of formal research projects. This is known as replication. If the results of a project were unique to a single study, we would conclude they may be biased, perhaps because of faulty sampling procedures or problems with the data-collection process. When study results are replicable, they provide accurate information for the population under study.

Returning to the focus group example, the results of focus groups are largely unique to a single study. Differences among groups arise because of differences in participants' experiences, opinions, observations, and the like. More important, researchers cannot know with certainty how accurate focus group results are because their findings lack external validity. Researchers commonly conduct multiple focus groups with similar audiences hoping to avoid highly unusual results that do not represent the characteristics of the population under study. When a formal survey is conducted using probability-based sampling methods, however, researchers can have a high level of confidence that the results of their project are not unique to their study, but reflect the characteristics of the population from which the sample was drawn. The ability of other researchers to replicate research findings is an essential characteristic of formal, scientific research.

A research project generally is considered formal to the extent that it incorporates the characteristics of objectivity, systematic collection of data, representative samples, and replicable results into its design. The following discussion of scientific research methods is designed to introduce you to the range of possibilities available for research projects. We begin with a review of survey research, followed by a discussion of experimental research designs, and media content analyses. Because of the wide application of survey research to public relations, more specific aspects of survey research design are discussed.

SURVEY RESEARCH OVERVIEW

Survey research is used extensively by organizations in different fields including all levels of government, political organizations, mass media corporations, educational institutions, entertainment conglomerates, financial institutions, and other product manufacturers and service providers. In public relations, the purpose of survey research is to collect accurate measurements of people's attitudes, beliefs, and behaviour by asking them questions. Organizations commonly turn to survey research when they want to understand their target audiences' awareness, opinions, attitudes, knowledge, behavioral motivations, media use, and other information necessary for successful campaign implementation or evaluation.

Research is useful at all stages of the Programme-planning, implementation, and evaluation process. Survey research, more specifically, often is used in the planning and evaluation phases of a campaign. In the campaign planning phase, precampaign surveys help practitioners establish target audience benchmarks so campaign goals can be set. If one of the purposes of a campaign is to increase target audience awareness of a client's product, for example, current audience awareness levels must be established so appropriate goals and objectives can be determined. In this way, precampaign research findings provide a point of reference for the campaign.

Postcampaign surveys are used as a part of campaign evaluation to help determine whether goals and objectives have been accomplished. If a Programme aims to increase target audience awareness of a client's product by 20%, a postcampaign survey is one of the ways practitioners can determine the campaign has met its goals. Simply put, campaign outcomes are determined by comparing postcampaign research results with precampaign benchmarks. Postcampaign research also may serve as "between-campaign" research. That is, many organizations simply transition from one or more existing campaigns to new campaigns without stopping to conduct new research at every point between campaigns. In these cases, postcampaign research may serve some precampaign research purposes when additional Programmes are in the planning or early implementation stages.

Sometimes surveys and other forms of research are conducted during a campaign to provide intermediate campaign evaluations. This monitoring helps determine whether a campaign is on course. In such a case, research results are used to monitor campaign progress and to make corrections in campaign strategies and tactics.

In addition, surveys generally fall into one of two broad categories. Descriptive surveys document current circumstances and conditions, and generally describe what exists in a population. The federal government, for example, uses its Current Population Survey to determine the total number of adults who are unemployed in the United States. Voters are regularly surveyed by political candidates, special interest groups, and the media to determine the level of support for a particular candidate or policy initiative, or to understand

and predict election outcomes. Most applied public relations research projects are descriptive in nature.

Analytical surveys, on the other hand, attempt to explain why certain circumstances, attitudes and behaviors exist among members of a specific population. This type of survey research is likely to rely on advanced forms of statistical analysis to test hypotheses concerning the relationship among a group of variables under study. Academic researchers, for example, commonly study the relationship between exposure to negative political advertising and attitudes about politics and political participation.

In many cases, surveys serve both descriptive and analytical purposes. In each instance, practitioners, or a PR research outfit, follow formal procedures and use a systematic process to ensure the data collected are objective, reliable, and accurate. Regardless of the use of a survey, most survey research projects generally follow the same planning process. Initially, researchers determine the objectives of the research project. Next, researchers design the study. During this phase of a survey they determine the population and sampling procedures used in the project, select a specific interview method, and design and pretest the survey instrument or questionnaire. Then, the research team collects, edits, and codes data. Finally, researchers analyze and interpret results.

Survey Planning

Initially, the most important aspect of survey research planning involves identification of the goals and objectives of the research project. This normally involves identifying a research problem and the potential hypotheses and research questions a project will address. Campaign practitioners often give this aspect of a research project relatively brief attention because they are busy, and purposes of many projects appear obvious. However, the most successful research projects are those that have a high degree of direction. Surveys that lack direction often fail to live up to their potential as a planning or evaluation tool. For this reason, although applied research projects typically use research questions, practitioners may find it useful to think about expected research outcomes as a way to formalize their expectations concerning the results of a research project.

Survey Sampling

Sample selection procedures depend on survey objectives. Sampling procedures range from convenient to complex. They also vary in terms of their trustworthiness. A scientific technique called probability sampling, usually provides an accurate and reliable understanding of the characteristics of a population when sampling methods are used correctly. For this reason, the use of proper sampling methods is one of the most critical aspects of any research project and an especially important characteristic of scientific survey research.

DETERMINING THE DATA-COLLECTION METHOD

The three primary means of collecting survey data are personal interviews, mail surveys, and telephone surveys. Computer-assisted data collection, through online bulletin boards for example, also is growing in usage as informational needs and technology resources make its use practical. Selecting a proper data-collection method is critical to the success of a research project, and each method of data collection has its own strengths and weaknesses. There is no single best survey research method, but there is almost always a best survey research method to use given the limitations and requirements of a research project.

The choices at first may seem overwhelming. If the purpose of a project is to interview business professionals working in telecommunications industries, for example, telephone and interpersonal interviewing probably are poor choices because participants will be too busy to respond to a researcher's request for information. Respondents can fill out mail surveys at their convenience, however, so this method shows more promise with this group of respondents. In addition, mail surveys tend to cost less. If time is a major concern, however, regular mail surveys might not be the best research method because it takes longer to complete a project. Completion times for mail surveys typically range from a few weeks to several weeks or more if multiple mailings are necessary. Given time concerns, an electronic-mail survey may be a viable option for data collection. There may be significant sampling limitations in the use of such a survey, however, making it less appealing. There also may be other research methods to consider.

Research professionals must address various important issues when considering data-collection methods. Selecting an appropriate survey method is crucial to the successful completion of a research project.

Questionnaire Design

Proper questionnaire design contributes significantly to the trustworthiness of survey results. Good survey questions, when combined with appropriate data-collection methods, produce accurate responses. Poor survey questions, or inappropriate data-collection methods, produce untrustworthy results that can misinform public relations managers.

Poorly designed questionnaires often bias participants' responses. In this case, researchers are no longer measuring respondents' true attitudes, opinions, and behaviors, but instead are measuring manufactured participant "responses" they have created through a poorly designed questionnaire. These responses are not useful because they simply do not represent the true responses of research participants or the target publics they represent. A public relations campaign or other Programme based on such erroneous information is likely to fail. Erroneous information may worsen situations in which practitioners use research as the basis for problem solving.

Several questionnaire characteristics that seem relatively unimportant can bias participant responses, including question wording, question response categories, and question order. In addition, when interviews are administered by another person either face to face or over the telephone, interviewers can bias survey results as they interact with participants.

Data Collection

Data collection typically is the next step in the survey research process, and in many respects it is the beginning of the final phase of a research project. By this point, the researcher has made many of the most difficult decisions, and, although there may be surprises, research projects that are well designed tend to run relatively smoothly. Practitioners' levels of involvement in data collection range from managing all aspects of data collection to leaving all aspects of data collection to a research project manager or field service provider. Although practitioners may leave projects in the hands of capable managers with relative confidence, it generally is in their best interest to monitor data collection at least to some extent. Occasionally, practitioners need to make critical decisions concerning data collection. When survey response rates appear unusually low or respondents do not understand a question, for example, practitioners should be involved in determining the best solution. A minimum level of practitioner involvement is warranted during data collection to help ensure the knowledge gathered will best serve the purposes of the research project.

Editing and Coding

Editing and coding are the processes used to translate the information collected in questionnaires into a form suitable for statistical analysis. When a computer-assisted telephone interviewing (CATI) system is used, editing may not be necessary. When interviewers record participant responses using paper and pencil, however, some editing is usually necessary. Editing questionnaires typically involves checking responses to eliminate or correct incomplete or unintelligible answers. Questionnaires should be edited by a supervisor during data collection to detect errors and provide rapid feedback to their source (often an interviewer who is not paying careful attention). Particular attention should be given to missing answers and inconsistencies or a lack of uniformity among interviewers, because interviewer differences in wording questions or recording participant responses introduces error.

Editing may be necessary when a questionnaire has open-ended responses or other data that need categorization. Editing is best conducted by a few trained supervisors working with a fixed set of rules. Using these rules, editors typically place responses into mutually exclusive and exhaustive categories to facilitate data analysis. Often unseen intricacies are involved in this type of editing, requiring a high degree of consistency among editors to generate reliable results.

Coding is the process of preparing the data for computer analysis. The essential task in coding is to translate survey data into quantified form so it can be easily accessed and analyzed. Each survey project should have a code book, which is a column-by-column explanation of the responses and their corresponding code numbers. Coding questionnaires consists of reading each question, referring to the code book, and assigning the appropriate code for the respondent's answers. These data are then put into a computer for analysis.

Analysis and Interpretation

Statistical analysis and interpretation is the next step in survey research. Although a thorough discussion of statistical procedures is beyond the scope of this text, a brief review of commonly used analytical techniques appears.

Survey Critique

Survey research can be an interesting and effective means of studying public relations issues and publics. A primary advantage of survey research is that a project can be conducted relatively quickly. As noted, not all research methods are quick, but telephone surveys and some forms of personal interviews may be conducted in a relatively short time. Cost may be an advantage, as well. The cost of most survey research is reasonable considering the amount of information gathered. In addition, different methods of data collection provide for cost control through the selection and implementation of more or less expensive survey methods. The relatively low cost and ease of implementation make survey research attractive to communication managers.

Nevertheless, no research method is foolproof, and survey research has its limitations. First, survey research cannot provide direct evidence of causation. When evaluating campaign outcomes, for example, survey research cannot prove with certainty that a campaign has had a particular effect on target audience opinions, attitudes, and behaviors. In addition, researchers occasionally attempt to specify causes when research results do not support such conclusions. For example, if survey research indicates boating accidents increase as ice cream sales increase, we might be tempted to conclude ice cream is a culprit in boating accidents. Of course, nothing could be further from the truth. Both ice cream sales and boating accidents simply increase as the weather warms up, and they clearly are not related in terms of a cause-and-effect outcome. Although this example is absurd, researchers need to beware of making conclusions that are equally, if perhaps more subtly, absurd using research data that do not support their "findings."

Other weaknesses of survey research are specific to the data-collection method used in a project. Large personal interview surveys may be costly, for example, requiring researchers to train field supervisors and interviewers, as well as covering travel expenses and other costs associated with interviews. Similarly, mail surveys typically take longer than other survey research methods to complete because of the time associated with mailing the questionnaires to a sample and receiving responses back from participants. It is important to know the specific strengths and weaknesses associated with each method of data collection, and these are discussed in detail.

Other concerns associated with survey research apply in some way to all survey data-collection methods. Sometimes respondents are inaccurate in the answers they provide, for example, whether in a direct interview or on a mailed questionnaire. These responses introduce error into survey results. The reasons for this problem are variable. Sometimes, respondents simply do not remember information about themselves or their activities. Rather than admit they do not know the answer, they may simply make up a response. This also is a problem when respondents lack knowledge regarding the subject of a question, but answer the question rather than admit they do not know.

Respondents may also provide incorrect answers in an attempt to find favor with interviewers. Some survey questions include responses that are more socially desirable than alternative choices. In other instances, participants may simply choose to deceive researchers by providing incorrect answers to questions. At times, respondents may attempt to determine the purpose of a survey and provide the responses they think researchers are looking for. Survey results concerning complex subjects are further complicated by respondents who find it difficult to identify and explain their true feelings. As a result, practitioners should consider the potential drawbacks to the successful completion of a survey before a research project is started.

Despite the weaknesses of survey research, its benefits outweigh its drawbacks for many research projects. Survey research is particularly useful for description and association, a necessity given the largely exploratory and descriptive nature of many applied projects. A carefully prepared questionnaire contributes to results that are reliable and accurate. Telephone surveys, in particular, enable collection of a large amount of data within a short time at a reasonable cost. Given the needs of data collection, and the time and budget constraints placed on many research projects, survey research often is an excellent research method choice. This is why it is the method of formal research used most often by communication managers.

EXPERIMENTS

In the most basic sense, an experiment involves taking action and observing the consequences of that action. In a sense, experiments are a natural part of public relations because in most cases, practitioners take action of one sort or another and then gauge the effect of that action (in experimental language called a "treatment") on target audience opinions, attitudes, or behaviour. Although various study designs exist, generally an experiment requires at least one group of participants to receive a treatment (such as exposure to part of a public relations campaign). The effect of that treatment can be determined by comparing participants' before-treatrnent responses with their after-treatment responses on a series of questions designed to measure their opinions or attitudes, for example.

Experimental research designs can provide important contributions to public relations Programme planning and evaluation because they allow practitioners to isolate campaign variables and control them. This high degree of control allows researchers to use experimental designs to systematically examine variables that may or may not influence target audience members. If campaign planners want to determine voter responses to potential campaign advertisements, for example, they might measure the attitudes and projected voting behaviors of a relatively small sets of voters (perhaps 40 or 50), expose them to the advertising, and measure their attitudes and projected voting behaviour again. If no other variables were introduced in the process, the changes that took place from the first measurement to the second measurement would be due to the advertising.

In an applied setting, the use of true experiments is relatively rare. Given the previous political advertising example, campaign managers are more likely to conduct a focus group and get participant feedback on different advertising executions (called copytesting in advertising) than to conduct an experiment. As a rule, informal research methods such as focus groups produce results that are low in external validity and reliability, and there is no scientific basis for understanding the potential inaccuracies that exist in informal research. The result is that incorrect findings could be used as the basis for making important campaign decisions.

Controlled experiments, on the other hand, are the most powerful means of determining campaign effects because they can be used to determine causation. This is the primary benefit of experiments. From a scientific perspective, three conditions are necessary to determine causation. First, the cause (variable A) must precede the effect (variable B) in time. Second, a change in the first variable (A) must produce a change in the second variable (B). This is called concomitant variation, and the idea is that a change in one variable depends on a change in another variable, such as summer "causing" popsicle sales and boating accidents. Third, all other possible causes of an effect must be eliminated or controlled in the experiment. This ensures that the relationship between the variables is not caused by a third variable. By using experiments, researchers can examine and understand variable relationships under uncontaminated conditions. This allows them to develop greater insight into variable relationships, such as the effects of political advertisements on voters.

Researchers use systematic procedures when they conduct experiments. Initially, they select the setting for the experiment. Next, they design or plan the project. In this phase researchers decide how to measure and manipulate variables, select a specific study design, and develop and pretest the materials used in the experiment. Finally, researchers collect, analyze, and interpret data.

Settings

The two main settings in which researchers conduct experiments are in a research laboratory or similar facility used for research purposes and in the field. A laboratory setting is advantageous because it provides researchers with the ability to control almost all aspects of an experiment. By controlling outside influences, researchers can make exact determinations regarding the nature of the relationships between variables. Generally, the more controlled and precise an experiment is, the less error that is present. By controlling the conditions under which an experiment occurs, researchers can reduce the risk of contamination from unwanted, unplanned sources.

The artificial nature of research laboratories or similar facilities have disadvantages. Isolated research environments that are highly controlled to exclude potential interference are different from most real-life circumstances. In measuring voters' responses to televised political advertisements, for example, it would probably be better to test voters at home where they normally watch television. This environment is a natural setting that is likely to contain all the distractions and other influences people encounter when they watch television. It is in this environment that we would most likely get participants' most natural responses. Unfortunately, these distractions and other influences also are likely to change research results. This contamination makes the determination of causation nearly impossible.

Practitioners have to balance these advantages and disadvantages when choosing a design. When researchers pull people out of their natural settings and place them in controlled environments such as laboratories, they may react differently to the materials used in the experiment (televised political ads in this example) because this is not their normal viewing environment. Ultimately, the controlled artificiality of research settings tends to produce results high in internal validity (when a measure precisely reflects the concept that it is intended to measure) but low in external validity (the generalizability of results from a sample to a population).

Field experiments are conducted in the environment in which behaviors concerning the subject under study naturally occur. In other words, the "field" is the environment in which participants live, work, or relax. The dynamics and interactions of small groups, for example, may be studied at places where small groups of people naturally congregate such as common meeting areas in college dormitories. Field experiments tend to have a higher degree of external validity because the real-life settings used in field research are normal environments. The control available in field experiments, however, is rarely as tight as that available in laboratory experiments, because of the uncontrollable factors that exist in any natural environment.

Terms and Concepts

Before we discuss specific designs, we should briefly examine (or reexamine in some cases) some important terms so you have a better understanding of the research designs to be discussed. The basic purpose of an experiment is to determine causation. In an applied public relations setting, practitioners might be interested in determining the effect of a public relations campaign or Programme on the opinions, attitudes, and behaviors of target audience members. Each of these represent variables we are examining. In its simplest sense, a variable is a phenomenon or event that can be measured or manipulated.

In this case, the public relations Programme being tested is the independent variable. The independent variable is the variable that is manipulated in an experiment to see if it produces change in the dependent variable. Changes in the dependent variable depend on, or are caused by, the independent variable. If we wanted to examine the effects of potential campaign messages on target audience members, the messages are the independent variables. As independent variables, the campaign messages affect the dependent variables in the experiment, the opinions or attitudes of target audience members toward our organization.

In addition, we might manipulate the independent variable (the content of a campaign message) to determine how to make it more effective. We might consider a humorous message versus a serious message, for example. In this case, variable manipulation is a critical aspect of study design. We must make sure our humorous and serious messages are equal in terms of key points and features, so the only difference between the messages is the existence of humor or the lack of humor. If all other message characteristics are equal, any differences in participants' responses to the messages likely will be due to humor. This controlled experiment allows us to test the effect of humor on participants' responses to our message and gives us the scientific basis for determining cause and effect.

Initially, you may notice that in experimental research designs, subjects are assigned to a condition. A condition consists of all the people in an experiment who are treated the same way. In a source credibility experiment, for example, some participants are exposed to a message delivered by a high-credibility spokesperson, while other participants are exposed to a message delivered by a low-credibility spokesperson. Each group exposed to the same spokesperson in our example is part of the same condition.

Participants in the same condition are exposed to the same treatment. A treatment occurs when the participants in a condition are exposed to the same material, or stimulus, which typically contains the independent variable. Although it sounds confusing, it is really very simple. In the credibility experiment, for example, the message from a high-credibility source is one stimulus, and each participant who receives that stimulus receives the high-credibility treatment (these participants are in the same condition). In the same way, the message from a low-credibility source is a different stimulus. Participants exposed to the message from the low-credibility source receive the low-credibility treatment and are in the same condition.

Some participants may be placed in a condition in which they receive no treatment, or at least a meaningless treatment. These participants are in the control group or control condition. The control group contains people who are not exposed to any meaningful stimuli. Members of the control group can be used for comparison in an experiment because they receive no treatment; they are not exposed to an independent variable in any form. By using a control group, researchers can understand and control the effects of simply conducting the experiment on participants. In medical research, for example, one group of participants may receive an actual drug, whereas the control group members are given a placebo (sugar pills are commonly used). This allows researchers to determine the amount of patient improvement due to the new drug versus the amount of patient improvement due to other factors, including participants' improved mental outlook perhaps caused by the special medical attention they are receiving.

Finally, participants should be assigned to either a treatment condition or a control condition in a random manner. When random assignment is used, each participant has an equal chance of being included in a condition. Random assignment helps to eliminate the potential influence of outside variables that may hinder the determination of causation. If participant assignment is not random, researchers cannot be sure the participants in each condition are equal before exposure to experimental stimuli. When the participants in each condition are not equal, this is called selectivity bias. Random assignment helps ensure the differences detected in an experiment are caused by exposure to the stimuli and are not caused by differences among participants.

Research Designs

There are several potential ways to design an experiment, and, as long as an experiment allows for the determination of causation and addresses the need for internal and external validity, no single design is best. Instead, the best experimental design typically depends on the hypothesis or research questions, the nature of the independent and dependent variables, the availability of subjects, and the resources available for the project. The three experimental designs with the widest acceptance among social scientists are the pretest-posttest design with a control group, the posttest-only design with a control group, and the pretest-posttest design with additional control groups, commonly referred to as the Solomon four-group design.

The pretest-posttest design with a control group is a fundamental design of experimental research. It is widely used and applicable to a variety of different settings. When researchers use the pretest-posttest with control group design, they randomly assign subjects to two groups, or conditions, and initially measure the dependent variable (this is the pretest) for each group. An independent variable manipulation is then applied to one of the groups, followed by further testing to determine independent variable effects. The order of the research procedures, random assignment of subjects to conditions, and use of a control group helps eliminate or avoid many of the potential problems that threaten to ruin the internal validity of the experiment. Although a detailed discussion of these problems (called threats to validity) is beyond the scope of this book, readers may be interested in reading a short but important book by Campbell and Stanley (1963). Because each condition is the same and only one condition receives an experimental treatment, any significant differences that exist between participants in the conditions after the experimental manipulation have been caused by the treatment.

A second design that is commonly used in experimental research is the posttest-only design with a control group. In this research design, there is no pretest. Instead, subjects are randomly assigned to separate conditions. One group is exposed to the experimental manipulation (treatment). The treatment is followed by a posttest of both groups, and participants' dependent variable scores are compared. Pretesting, though an important part of experimental research, is not required to conduct a true experiment. Instead, the random assignment of participants to conditions allows researchers to assume participants in each condition are equal at the beginning of the experiment. The random assignment of subjects controls for selectivity biases. This design is especially useful to researchers when pretesting is unavailable or inconvenient, or may somehow interfere with the experiment.

The Solomon four-group design is a combination of the first two designs. The Solomon design uses four conditions, in conjunction with random assignment, to help control threats to validity and to allow researchers to determine unwanted effects of pretesting. Participants in the first condition receive a pretest, a treatment, and a posttest. Participants in the second condition receive a pretest and a posttest with no treatment. Those in the third condition receive no pretest, a treatment, and a posttest. Those in the final condition receive only a single measurement, the equivalent of a posttest. The Solomon four-group design is the most rigorous of the experiment designs, allowing researchers to separate and identify treatment effects independently of the effects of pretesting. In other words, researchers can figure out whether posttest scores changed because people learned how to answer the questions better from taking a pretest, as opposed to whether the experimental treatment explains the difference in posttest scores. The biggest drawbacks to the use of the four-group design are practical. Four groups are required to properly execute the design, requiring a high number of subjects and increased costs.

Various other designs may be used that are considered something other than fully experimental. These designs are most commonly considered preexperimental or quasiexperimental and include case studies and the one-group pretest-posttest design, among other design possibilities. Quasiexperimental studies suffer from design flaws because they lack control conditions and/or researchers use nonrandom procedures to assign participants to different conditions in an experiment. Quasiexperimental designs may be used for various purposes including exploration, but their methods cannot be considered scientific and their results, therefore, are not trustworthy.

It is often impossible or impractical to use probability sampling methods when recruiting research participants for studies. Instead, researchers commonly select participants using incidental, or convenience, samples in research experiments. Because research participants may not be completely representative of a target audience or other population, the results of an experiment may lack external validity, or generalizability from the sample to the population. In general, this is not as detrimental for explanatory research such as experiments as it is for descriptive research such as surveys.

Social processes and patterns of causal relationships are generally stable across populations and, because of this, are more generalizable than individual characteristics. In reality, the samples used in experiments are so small they would not be highly representative even if probability sampling were used. With this in mind, convenience sampling normally suffices in experiments when probability sampling is impossible or impractical. Even though probability sampling may be impossible, researchers use random assignment to ensure participants are equal in each condition in an experiment.

As with any other research or communication project, pretesting variable manipulations, measurements, and the procedures used in an experiment is necessary before data collection begins. Pretesting allows researchers to correct any deficiencies in the procedures used for data collection, as well as providing a check of independent variable manipulations. A manipulation check is particularly important in helping ensure the success of a study. A manipulation check is a procedure that ascertains whether something that was supposed to happen actually did happen. For example, if one community was supposed to see a scary type of public service announcement and another community was supposed to see a humorous type of announcement, a manipulation check would determine whether the people in the communities thought the scary message was actually scary and that the humorous message was actually funny.

Finally, researchers must develop a procedure for telling participants what the purpose of the study is and how the study's results will be used. Participants' questions are answered at this time, in a process called debriefing. Debriefing allows researchers to eliminate the potential harms, however small, that may result from research participation. Debriefing should be comprehensive enough to remove any effects on participants that may have been created during a research project.

Bias in Data Collection, Analysis, and Interpretation

It is essential for researchers to collect, analyze, and interpret data in a careful manner. Practitioners should pay particular attention to the introduction of bias during data collection. Bias may be introduced in several ways, including through the behaviour of researchers. Any changes in participant behaviour due to the actions of researchers introduce bias into the experiment, unless the behaviour of the experimenter is intended to be part of the study. Researchers may inadvertently encourage a behaviour they are looking for through demonstrations of tension or relief, for example. One way researchers control unintended experimenter influences is through the use of automated procedures and equipment such as VCRs and videotapes. Experimenter bias may also be minimized by using researchers who are unaware of the purpose of a study, or researchers who have differing expectations regarding experimental outcomes.

Experiment Critique

When conducted properly, formal experiments allow researchers to isolate variables and establish causation. This is a powerful benefit that is provided only by properly designed and executed experiments. In laboratory experiments, researchers have a high degree of control over the research environment, independent and dependent variables, and the selection and assignment of subjects. This high degree of control and isolation of research environments provides conditions that are free from the competing influences of normal activity and ideal for examining independent and dependent variable relationships. Although field experiments do not allow as high a degree of control as laboratory experiments, they generally provide enough control for researchers to make determinations of causation when properly conducted.

Another benefit of experiments to practitioners is their ease of replication. Since the variables and manipulations used in experiments are typically made available to other researchers, it is common for social scientists to replicate research findings. Replication may take the form of an identical experiment or one that provides replication under slightly different conditions. The successful replication of research findings contributes to increased confidence in the validity and generalizability of research findings.

Finally, the cost of experimental research can be low when compared with other research methods. Laboratory research, in particular, tends to be limited in scope requiring relatively little time and relatively few subjects. These requirements often combine to provide a high degree of power at a relatively low cost.

There are two primary disadvantages to using experiments: the artificial situation and the introduction of bias. Although isolation and control are necessary in the determination of causation, research environments may be so isolated and so controlled that they do not represent environments found in natural social settings. Here, the external validity, or generalizability, of research findings may be hindered. The artificiality of laboratory research settings presents a particular problem in applied campaign studies because it does not reflect the busy, competitive environment in which most communication campaigns are conducted. In this instance, the generalizability of research findings from laboratory experiments to public relations campaign settings may be limited.

A second disadvantage of experimental research is the potential for introducing bias. Bias may be introduced through various sources during an experiment. The result is that research outcomes are inaccurate and provide a poor basis for campaign planning and execution.

Finally, experiments can be challenging to conduct. It can be difficult, for example, to measure complex human processes using a series of simple questions. It may be that participants have never considered the reasons for some of their attitudes and behaviors, and they may find it difficult to identify their responses. Sometimes, participants simply are unable to express their feelings, even if it only involves answering a few questions. It also can be difficult to manipulate the stimuli used in experiments or execute procedures with the care necessary to determine causation. In fact, it is possible to plan an experiment that is virtually impossible to conduct. Experiments, like all research methods, are useful only for specific situations, and their limitations should be considered carefully.

CONTENT ANALYSIS

Content analysis is a scientific research method used for describing communication content such as message characteristics in a quantitative, or numerical, form. Many public relations practitioners work to place messages in the media on a regular basis and continually monitor and track media coverage concerning issues, events, and clients. Right or wrong, public relations clip files have long served as the basis for evaluating public relations campaign success and often are seen as a critical measure of practitioners' achievements. Evaluating the contents of a clip file or other important media messages—including the messages of competing organizations—often is difficult. The sheer volume of material can make even a basic description and analysis a daunting task. When additional information is desired concerning specific content attributes of different stories, the tone of media coverage, or the balance of media portrayals, for example, the task becomes seemingly impossible.

Content analysis is a research technique used for the objective, systematic, and quantitative description of specific aspects of communication. Content analyses are objective because their results are not based on the informal observations and biases of those conducting the study, but instead rely on an objective classification system. They are systematic because a set of procedures is established and a formal process is followed when media content is analyzed. Content analyses are quantitative because the results of the classification process produce numerical classifications of content that are subjected to appropriate statistical analyses. The result is a scientific (that is, trustworthy) description of communication content in terms of specific themes, styles, and techniques.

If an organization wanted to better understand the ways it was portrayed in the media, for example, it might decide to have an employee comb through a collection of media to determine frequency of coverage, evaluate the general tone of the stories, and note recurring themes and major issues. Alternatively, the organization could conduct a formal content analysis. In this case, researchers would determine the aspects of media coverage most important to the company, and the media content would then be categorized and analyzed quantitatively based on the critical components of media coverage. The results and conclusions from such a study would be both sophisticated and accurate, and would provide an unbiased assessment of the media coverage concerning the organization. Study findings could serve as the basis for future media relations efforts or might be part of an analysis of the messages of competing organizations. The results also might serve as a benchmark if the company decided to undertake an effort to improve its media coverage.

Content analyses typically require several steps similar to those used in survey research. In fact, a content analysis is a lot like a survey, except that researchers collect samples of messages rather than of people. Initially, investigators identify a research problem and develop research questions or hypotheses. Next, they choose an appropriate media sample. Then, they determine procedures and categories for coding the content. Researchers must train those who code the data, and they usually conduct a small pilot study (the equivalent of a pretest) to ensure the study is well designed. Content coding takes place once the pilot study proves successful, followed by the data analysis and interpretation.

Research Problem and Questions/Hypothesis Development

As with any other research project, investigators should clearly map out the purpose of the study, including any problems that they must address, in the first phase of a content analysis. This helps researchers design a useful study with realistic procedures. A good research design clearly integrates the procedures for selecting the sample, the content categories and other aspects of the analysis, and study design into a comprehensive plan. By implication, an investigator must determine the reason for the study, specify the evidence needed to test ideas or relationships, and know the methods of analysis that will be used once the data are gathered and coded.

Content analysis can apply to almost any form of communication. Researchers most often use it to address research questions or hypotheses concerning specific message attributes. This may include an analysis of messages over time, or an analysis of messages directed to different audiences (such as trade publications versus general interest magazines). Often, analysts examine the relationship between two or more variables, such as the mention of a campaign theme along with the tenor of a message.

Researchers sometimes go beyond description to make inferences about the origins of messages based on the results of a content analysis. Such analyses generally focus on the author of a message to associate authorship with meanings and values inherent in the messages analyzed, such as to determine whether certain reporters or media outlets favor particular types of story themes. Finally, too often researchers erroneously use content analyses to make inferences about the effects of messages on receivers, such as effects of violent content on children's behaviour. Content analyses conducted for this purpose are fatally flawed because they make several untenable assumptions. As explains, people interpret similar messages differently. Exposure to a message does not lead to uniform message effects. Simply put, content analyses do not allow researchers to determine causation.

Sample Selection

Researchers must select the messages to analyze after they have determined research questions, hypotheses, or both. First, they determine the body of messages, or population, from which the sample will be drawn, just as the survey designer chooses a population of people to study. In this process, also known as defining the "universe" or "sampling frame," investigators choose the body of content from which they will draw their sample, such as popular magazines published during the past six months. Just as with survey research, content analysts usually do not try to analyze all relevant messages (this would be a census). The sheer volume of potentially relevant messages almost always makes some form of sampling necessary, especially given the time and monetary limitations that accompany most research projects. Researchers should make sure the message population is comprehensive and logically consistent with the purposes and goals of the study.

It is important to distinguish between all the content potentially relevant to a study and a subset, or sample, of content needed to answer research questions or test hypotheses. Various techniques lend themselves to the selection of materials for analysis.

Content analyses may require some type of multistage sampling involving sample selection procedures at two or more levels. At the initial stage of sample selection researchers might select specific media sources—daily newspapers during an election cycle, for example—from among all possible sources. At a second stage of sampling, researchers might select specific stories from each selected newspaper. Additional stages may be necessary, as well. Researchers may find it advantageous to first select specific pages, for example, and then select specific stories as an additional sampling stage.

Units of Analysis

Researchers must determine the unit of analysis and content categories used in a study before data collection begins because content can be analyzed in different forms. Each form of content analyzed is reduced to a unit for measurement and evaluation. A unit of analysis is an individually distinct portion of content, meaning the element researchers actually count. Units of analysis can include stories or articles, words or terms, themes, paragraphs, characters, and more.

In a study designed to examine the media's portrayal of an organization, for example, the units of analysis may include positive, negative, or mixed stories about the corporation, specific aspects of the corporation's image in stories, the mention of specific corporate Programmes in stories, the names of competing organizations mentioned, and other relevant information. Specification of the units of analysis can present challenges and generally requires pretesting through trial and error. Often researchers begin with a rough-draft definition of a unit. Then they analyze a sample of representative content to determine problems in identification. Such a procedure typically results in the modification and further refinement of unit descriptions.

Categories of Analysis

Researchers code and classify units of analysis, placing them into categories created for a study. For example, each article may be labeled as favorable or unfavorable. Well-constructed categories are essential, forming the substance of an investigation. Researchers who develop content categories that are vaguely drawn or poorly articulated will produce a study with inferior quality and limited usefulness. To be effective, category systems should be mutually exclusive, exhaustive, and reliable.

Categories are mutually exclusive when a unit of analysis can be placed into only one category. If a unit simultaneously falls into more than one category, revisions are necessary for either or both categories. One means of avoiding problems related to exclusivity is to have category definitions that possess a high degree of specificity. When category units are well defined, fewer questions are likely regarding unit placement among categories.

Categories must be exhaustive, in addition to being mutually exclusive. Categories that are exhaustive provide space for every existing unit of analysis. It is necessary to expand content categories when units are discovered that are not covered by existing categories. When only a few miscellaneous units are not covered by existing category systems, researchers may use an "other" category.

Finally, the category system must be reliable. To be considered reliable, different coders should agree on the placement of units of analyses within categories most of the time. This is called intercoder reliability. Content categories that are poorly defined and lack specificity generally suffer from low intercoder reliability. Conversely, weld-defined category systems increase intercoder reliability. The extensive pretesting of sample data for unit placement win helps researchers develop and refine categories until they are mutually exclusive, exhaustive, and reliable.

Coding Content

Coding content involves the placement of units of analysis into content categories. This process is generally the most time-consuming aspect of content analysis, requiring researchers to train coders, develop a pilot study, and code the data. Reliability is critical in content analysis because content analyses are supposed to produce objective results. Researchers must use reliable measures to produce study results that are objective (Wimmer & Dominick, 2000). The measures used in a study are reliable when repeated measurement of the same material produces the same results. Normally, the same set of data is coded by two coders working independently. Analysts can compare the results of each coder's work using a sample of data to determine the level of accuracy between the coders. This produces a test of intercoder reliability. Intercoder reliability can be calculated using one of several methods.

In this formula, M represents the number of coding decisions agreed on by coders, and each n refers to the total number of coding decisions made by the first and second coder, respectively. This formula has some limitations, but it is simple and easy to use. Readers may be interested in using other formulas depending on their need for a more sophisticated measure of reliability, but Holsti's method is generally acceptable in most content analyses.

The thorough training of coders generally results in a more reliable analysis. It is helpful to have several training sessions in which coders work on sample data. The results are compared between coders and differences are discussed and possibly recoded. Detailed instruction sheets should also be provided to coders. Rigorous training efforts result in higher intercoder reliability. After a thorough training period, a pilot study may be conducted to check intercoder reliability. As a result of the pilot study, researchers may need to revise definitions and category boundaries, and coding sheets may need to be altered. This process should continue until coders are comfortable with the materials and procedures, and a high degree of reliability is maintained.

Finally, the content is coded. The use of standardized score sheets developed during training aids in the quick and accurate collection of data. Templates may also be used to measure media space. Broadcast media used for analysis is often taped allowing coders to start and stop the tape at their convenience. As a final note, researchers can enhance data collection with the use of computers, which they also can use to tabulate results.

Content Analysis Critique

The objective and systematic nature of this research method often helps researchers produce content descriptions and analyses that are high in validity and reliability, and avoid the subjective interpretations of less rigorous methods of analyzing content. In addition, many content analyses are inexpensive to conduct and can be used to examine content as it evolves over long periods. This gives researchers an important perspective not easily available in other scientific methods of research. Further, although most research methods typically pose little risk to participants, content analyses involve even less risk because human participants are not part of the population under investigation. Together, these benefits make content analysis an attractive and useful research method.

Content analysis should be used carefully despite its potential usefulness. Kerlinger (1973) suggested that content analysis is not an easy method to use correctly. The primary concerns include problems of reliability, validity, and inference. The concept of reliability is of maximum importance in content analysis. A high degree of reliability may be particularly difficult to achieve when analyzing content such as negative political advertising. Determining whether a negative advertisement contains a direct attack on an opponent, for example, may involve making several slight distinctions between ads.

Does an ad in which a candidate is referred to, but not named, contain a direct reference? Do ads that refer to a candidate's political party and/or position without mentioning the candidate by name contain a direct reference? Do ads that contain negative testimonials without naming a candidate contain direct references? Even determining whether an ad is negative or positive often involves making judgment calls. These types of difficulties are common in content analyses. They typically create problems for coders and contribute to low levels of reliability in content studies.

Validity in content studies is typically determined by the degree to which an instrument actually measures what it is supposed to measure. Validity is directly connected to the procedures used in content analysis. When sampling designs are incorrect, if categories are not mutually exclusive and exhaustive, or if reliability is low, the results of a content analysis possess a low degree of validity.

The final concern regarding the use of content analysis involves problems associated with inference. The strength of most content analyses depends on their ability to provide a precise description of communication content. Content studies often purport, however, to present conclusions and interpretations of wider application than the content itself. Such interpretations are untrustworthy. Practitioners purchasing content analytic services from an agency should carefully evaluate the claims made. Several reputable firms, such as Ketchum Public Relations's Publicity Tracking System, offer specialized and sophisticated content analysis techniques. The problem comes when a company equates content analysis with public opinion analysis. Remember that public opinion resides in the public, not in the content of media messages.

Formal research methods provide essential information for the public relations manager. Because formal methods offer objectivity, systematic data collection, representative samples, and replicable designs, they provide trustworthy information. Only dependable information can help practitioners accurately describe situations and publics, predict the outcome of an election, understand the reasons why public opinion seems to have turned against an organization, and exert some control over what happens in the future.

Each formal method has its strengths and weaknesses, which means that each method can be used well or misused badly. As a result, a good understanding of the benefits and limitations of each method can help the managers do independent, in-house research. It also enables managers to knowledgeably weigh the promises and strategies of research firms, and to purchase reputable services that provide useful information at a reasonable cost.

Chapter 10

Survey Research

A survey is a method of collecting information directly from members of a population. It usually involves interviews and questionnaires that participants fill out alone or with the assistance of an interviewer. This method of research has experienced an enormous surge in usage over the past several years and today is a regular part of many organizations' public relations Programmes. Survey research is an indispensable part of organizations' attempts to monitor their internal and external environments; solve complex problems; understand the opinions, attitudes, and behaviors of key target audience members; track public opinion; engage in sophisticated public relations campaign planning and evaluation; and, in some cases, seek media attention for an organization or client.

What is responsible for the rapid increase in the use of survey research? Organizations have increasingly felt the need to understand the opinions, attitudes, and behavioral motivations of their key target audience members, including legislators and government regulators, community members, consumers, employees, and other important groups. The environments in which organizations operate are more competitive; target audiences are more sophisticated and, in some cases, given to greater activism. Single-issue activist groups, employees, and others are more likely to use the media to engage organizations in public "debates" using publicity and promotion techniques to gain the attention and support of the media, community watchdog groups, government regulators and key target audiences.

Practitioners want to ensure a high level of performance for their Programmes and campaigns, particularly as the costs of a campaign or Programme increase, or as organizational certainty about a campaign or Programme decreases. In this case, survey research serves as a kind of insurance, providing critical information to practitioners as they plan and implement public relations Programmes and campaigns. Valid, reliable information replaces practitioners' reliance on past practices, hunches, industry standards, as previously noted. In these circumstances, survey research is an invaluable part of public relations planning and problem solving.

Finally, organizational management wants to know how resources are being used and the return on investment they provide to an organization. Practitioners commonly have used favorable media coverage, key story placement, media clip counts, and similar methods to communicate the value of their publicity and promotions work to organizational management and clients.

Clients and managers are initially impressed when practitioners bring in large clip-filled binders and low cost-per-impression numbers. They grow skeptical, however, when larger, more important questions are asked about the effect of public relations activities on the attitudes and behaviors of key target audience members. In this instance, survey research provides a more sophisticated means of tracking changes in the opinions, attitudes, and behaviors of target audience members, and it is an indispensable tool for practitioners communicating the benefits of public relations activities to organizations and clients.

These are among the most critical issues practitioners face and are a large part of the reason practitioners' use of survey research has increased so rapidly over the past several years. As noted, surveys generally are descriptive or analytical in nature. Descriptive surveys characterize conditions and circumstances as they exist in a population, and analytical surveys attempt to explain why current conditions exist. In fact, many surveys serve both purposes, and this often meets practitioners' and organizations' needs for information. As a group, survey research methods also possess several advantages in the collection, analysis, and interpretation of information.

Researchers primarily use mail, telephone and personal interviews to conduct surveys, and are increasingly using electronic surveys in different forms. Researchers can use each method in a relatively straightforward approach or adapt a method to reach new audiences or to meet the demands of a particular research situation. In addition, technology such as the Internet is contributing to the development of new survey research methods. In a typical survey, researchers initially set objectives for a research project, and then design the study. When researchers design a study, they normally select a population and establish sampling procedures, select a survey method, and design and pretest a questionnaire. Next, members of a research team typically collect, edit, and code data. Finally, researchers analyze and interpret the results.

Clients and organizations, often looking to make quick decisions, frequently want to identify the single "best" survey research method. The reality is there is no best method of survey research, and it is a risky oversimplification to sort methods based on a scale of "goodness" or strengths and weaknesses. The method that is best for a project depends on various factors. Beyond the informational requirements of a project, researchers must consider the target audience, the survey topic or topics, and the importance of reliability and validity. In addition, a project's budget and time frame often have a disproportionately large effect on survey-method selection.

As Dillman pointed out, the question of which method is best cannot be answered in abstract terms. The potential advantages and disadvantages of each method do not apply equally, or even at all, to every survey situation. Choosing the most appropriate research method is critical, and, for this reason, the use of a survey method must be considered in relation to the needs and constraints of each situation.

With this in mind, it is beneficial for practitioners to understand each survey research method. The flexibility and adaptability of different survey methods inevitably leads to conflicting suggestions from researchers or others concerning the "best" survey method to use for a project. Practitioners serve their own interest by understanding at least some of the key issues associated with the use of one survey method over another in a research situation, as well as other critical aspects of survey implementation such as issues associated with the use of probability versus nonprobability sampling. This understanding allows them to make an informed decision and makes them sophisticated consumers of the research products they, in effect, purchase. The remainder of this chapter presents each of the primary survey research methods broadly and includes information about the potential benefits and limitations of these methods.

MAIL SURVEYS

Mail surveys are conducted by mailing a questionnaire to a sample of individuals. Participants fill out the questionnaires on their own and mail the surveys back to the researcher. A cover letter is mailed with the questionnaire to explain the purpose of the survey and encourage sample members to respond. Stamped, addressed reply envelopes typically are enclosed to encourage respondents to complete the surveys and mail them back to researchers. Researchers often use mail surveys because of their low cost and ease of administration. If a mailing list is available (and it often is), it is relatively easy to use it as the source of a probability-based sample.

Several challenges face researchers using survey research including the length of time it takes to complete a project and the relatively low response rates. Despite these concerns, the low cost and ease of administration of mail surveys are among the advantages that make them an attractive choice.

Mail Survey Considerations

There are many nuanes of successful survey research, and this is especially true of mail surveys. A mail survey is a self-administered questionnaire. This requires that the cover letter and questionnaire be carefully constructed and written to optimize the participation rate of sample members. Unfortunately, no matter how well a questionnaire and cover letter are written, this is not enough to ensure the success of a mail survey. The result is that mail surveys often suffer from the lowest rates of response among the primary survey research methods, despite researchers' best efforts to encourage participation. Although there are many keys to a successful mail survey project, practitioners should pay special attention to the cover letter and questionnaire, and the sampling method and response rate to ensure the success of mail survey.

A well-written cover letter is critical to the success of a survey because it must introduce a survey to potential respondents who are busy and uninterested, and motivate them to fill out the survey and return it immediately. A cover letter usually is the only opportunity a researcher has to pique the interest of sample members, establish a minimal level of rapport, and anticipate and answer key questions. The difficulty of writing a good cover letter is increased because a long, dense letter that satisfactorily answers everyone's questions will discourage careful reading, or worse, will cause potential respondents to simply throw the questionnaire in the trash with the day's junk mail.

The first two paragraphs of a cover letter usually explain who is sponsoring the study and what the study is about, and convince the reader the study is useful. Later paragraphs are used to convince readers that their response is critical and assure them of confidentially. All of this must be accomplished without biasing participants' responses. Writing an effective cover letter can be difficult and perplexing. Given the importance of the cover letter to the success of a mail survey, researchers should draft and pretest different letters to ensure they have written a compelling letter.

Mail surveys also require the use of carefully written and pretested questionnaires. The mail questionnaire requires more careful writing and construction than any other type of questionnaire, because it must be completely self-explanatory. An attractive questionnaire of reasonable length with plenty of white space and clear, simple instructions is a good start. The absence of an interviewer means no opportunity for interviewers to encourage survey response, gloss over poorly written questions or instructions, or answer even basic participant questions.

Although a telephone number or E-mail address can be provided for such purposes, participants rarely use them. In fact, participants should not need to contact researchers to understand questions and instructions. Instead, the instructions and questions used in mail surveys must be written so they are uniformly understood by as many potential respondents as possible. Poorly written questions decrease the reliability and validity of survey results, and sample members who do not understand questions or instructions are unlikely to participate, resulting in low response rates.

Pretesting a questionnaire is essential to ensure that readers understand survey instructions, questions, and response categories. When a questionnaire is pretested, individuals who are similar to sample members in terms of key sample characteristics—such as age, education level, work experience, or other relevant qualities—actually complete the survey, making note of confusing or unclear questions and instructions. Other aspects of the questionnaire also are noted and discussed at length with researchers such as length of time needed to complete the survey and various features of questionnaire design. There are many ways to pretest a questionnaire, and no single method is particularly advantageous. The key is to pretest all written material potential respondents will receive, preferably several times. Experience shows that problems can sneak into even the most comprehensively tested questionnaires. Most survey problems, however, are caught and corrected through multiple pretests.

Even when mail surveys are well written and comprehensively pretested, they often suffer from low response rates, typically the lowest response rates of the primary survey research methods. Although there are different formulas for determining survey response rates, the response rate generally is the percentage of sample members who, once contacted, actually participate in the survey. A low response rate raises concerns of nonresponse bias. Nonresponse bias is the potential distortion of survey findings that results from differences between those who participate in a survey and those who do not. Simply put, when enough sample members choose not to participate in a survey, their lack of participation ruins the external validity, or generalizability, of a study's results, and accurate generalization from the sample to the population is not possible.

Surveys that are well designed help increase participant response rate. Although each project is different, there are several elements to a successful project and a number of ways researchers work to increase mail survey response rates. Dillman noted that integration and consistency among the individual elements of a mail survey are keys to increasing mail survey participation. These most commonly include the use of prenotification and reminder cards or letters, as well as sending new cover letters and an additional copy of the questionnaire to nonrespondents.

Initially, a prenotification card or letter can be an effective way to prepare respondents for survey participation. Typically, sample members receive this mailing one or two weeks before the questionnaire and cover letter are sent, and it is used to create understanding and even a small degree of anticipation among sample respondents. The cover letter and questionnaire are mailed next. The cover letter and questionnaire typically are followed by a reminder card or letter, or even better, a new letter and questionnaire, two or three weeks later. This process often is repeated more than once to offer potential respondents as many opportunities as possible to participate in the survey.

Research suggests that follow-up mailings are an effective way to increase mail survey participation. In general, the longer sample members delay responding, the lower the likelihood that they will participate. Properly timed follow-up mailings provide additional encouragement to respond. Various other ways help increase mail survey response rates, as well. Research suggests that other techniques generally produce higher response rates such as sponsorship by a university or other respected institution; questionnaires mailed in envelopes with stamps rather than metered or bulk rate markings; the enclosure of a stamped, self-addressed return envelope with the survey; and the use of monetary incentives such as $1 or other small inducements (sometimes small gifts are used such as a pencil or pen).

There are other ways to increase response rate as well, but some attempts to increase response rates are not successful and even may reduce participation in some cases. Using personalized envelopes or questionnaires, for example, when respondent anonymity is important or the topic of a survey is sensitive is ineffective. It is critical for researchers to understand as much as possible about the topic and sample members, and to pretest all aspects of a survey to increase their ability to obtain valid, reliable results from sample members.

The representativeness of mail survey results is increased through probability sampling methods. One benefit to mail surveys is that the names and addresses of randomly selected members of a population can be purchased from vendors who sell samples, often at a reasonable price. In addition, these same companies typically can provide highly specialized samples at a higher price. Such samples often are invaluable because they allow researchers to complete a survey using a probability-based sample, helping to increase the reliability and validity of survey results. Some organizations and associations use their own mailing lists as the basis for a probability sample. The mailing list serves as the sampling frame (a list of population members from which a sample is drawn), and researchers can randomly draw names and addresses from the list to form the sample. In this way, it is a relatively simple process for researchers to generate a probability-based sample to use when conducting a mail survey.

Practitioners should take care in the interpretation of research results, however, when mailing lists serve as the basis for a sample. Even though the sample is probability based, the results are only directly generalizable to members of the mailing list. Ideally, a mailing list contains all of the members of a population. In this case, the results of the survey are likely to represent the true opinions and attitudes of all population members (given a certain range of error at a specific level of confidence).

In other instances, however, a mailing list is not a complete list of all members of a population. This might be the case, for example, if you were trying to survey members of a professional association using the association's mailing list. Any sample generated using such a mailing list would produce results that were directly generalizable only to members of the association, and not to all members of the profession. This matter may seem small and technical, but it is significant. Research results are only as trustworthy as the sample on which they are based. Researchers should use mailing lists with care and consider the ramifications of sampling decisions before plunging into data collection. There is no way to increase the generalizability of a survey's results once a study is complete.

Finally, one of the newest approaches to survey research is to use computerized self-administered questionnaires (CSAQ). When CSAQ interviews are conducted, a respondent receives the questionnaire by way of a floppy disk, bulletin board, or other means, and runs the data-collection software, which asks questions and records answers. Researchers may E-mail a questionnaire to sample members directly, for example, or notify them they have been selected to participate in a survey via E-mail and ask them to access a questionnaire on a bulletin board. Such surveys generally have all the benefits of regular mail surveys with some additional advantages. In particular, electronic surveys commonly cost even less than regular mail surveys because of the lack of postage and production costs, and immediate delivery shortens the time it takes to complete a project.

CSAQ interviews also have some significant disadvantages. Perhaps most important, a sample is limited to persons with computers and/or on-line access. Although the use of technology is rapidly expanding, much of the population does not have computers and/or online access. In addition, when surveys are posted on bulletin boards, it may be difficult to control who actually completes a questionnaire. Ultimately, the reliability and external validity of a survey's results may be extremely low as a result of these limitations. In addition, online communication is far from problem free.

Documents and attachments sent via electronic mail commonly suffer a host of problems. They may end up reformatted to such an extent that they are difficult or impossible to read, or sample members may be unable to open them at all. Electronic survey research still is being developed. Although this kind of research has much potential, practitioners should be careful before undertaking an important project using largely untested research methods.

Mail Survey Critique

Mail surveys are generally the least expensive survey research method. This benefit alone contributes greatly to their popularity as a research method. Although there are situations in which other survey methods may cost less, in most instances, mail surveys provide the ability to cover a large geographical area at the lowest cost per respondent. For many surveys, the costs of developing and producing a questionnaire, securing a sample, and analyzing and interpreting the results are similar. Two methodological benefits significantly reduce the cost of mail surveys relative to other research methods.

The first is postage; sample members can be reached for the same cost whether they are across town or across the nation. Although telephone surveys can also be inexpensive, mail surveys consistently enjoy a cost savings because of mail distribution. The second cost-savings benefit results from lower administrative costs. The data are not collected by interviewers, and mail surveys generally require fewer people to manage the data-collection process. Although a knowledgeable staff is needed to assemble materials, track responses, mail follow-ups, and edit and code returned questionnaires, mail surveys almost always require fewer administrative resources than other survey methods.

Mail surveys also are useful for reaching widely dispersed sample members. Although other methods can be adapted to reach dispersed sample members, often at increased costs, mail surveys easily address this issue. In addition, mail surveys allow for selective probability sampling through specialized mailing lists. Although researchers must be concerned about the limited generalizability of survey results when lists are used as the sampling frame, mailing lists can make excellent sampling frames in appropriate research settings. Researchers may use a selected list, for example, when they need to sample a highly specialized professional population. Mail surveys also may be used to collect information from sample members who are busy and unlikely to participate in a telephone or personal interview.

Researchers may use mail surveys when a high degree of respondent anonymity is desired. Respondents are more likely to provide candid answers to questions concerning sensitive subjects because they are not speaking directly to an interviewer. Research suggests, for example, that respondents can more easily answer questions about highly personal issues such as drunk driving convictions or personal bankruptcy using self-administered questionnaires. In addition, researchers generally are less concerned over the introduction of interviewer bias into study results when mail surveys are used.

Respondents typically are sensitive to both verbal and nonverbal cues during the interview process, and sometimes interpret these cues as supportive or unsupportive of their opinions, attitudes, and behaviors. They may change their responses as a result. Survey results concerning racial prejudice, for example, would be ruined if participants changed answers because they sensed interviewer disapproval for their prejudicial opinions and attitudes. Instead of an accurate measure of racial prejudice, study results would be skewed by participants who provide socially desirable responses because of apparent interviewer influence. Researchers who are studying sensitive subjects or who have concerns regarding the potential for interviewer bias can use mail surveys to eliminate such problems.

Perhaps the greatest concern in the use of mail surveys is their low response rates. It is not uncommon for mail surveys to have response rates ranging from 10% to 40%. A low return rate casts doubt on the validity and reliability of a survey's findings by introducing nonresponse bias. Mail surveys with enough follow-up to obtain a high response rate typically require at least 8 weeks conducting regardless of a sample's size or its geographic location. In many instances, 8 weeks is too long to wait given the time constraints that typically accompany research projects, particularly when telephone surveys can be conducted in less than half that time. In addition, the need for incentives and multiple mailings increase survey costs.

Another significant problem with mail surveys is that questionnaires must be self-explanatory and relatively short to encourage survey participation. Because no one is available to explain questions or provide additional information, survey instructions, question wording, and question skip patterns—necessary when certain questions apply to some but not all participants—must be extremely simple and clear. Even when questions and instructions are clear, some respondents skip questions or even entire sections of a questionnaire for any number of reasons. Additionally, researchers can never be sure who has actually filled out a survey. Despite the fact that surveys usually are directed to specific individuals, individuals other than selected sample members may be asked or allowed to fill out questionnaires. Finally, returned surveys are less likely to be received from respondents who are of low education, who do not like to read or write, and who are not interested in the survey subject. Any of these concerns, working individually or together, may introduce bias and threaten the reliability and validity of study results.

TELEPHONE SURVEYS

Telephone interviewing involves contacting respondents and conducting personal interviews by telephone. This method of data collection represents a middle ground between personal interviews and mail surveys. Telephone surveys offer many of the advantages of personal interviews at a cost that is often competitive with that of mail surveys. Although not offering the degree of flexibility present in personal interviews, telephone surveys offer more control and generally higher response rates than most mail surveys, and they often can be completed in less than half the time it takes to complete a mail survey. In many research situations, telephone surveys can provide substantially the same information as a face-to-face interview at about half the cost. These benefits have contributed to a rapid increase in researchers' use of telephone survey research.

Telephone Survey Considerations

Telephone surveys require interviewers to introduce the survey to sample members; obtain cooperation; present instructions, questions, answer categories, and other relevant information; motivate participants to answer questions, answer any questions participants have; and administer the survey and record answers. Throughout this process, an interviewer ideally operates as a neutral vehicle through which a respondent's answers are communicated to researchers. It is a complex process that requires carefully trained interviewers. Telephone surveys require well-written questionnaires and instructions because they rely solely on verbal communication. Because of this, survey design and construction are based on utility rather than on aesthetics.

The interviewers' job is made more difficult, and quality of the data collected is lowered, if instructions, questions, and response categories are unclear. Problems also are likely if question order does not proceed in an obvious manner with the aid of transitional statements, if question placement is irregular or lacking apparent topical organization, or if the survey lacks easily understood instructions. Interview questions and survey design issues often revolve around the needs of an interviewer to attract and keep a potential respondent's attention.

Questionnaires typically flow from "warm-up" questions designed to maximize respondent interest; to issue-oriented questions that provide critical information about respondents' opinions, attitudes, and behavioral motivations; and conclude with routine demographic questions. Open-ended questions, which require interviewers to record a respondent's answer verbatim are used sparingly because they take time, interrupt questionnaire flow, and require additional coding during data analysis. Given the importance of a well-designed survey instrument, questionnaire pretesting and comprehensive interviewers training are a pivotal part of telephone survey success.

Although each survey is different and typically requires specialized interviewer training, there are common threads to successful training of telephone interviewers. First, researchers want interviewers to pay particular attention to the survey introduction because this is the first point of caller contact. Then, interviewers need to learn to read questions exactly as they are written; practice answering respondents' questions; practice selecting survey participants after initial phone contact has been made, if necessary; and learn how to help certain respondents use appropriate response categories.

All of this must be accomplished while providing neutral feedback and probes so participant responses will not be influenced. Interviewers also must be prepared for difficult skip patterns or survey questions that, though necessary, are unusual or potentially bothersome to respondents, such as questions concerning their age or income. Finally, interviewers must complete a call record. This is a record of the result of each call attempt, and it provides researchers with information they need to determine sample members who receive additional call attempts and the response rate for a survey. The number and complexity of these and other issues necessitate thorough interviewer training before ever calling sample members.

In addition, precontact in the form of letters or cards effectively increases response rates in a manner similar to mail survey research. Prenotification letters or cards also can help legitimize a study by providing information about why sample members will be contacted, what kind of information will be requested, and what the benefits are of participation. Providing general information concerning the timing of survey phone calls helps to reduce the surprise associated with receiving an unanticipated phone call from an unknown source. Depending on the sample, many survey calls are placed on weeknight evenings (excluding Friday) from 6 p.m. to 9 p.m. Finally, callback attempts help increase participant contact and response. Callbacks typically are made to sample members who were not contacted during an initial call attempt. Although the number of callbacks differ according to survey characteristics, Wimmer and Dominick reported that three callbacks produce contact about 75% of the time.

As with all research methods, the external validity, or generalizability, of telephone survey results depends on the use of probability-based sampling methods, which are explained. One benefit of telephone survey research is that, similar to mail surveys, names and phone numbers of randomly selected members of a population can be purchased from commercial sample vendors, allowing researchers to complete a survey using a probability-based sample relatively easily. These same companies typically can provide specialized samples at a higher price.

When researchers choose not to purchase a sample, they often can use telephone directories, typically available for free or low cost, as the basis for sampling. Of course, no telephone directory is entirely representative of a population because of the households with unlisted telephone numbers. In some communities, the proportion of households with unlisted telephone numbers exceeds 50%, leaving a large portion of the population unavailable for sampling from a telephone directory, particularly in urban areas. Researchers typically use a random digit dialing (RDD) technique to overcome problems with unlisted telephone numbers.

RDD theoretically provides an equal probability of reaching a household with a telephone access line regardless of whether its telephone number is listed or unlisted, and it replicates what would occur if a complete sampling frame existed. There are several RDD techniques including some that are computer based. Most RDD techniques rely on standard area codes and telephone number prefixes that correspond geographically to a desired population, and they use a randomization technique to produce a telephone number suffix.

In some of the more common but cumbersome RDD techniques, research staff members draw telephone numbers out of an appropriate telephone directory by hand and randomly change the last four digits to create a new number. They may add a number between 1 and 9, for example, to the last digit of a phone number. The added digit can be a constant or can be assigned randomly to each new number. In the "plus-one" method, 1 is added to the last digit of a telephone number suffix to produce a new telephone number. So, if staff members draw the telephone number 441-7165, they dial 441-7166. In a common variation of this technique, researchers use a table of random numbers to generate numbers used to replace one or more telephone number suffix digits. Although such techniques produce unusable telephone numbers such as businesses or government offices, which adds to survey costs, they also produce a probability-based sample that provides coverage of unlisted telephone numbers.

Once initial telephone contact is made, some studies require randomization within each household contacted. If the household itself is the unit of analysis, any adult member can provide the information needed and within-household selection procedures are not necessary. When researchers seek results that are generalizable to an entire population of adults rather than households, however, interviewers must use a systematic process for selecting the member of the household to interview. If staff members do not use selection procedures, the resulting sample may include disproportionately high numbers of women and older adults, who are most likely to be home when interviewers call.

Scholars and research practitioners have developed various selection procedures to avoid possible bias resulting from interviewing the person who answers the telephone. Unfortunately, they can be complex and unwieldy to use. When such selection procedures are used, they typically increase survey costs because of the extra time required to identify and select respondents and the need to make additional callbacks when selected respondents are unavailable. In addition, interviewers may experience additional refusals because interviewees are confused or frustrated by complex procedures that must be followed before an interview begins. One method that has gained widespread acceptance for randomizing respondent selection is to ask for the eligible person in the household whose birthday was most recent or who will have the next birthday. Although there are concerns that these methods do not always produce a completely randomized sample, the birthday-selection methods have been widely embraced by both scholars and research practitioners because they are generally effective, easy to use, not time consuming, and not intrusive.

Finally, computer-assisted telephone interviewing (CATI) has become common among universities and commercial research firms and is perhaps the most significant technological advancement to telephone interviewing. When CATI systems are used, computers are used by interviewers to facilitate nearly every aspect of the interview process. The computer dials the telephone number and the interviewer reads the introduction, respondent-selection procedures, and questionnaire off the screen. Interviewers use the computer to record and code responses, and to help with statistical analysis at the end of the day. A CATI system is particularly useful if a questionnaire has complicated skip patterns or if the randomization of questions within a survey is desirable. The development of computer technology in connection with data collection is growing rapidly, and when a research organization properly implements a CATI system, it has the ability to improve the quality of telephone survey research.

Telephone Survey Critique

The benefits of telephone survey research have contributed to an increase in the popularity of this type of data collection. In particular, telephone surveys are relatively cost effective. Although they are generally more expensive than mail surveys, they often are less expensive than personal interview surveys. In addition, the short time in which researchers can complete a telephone survey is highly advantageous. Given the importance of cost and time factors in many research project decisions, these factors make telephone surveys the frequent choice of research professionals and public relations practitioners.

In addition, telephone survey data-collection methods have improved over the past several years to the point that telephone survey research compares favorably with other methods of data collection in terms of data quality. Research staff can collect data from a widely dispersed sample and ensure the representativeness of the data relatively easily. If a list suitable as a sampling frame is available, research staff can draw a probability-based sample. If a suitable list is not available, staff members often can use random digit dialing to produce a probability-based sample. Either way, researchers use telephone surveys to produce data with a high degree of reliability and external validity.

Telephone surveys also tend to have strong response rates, often much higher than mail survey response rates. Although there is concern that response has been falling, telephone survey response rates commonly range from 60% to 90%. Telephone surveys are especially likely to enjoy strong respondent participation when research staff members write and pretest survey introductions and questionnaires carefully; send prenotification cards or letters; use callbacks as needed; and when the project is sponsored by a university or respected institution. Interviewers who are well trained and experienced also help increase response rates and increase the quality of the data collected.

Interviewers help provide some degree of question flexibility in telephone surveys. Although telephone surveys are not as flexible as personal interviews, interviewers are available to clarify terms, explain questions to reduce respondent confusion, negotiate complex skip patterns, and help the data-collection process move forward in a smooth and orderly fashion. In addition, interviewers may be able to establish rapport with respondents that helps them obtain complete and accurate information, and sometimes convince respondents to complete an interview.

At the same time, the use of interviewers raises concerns about the potential for introducing bias into survey results. Interviewers should have no influence on respondents' answers, but instead serve simply as a means of data collection. Interviewers require thorough training to learn how to provide neutral feedback and answer respondents' questions in a nonbiasing manner. In addition, interviewers should have a high level of experience when there is concern about the potential for bias.

Survey results also can be biased through sampling limitations. According to Czaja and Blair, in 1990 approximately 5% of the households still were without telephones. Although a relatively small number, rural areas, some areas in the southern United States, and areas that are economically depressed have higher percentages of houses without telephone access. Residents who do not have telephone access are unavailable for survey purposes, and telephone survey results cannot accurately represent their opinions, attitudes, and behaviors.

In addition, answering machines, call waiting, call forwarding, caller identification, and other technological marvels hinder telephone interviewing. They often require multiple call attempts and make it harder to reach potential respondents. Even after initial contact is made, respondents may suspect they are the target of a sales attempt, or simply resent an interruption, and terminate an interview before it is completed. Ultimately, these obstacles reduce the external validity and reliability of telephone survey research findings.

Finally, telephone interviews are limited in some respects. Perhaps most obvious, researchers' use of visuals and similar interview aids is severely hampered. In addition, instructions, questions, and response categories must be easy to understand because they are being read over the telephone to a respondent. Participants must be able to remember the question and the appropriate response categories; they also typically have no time to examine personal records or other information before responding to a question.

Open-ended questions are difficult to use in a telephone survey because they require the interviewer to record a response verbatim and often result in short answers that are difficult to interpret without some discussion. In addition, researchers have no control over the survey environment. Incoming calls, the doorbell, children, or a loud television commercial commonly interrupt an interview, sometimes requiring interviewers to schedule a callback that may result in an incomplete interview.

Interviews also must be kept relatively short. Most respondents are unwilling to spend a great amount of time on the phone answering questions from a stranger. Although 30 minutes or less is an acceptable interview length, many market researchers try to keep an average interview under 10 minutes. It can be difficult or impossible to collect a large amount of high-quality data in such a short interview. Despite these difficulties, telephone survey research is a proven research method that is used frequently by scholars and market research practitioners.

PERSONAL INTERVIEWS

When personal interviews are conducted, interviewers typically collect information in a respondent's home, office, or other convenient location. Research staff members administer questionnaires in a face-to-face interview, recording respondent's answers and possibly collecting other information. There generally are two types of personal interviews: unstructured and structured. In an unstructured, in-depth interview, interviewers ask broad questions and respondents are given freedom to respond as they wish. The results of these interviews typically lack a high degree of validity and reliability because of the unstructured nature of the interview and sample limitations. The result is that in-depth interviews are largely an informal research method.

In a structured interview, questions are asked in a predetermined order and interviewers have less freedom to deviate from the questionnaire, also called a survey schedule. The result is a flexible interview process that often produces high-quality data, has a strong response rate, and lends itself well to various topics and question types. For these reasons, many scholars and market-research professionals have historically favored personal interviewing as a survey research method.

Several issues, however, have reduced personal interviewing for survey research purposes. Factors such as a high cost per completed interview, the length of time needed for completion of a research project, and the need for a high degree of administration and coordination have contributed to a decline in the large-scale use of personal interviews. Nevertheless, personal interviewing is a flexible and effective survey method that serves many survey research projects settings.

Personal Interview Considerations

In many research situations, several important benefits result from having an interviewer collect data in a one-on-one meeting with a survey participant. A face-to-face meeting allows interview staff to interact and build rapport with potential participants, helping to increase survey response rates. In addition, after an unsuccessful contact attempt at the household of a sample member, an interviewer may visit with neighbors or generally observe the characteristics of a household or neighborhood to determine a better time to return for an interview. As a result, personal interview surveys historically have the highest response rates of any of the primary research methods, typically ranging from 65% to 95%.

A high level of personal interaction also increases the likelihood that interviewers will get complete and accurate information by creating a comfortable interview atmosphere. This factor is important when interviews are long or questionnaires contain complex questions and/or skip patterns. In this instance, the interviewer has a great deal of influence over the administration of the questionnaire and other aspects of the data-collection process. Personal interviews also are highly flexible, much more so than other survey methods. Research staff can answer respondents' questions; seek additional information to clarify ambiguous responses; show charts, pictures, or graphs; and even estimate respondent information such as general appearance or general living conditions.

Finally, personal interviews do not depend on the literacy or education level of respondents, nor are they limited to persons with telephones, computers, or online access. Although this does not eliminate sampling bias concerns in personal interviews, it does address some sampling bias concerns. Ultimately, the use of face-to-face interviews can significantly improve the reliability and external validity of survey results.

Personal interviews, however, are susceptible to bias. Interviewer-related bias, or error, occurs in face-to-face interviews when participants vary their answers because of the person conducting the interview. Participants who sense that interviewers agree or disagree as they respond to certain questions, for example, may wittingly or unwittingly alter their answers to survey questions. Respondents also may hesitate to report sensitive information and are more likely to provide socially desirable responses in personal interviews.

In research concerning racial attitudes, for example, participants are more likely to give socially desirable responses when the interviewer and interviewee are of different races.

The need for extensive interviewer training and standardized interview techniques is important in personal interview surveys, given the importance of the interviewer in the data-collection process. Although it is difficult to accomplish, a standardized interview process in which all interviewers conduct their work in a consistent manner reduces interview-related error.

Two aspects of personal survey administration merit special attention. The first is the need for thorough interviewer training. A well-trained research staff is critical to the success of personal interview surveys. Well-trained staff members help encourage survey participation among sample members; draw thoughtful, relevant information to survey questions; and produce data that are high in accuracy, reliability, and external validity. Poorly trained staff members, on the other hand, are more likely to collect poor quality data and even bias survey results through their actions and statements.

Problems may occur when poorly trained interviewers fail to probe inadequate answers, record respondents' answers incorrectly, ad lib questions rather than reading them as written, and behave in a way that could bias respondents' answers. There is no standard training Programme because there is no standard survey. The type and intensity of training depends on the goals of the study, the number of interviewers, their previous experience, the study's time frame, and the complexity of the questionnaire, among other things. Most training sessions attempt to communicate the goals of the study, develop basic interviewing skills, familiarize interviewers with the questionnaire and objectives for each question, and help interviewers learn to manage difficult interview situations.

The second aspect of personal survey administration that merits special attention is appropriate supervision. Proper training must be combined with effective supervision to contribute to a highly successful personal interview project. Field supervision takes place where training leaves off and occurs during actual data collection.

The importance of field supervision is heightened in personal interview studies because data collection is decentralized. That is, interviewers are necessarily spread over a relatively broad geographic area. Some of the most critical aspects of field supervision include organizing work groups for neighborhoods or other geographic locations, arranging work assignments for research staff members, establishing production quotas for interviewers, reviewing completed work, serving as a liaison with the research office, and helping maintain a high level of commitment to the study among interviewers.

Accomplishing these tasks requires strong organizational skills. Fowler and Mangione suggested that organizations pay attention to five critical aspects of each interviewers' work: the number of interviews each interviewer conducts during a period; the number of hours each interviewer works; the response rate of each interviewer; the quality of each interviewer's completed interviews; and the overall ability of each interviewer, including interactions with survey participants. Given the key role of interviewers in the data-collection process and the decentralized nature of personal surveys, interviewer training and effective field supervision contribute greatly to the success of these projects.

PERSONAL INTERVIEW VARIATIONS

Group-administered surveys combine some of the features of personal interviews and some of the features of mail surveys. The survey is given to members of a group who complete the survey individually, usually with minimal input from a survey administrator. Research staff members typically give group-administered surveys to existing groups of people who are part of a selected sample. Groups such as students, employees, or members of the armed forces typically are used for samples. Sometimes, participants are recruited at shopping malls and taken to a vacant store location or in-mall research facility where they are given a survey.

In this case, participants typically are thanked for their participation with a small inducement, similar to mail surveys. In each case, research staff members administer the survey in a group setting. Group-administered surveys also may be given at conventions or meetings. In fact, technology has made it possible to measure participants' responses immediately, providing the basis for group discussion and feedback. Elway Research in Seattle, for example, uses what it calls a "group interaction system" to collect and monitor participants' responses to questions.

Questions are asked of the group and participants can respond using 'a handset that transmits their opinions to a computer. The data are saved and analyzed instantly. Survey results can be projected for viewing by all participants to see and discuss, or displayed to meeting organizers on a monitor in a separate room. This system makes it possible to determine and discuss participants' opinions immediately, and sample members can participate equally in an anonymous fashion.

This raises some of the concerns of group-administered surveys, however. In some cases, group members may feel coerced to participate. If participants' anonymity is compromised, they may not answer questions honestly. In addition, most group-administered surveys require the permission of organizational management since they typically take place on organizational property. If the survey is an instrument of organizational management and not independently sponsored, or if participants suspect this is the case, they may be less likely to answer question honestly. In addition, many preexisting groups do not lend themselves to probability-based sampling procedures.

Although it is possible to use probability sampling for group-administered surveys, in particular, cluster sampling—such sampling may be difficult to execute. When probability-based sampling is not used, survey results generally suffer from limited reliability and external validity. Group-administered surveys have useful applications, but like all research methods, researchers should use them carefully to produce data that are accurate and reliable.

MALL INTERCEPT SURVEYS

Mall intercept surveys, or simply mall intercepts, are a common method of collecting data in a personal interview format. Well-dressed interviewers, typically wearing matching-colored blazers and carrying clipboards, are a common sight in most malls today. Researchers also use other locations for intercept studies, including downtown areas, college campuses and other areas that attract large numbers of people.

When mall intercepts are conducted, interviewers stand at strategic locations throughout a mall and orally administer a survey to shoppers. Shoppers may be asked to fill out a survey in a manner similar to group-administered surveys. An inducement may be used, depending on various considerations, including the topic and length of the survey, the need for a quick completion time, whether shoppers or others typically will complete a questionnaire without an inducement, and the study's budget.

Mall intercepts offer several benefits that have made them relatively popular, particularly among market researchers. Perhaps most important to many market researchers, the method can be used quickly if necessary and is inexpensive relative to other research methods. Combined, these two benefits make mall intercepts an attractive research method given the time and budgetary constraints that hinder many research projects. In addition, the method is relatively uncomplicated and provides some flexibility in data collection.

Mall intercepts have some key limitations that researchers should consider before undertaking a project. Perhaps most important, although a probability-based sampling method is possible in an intercept study, it is difficult as a practical matter. Even if researchers used a probability-based sampling method, the results would only be directly generalizable to shoppers at a single location.

For these reasons, nonprobability sampling methods are commonly used that, although convenient, limit the external validity and reliability of the study's findings. In addition, many shoppers avoid mall interviews raising further concerns about the validity and reliability of study results. Interviews typically suffer from poor interview conditions because of noise, foot traffic, and other distractions, and researchers must keep questionnaires short and to the point. Although intercept studies are useful in certain circumstances and popular among research practitioners, researchers should use them carefully and remember their results suffer from limited reliability and generalizability concerns.

PERSONAL INTERVIEW CRITIQUE

Researchers use personal interview surveys for several reasons, many of which concern data quality. Researchers conducting face-to-face surveys can achieve high response rates, often 65% or higher. These response rates, which are enhanced by the use of prenotification letters and the ability of interviewers to interact with sample members, help reduce bias due to nonresponse. In addition, interviewers usually can establish a strong rapport with survey participants. This provides them with an opportunity to probe respondents' answers when they are inadequate or unclear. Personal interviews typically take place in sample members' homes.

This allows them to consult personal records or locate other information. The home also is a comfortable interview environment and tends to make respondents less sensitive to questionnaire length. In addition, sampling frame bias is low when Census Bureau data are used as a basis for the sampling frame because all individuals in a population have a chance, at least in theory, of being included in the sample. As a result of these characteristics, researchers can use personal interview surveys to produce high-quality data.

Personal interview surveys also offer interviewers a high degree of flexibility in obtaining research information. One-on-one interviews lend themselves to questions requiring high degrees of depth or detail, and the interviewer can use visual aids or other interview devices if necessary. Interviewers can also explain questionnaire items that are confusing to respondents, particularly if the respondent misunderstands the intent of a question or is confused by a response category. Researchers can even estimate some information, although this should be done sparingly because of the potential to introduce error into survey results. The flexibility of one-on-one interviews also allows researchers to use complex questionnaires with difficult skip patterns. The flexibility and quality of data produced through personal interview surveys have historically made this research method highly desirable to researchers.

Unfortunately, personal interview surveys suffer from significant drawbacks that have limited the use of this survey method. Probably the greatest drawback to personal interview surveys is cost. Personal interviews generally are the most expensive survey research method. Although cost comparisons are not always available, Czaja and Blair (1996) estimated that a national personal interview survey would cost more than twice as much as a similar telephone interview survey, often at least $250 per hour-long interview.

These costs result from the need for field supervisors and extensive interviewer training, as well as travel expenses and other costs. In addition, personal interviews generally take longer than telephone interviewing because of logistical complexities. The administration of a personal interview survey can be costly and complex when sample members are geographically dispersed. These are significant limitations given the importance of time and cost factors in many research decisions.

Another significant disadvantage in the use of personal interviews is the possibility of interviewer bias. The physical appearance, age, dress, race, sex, and verbal and nonverbal communication skills of the interviewer may influence respondents to provide answers that do not accurately reflect their feelings. In addition, participants may be hesitant to report highly personal behaviour. The resulting bias ruins the reliability and generalizability of research results.

A high degree of careful interviewer training and field supervision is required to avoid interviewer bias, which also contributes to survey cost and length. Finally, some samples are difficult, or even dangerous, to access for a personal interview. Busy work schedules make it difficult to schedule interviews with many adults. In other cases, sample members live in areas with high crime rates. Each of these sample members is important as potential respondents and must be interviewed if possible, but reaching them presents a special challenge when personal interview surveys are conducted.

Survey research is an indispensable part of organizations' attempts to monitor their internal and external environments, solve complex problems, and plan and evaluate public relations campaigns. Despite suggestions to the, contrary, there is no best method of survey research, and the potential advantages and disadvantages of each method do not apply equally, or even at all, to every research situation.

The best method for a project depends on various situation-specific factors, and, because of this, the use of a survey research method must be considered in relation to the needs and constraints of each situation.

It is important for practitioners to understand each survey research method because of this. Practitioners serve their own interest by understanding the key issues associated with the use of one survey method over another in a research situation, as well as other critical aspects of survey implementation such as issues associated with the use of probability versus nonprobability sampling. This knowledge allows them to make informed research decisions and engage in sophisticated problem-solving and campaign-management activities.

Chapter 11

Sampling

Sampling is a powerful tool and a critical part of public relations research. Practitioners use sampling in partnership with the research methods they select to help them solve complex problems, monitor their internal and external environments, and engage in sophisticated campaign planning and evaluation. Sampling helps practitioners get accurate information quickly at a relatively low cost. It provides practitioners with a way to collect information from a limited number of target audience members, called a sample, and draw conclusions about the entire target audience. These processes are based on principles of statistical sampling and inference.

Although it sounds complex, it really is simple. If we want to know whether our spaghetti sauce needs more garlic, we usually take a small sample and taste it. It is not necessary to eat all of the sauce to determine whether more garlic is needed (and by the way, more garlic is almost always needed). Researchers sample people in the same way. It is not necessary to contact all members of a target audience to understand their opinions, attitudes, and behaviors. Instead, practitioners can learn this information from a properly selected sample of target audience members with a high degree of confidence that they are accurate. The purpose of this chapter is to explain basic aspects of sampling including both probability and nonprobability sampling methods and sample size calculations, in a simple, easy-to-understand manner. Math phobes should note that only a relatively small amount of math will be used. The emphasis is on developing a conceptual understanding of the principles of sampling and statistical inference.

SAMPLING BASICS

Even though sampling methods are relatively easy to understand and use, explanation of a few basic terms and concepts makes it easier to understand sampling practices. Although these definitions are not terribly interesting, they make it a lot easier to incorporate principles of sampling and inference. At a basic level, readers should know about the difference between a population and a sample. A population or universe consists of all the members of a group or an entire collection of objects. In public relations, a population most commonly refers to all the people in a target audience or public.

When researchers conduct a census, they collect information from all members of a population to measure their attitudes, opinions, behaviors, and other characteristics. These measurements, called parameters, are the true values of a population's members. A parameter is a characteristic or property of a population. Parameters contain no error, because they are the result of information collected from every population member. Often, parameters are expressed in summary form. If our research reveals that 59% of voters in King County, Washington, support a tax initiative, for example, this characteristic is a parameter of the population of all voters in King County.

It is often difficult or impossible for research professionals and social scientists to conduct a census that tends to be expensive and time consuming. More important, a census is unnecessary in most situations. By collecting information from a carefully selected subset, or sample, of population members, researchers can draw conclusions about the entire population, often with a high degree of accuracy. This is why sampling is such a powerful part of public relations planning and problem solving.

A sample is simply a subset of a population or universe. When researchers conduct a survey using a sample, they use the resulting data to produce sample statistics. Sample statistics describe the characteristics of the sample in the same way that population parameters describe the characteristics of a population. Statistics result from the observed scores of sample members instead of from the true scores of all population members, and they necessarily contain some error because of this. The amount of error contained in sample statistics, however, usually is small enough that researchers can estimate, or infer, the opinions, attitudes, behaviors, and other characteristics of a population from sample statistics, often with a high degree of confidence.

If you find all of this confusing, read this section again slowly and it will become more clear, although no more exciting (we suggest taking two aspirin first). This topic and chapter improve in terms of their ease of understanding, but it is important to have a basic understanding of sampling terminology and concepts before we discuss other aspects of sampling. It also becomes more clear as we move into discussions of sample representation, sampling techniques, and sample size calculations.

GENERALIZING FROM A SAMPLE TO A POPULATION

Researchers normally collect data to make generalizations. During a state gubernatorial election in Michigan, for example, a political campaign manager may survey a sample of registered voters to determine the opinions of all registered voters in the state. In this case, the campaign manager wants to generalize the results of the survey from a relatively small sample (perhaps consisting of no more than several hundred people) to all registered voters in the state. This process of generalization, when researchers draw conclusions about a population based on information collected from a sample, is called inference. Researchers generalize findings from samples to populations on a regular basis. How can researchers generalize in this way and be confident they are right? A sample must accurately represent the population from which it is drawn to allow investigators to make valid inferences about the population based on sample statistics.

An often-used example from the annals of survey research helps make the point. In 1920, editors of the Literary Digest conducted a poll to see whether they could predict the winner of the presidential election between Warren Harding and James Cox. Editors gathered names and addresses from telephone directories and automobile registration lists and sent postcards to people in six states. Based on the postcards they received, the Literacy Digest correctly predicted that Harding would win the election. Literacy Digest editors repeated this same general process over the next several elections and correctly predicted presidential election winners in 1920, 1924, 1928, and 1932.

Literacy Digest editors again conducted a poll to predict the winner of the 1936 election. This project was their most ambitious yet. This time, they sent ballots to 10 million people whose names they drew from telephone directories and automobile registration lists, as before. More than 2 million ballots were returned. Based on the results of its survey, the editors predicted that Republican challenger Alfred Landon would receive 57% of the popular vote in a stunning upset over Democratic incumbent Franklin Roosevelt. Roosevelt was reelected, however, by the largest margin in history to date. He received approximately 61% of the popular vote and captured 523 electoral votes to Landon's 8. What went wrong?

Simply put, the sample was unrepresentative. The sample was drawn from telephone directories and automobile registration lists, both of which were biased to upper income groups. At that time, less than 40% of American households had telephones and only 55% of Americans owned automobiles. The omission of the poor from the sample was particularly significant because they voted overwhelmingly for Roosevelt, whereas the wealthy voted primarily for Landon. Not only was the sample unrepresentative, but the survey method and low response rate (24%) contributed to biased results.

This often-told story illustrates a key point about the importance of sample representativeness. The results of research based on samples that are not representative do not allow researchers to validly generalize research results. It is unsafe for investigators to make inferences about a population based on information gathered from a sample when the sample does not represent the population from which it was drawn. It is a simple, but important, concept to understand.

In fact, George Gallup (of Gallup poll notoriety) understood the concept well. In July 1936, he predicted in print that the Literary Digest poll would project Landon as the landslide winner and that the poll would be incorrect. These predictions were made months before the Literacy Digest poll was conducted. He also predicted that Roosevelt would win reelection and perhaps receive as much as 54% of the popular vote. Gallup's predictions were correct, even though his numbers concerning the election were off. How could Gallup be sure of his predictions? The primary basis of his explanation was that the Literary Digest reached only middle- and upper-class individuals who were much more likely to vote Republican. In other words, he understood that the Literacy Digest sample was not representative.

As an additional note, for those who believe that a larger sample is always better, here is evidence to the contrary. When nonprobability sampling methods are used, sample size has no scientifically verifiable effect on the representativeness of a sample. Sample size makes no difference because the sample simply is not representative of the population. A large, unrepresentative sample is as unrepresentative as a small, unrepresentative sample. In fact, had a probability sampling method been used in accordance with an appropriate survey method, a sample size of less than 1% of the more than 2 million voters who responded to the Digest poll almost certainly would have produced a highly accurate prediction for both the Literary Digest editors and George Gallup.

SAMPLING METHODS

Sampling is the means by which researchers select people or elements in a population to represent the entire population. Researchers use a sampling frame—a list of the members of a population—to produce a sample, using one of several methods to determine who will be included in the sample. Each person or object in the sample is a sampling element or unit. When practitioners study target audience members, the sampling frame typically consists of a list of members of a target audience, whereas the sampling unit is an individual person. All the sampling units together compose the sample. If a nonprofit organization wants to examine the perceptions and opinions of its donors, for example, the sampling frame might be a mailing list of donors' names and addresses, whereas the sampling unit would be the individual names and addresses selected from the list as part of the sample. When researchers generate a sample, they select sampling units from the sampling frame.

A researcher's goal when drawing a sample is to accurately represent the population from which the sample was drawn. This allows them to make inferences about the population based on information collected from the sample. There are two types of samples: probability and nonprobability. Researchers select probability samples in a random way so that each member of a population has an equal chance, or probability, of being included in a sample. When researchers draw a nonprobability sample, an individual's chance of being included in a sample is not known. There is no way to determine the probability that any population member will be included in the sample because a nonrandom selection process is used. Some population members may have no chance of being included in a sample, whereas other population members may have multiple chances of being included in a sample.

When probability, or random, samples are chosen, scholars normally can make accurate inferences about the population under study based on information from the sample. That is, probability samples tend to produce results that are highly generalizable from a sample to a population. When researchers select samples in any way other than probability-based/random sampling, they cannot be sure that a sample accurately represents the population from which it was drawn.

In this case, they have no basis for validly making inferences about a population from the sample. Even though a nonprobability sample may perfectly represent a population, investigators cannot scientifically demonstrate its level of representativeness. For this reason, the results of research that use nonprobability samples are low in generalizability (external validity).

Why use nonprobability sampling if the research results it produces are not representative? In some cases, a nonprobability sample may be used because it is quick and easy to generate. At other times, the cost of generating a probability-based sample may be too high, so researchers use a nonprobability sample instead. The use of a nonprobability sample is not automatically a problem or even necessarily a concern. It is a significant limitation, however, in practitioners' application of research results to public relations planning and problem solving. Nonprobability samples are often used in exploratory research or other small-scale studies, perhaps as a precursor to a major study. In addition, some commonly used research methods, such as focus groups or mall intercept surveys, use nonprobability sampling almost exclusively.

The lack of generalizability should serve as a warning to public relations practitioners. Do not assume research results based on nonprobability samples are accurate. When practitioners want to explore a problem or potential solution in an informal fashion, get input on an idea, or obtain limited feedback from members of a target audience, a nonprobability sample normally is an acceptable choice. As editors of the Literary Digest discovered, however, nonprobability samples have limitations and should not serve as the sole basis for a practitioner's decision making about a major problem or solution, or serve as the primary means by which practitioners collect information about target audiences and develop Programme initiatives.

NONPROBABILITY SAMPLING METHODS

There are several methods of generating nonprobability samples. No matter how random the selection process appears in each of these sampling methods, researchers do not select sample members in a random manner. This means that population members have an unequal chance of being selected as part of a sample when investigators use these sampling methods. Some population members will have no chance of being included in the sample, whereas other population members will have multiple chances. The most common types of nonprobability samples are incidental (convenience) sampling, quota sampling, dimensional sampling, purposive (judgmental) sampling, volunteer sampling, and snowball sampling.

Incidental, or Convenience, Sampling

Researchers form incidental, or convenience, samples by using whom ever is convenient as a sample element. A public opinion survey in which interviewers stop and survey those who walk by and are willing to participate constitutes such a sample. Most mall intercepts use convenience samples because their sample consists of shoppers who happen to walk by and are willing to complete a questionnaire. Like all nonprobability samples, incidental samples do not generally provide accurate estimates of the attributes of target population. There is simply no way to determine the degree to which research results from a convenience sample are representative. Like all nonprobability sampling methods, incidental samples are most appropriate when research is exploratory, precise statistics concerning a population are not required, or the target population is impossible to accurately define or locate.

Quota Sampling

In this method, researchers interested in the subgroups that exist in a population draw their sample so it contains the same proportion of subgroups. Investigators fill the quotas nonrandomly, typically using sample members who are convenient. In practice, research staff members typically base quotas on a small number of population characteristics such as respondents' age, sex, educational level, type of employment, or race or ethnicity. An interviewer conducting a survey on a college campus, for example, might be assigned to interview a certain number of freshmen, sophomores, juniors, and seniors. The interviewer might select the sample nonrandomly by standing in front of the university library and asking people to complete a survey. The interviewer would stop surveying members of individual population subgroups as each quota was filled.

Dimensional Sampling

This method is similar to quota sampling in that researchers select study participants nonrandomly according to predetermined quota, but sample quotas are extended to include various population attributes. Generally, interviewers ensure that a minimum number of individuals are included for various combinations of criteria. Extending the college survey example, interviewers might nonrandomly select participants to meet additional criteria, or dimensions. Interviewers might have to interview a minimum number of males and females, traditional and nontraditional students, or married and unmarried students, for example, in addition to the class quota. Interviewers might use a seemingly endless number of potential attributes to broaden a sample.

No matter how many attributes interviewers use to determine samples, both quota and dimensional sampling rely on nonprobability selection methods. The result is that researchers cannot determine whether their participants fully represent the similarities and differences that exist among subgroups in the population. Ultimately, there is no scientific way to determine whether a nonprobability sample is representative and no scientific evidence to suggest quota sampling is more representative than other nonprobability sampling methods. Researchers correct the nonprobability selection weakness of quota sampling and dimensional sampling when they use stratified sampling, which we address shortly.

Purposive Sampling

In purposive, or judgmental, sampling, interviewers select sample members because they meet the special needs of the study based on the interviewer's judgment. A researcher's goal when using purposive sampling typically is to examine a specially selected population that is unusually diverse or particularly limited in some way, rather than to study a larger, more uniform population. If a product manufacturer wants to open a new plant in another country, for example, company management needs to learn the concerns of local business, government, and labour leaders. In this case, the sample is relatively small and diverse, and interviewers may simply select sample members using their own discretion to determine which respondents fit into the sample and are "typical" or "representative."

This creates situations in which sample-selection decisions may vary widely among interviewers. Even if the definition of the population is reasonably clear, the procedures used in drawing a sample may vary greatly among interviewers, limiting the comparability of sample members. These nonrandom selection procedures limit the generalizability of research results based on purposive samples, as is the case with all nonprobability sampling methods.

Volunteer Sampling

When media organizations ask viewers to write or E-mail their opinions, they are using a volunteer, or self-selected, sample. Instant, phone-in polls have become a common way for the media to determine and report "public opinion," for example, to attract and keep the interests of viewers and listeners. There are numerous potential sources of bias when research is based on a volunteer sample. First, sample representation is hindered because only the people who are exposed to the survey have an opportunity to participate.

All other potential respondents are unaware of the poll. Second, those who feel strongly about the topic of a poll may view the survey as an opportunity to "vote" for their viewpoint. Such individuals may respond more than once and/or encourage other like-minded individuals to respond in the same way. The result is that volunteer samples are not representative, and research results based on volunteer samples are highly untrustworthy. Organizations that use volunteer samples should use them for their entertainment value, not their scientific value.

Snowball Sampling

When researchers use snowball sampling, they collect data from a limited number of population members, and ask these individuals to identify other members of the population who might be willing to participate in the survey. The sample continues to grow as new research participants direct interviewers to additional sample prospects. The sample snowballs, starting from a small number of people and growing larger as each new participant suggests other potential participants.

Researchers may have no choice but have to rely on snowball sampling when they can locate only a few members of a population. If a social welfare organization wanted to learn about the particular difficulties of migrant workers, for example, it might start by interviewing those few migrant workers it could locate. After each interview was concluded, interviewers could ask participants to identify other migratory workers who might be willing to participate in the study. Interviewers hope the sample would grow to a desirable size through this process. Research results based on such a sample, however, have little or no generalizability, no matter how large the sample grows. A snowball sample uses nonrandom methods of selection, and because of this, there is no way to scientifically determine the degree to which it represents the population from which it is drawn. As with other nonprobability-based research results, research findings based on snowball samples should be interpreted and generalized carefully.

PROBABILITY SAMPLING METHODS

In probability sampling each element in a population has an equal probability of being selected as part of the sample. Researchers generate probability samples using a random selection process so each member of a population has an equal chance, or probability, of being included in a sample. The use of probability sampling normally allows investigators to make accurate inferences about a population based on information collected from a sample. Investigators' inferences, or conclusions, about the population are not perfectly accurate even when probability sampling is used.

Researchers calculate estimates of this error within a given level of probability. The result of this process is that research findings based on probability samples normally are highly representative. That is, they possess a high degree of generalizability, or external validity. The most common type of probability sample is simple random sampling. Common variations of simple random sampling include systematic sampling, stratified sampling, and cluster sampling.

SIMPLE RANDOM SAMPLING

Researchers must ensure that each member of a population has an equal chance of being included in a sample and select each sample element independently to produce a random sample. This is the most basic method of random sampling, and investigators use it to ensure that the sample they produce is representative of the population. Although true representation is never guaranteed unless a census is taken, the use of a random-selection process significantly reduces the chances of subgroup overrepresentation or underrepresentation, which helps eliminate sample bias. Researchers then can estimate, or infer, population parameters based on sample statistics. Although these inferences are not perfect—they have some error—investigators use statistical procedures to generate estimates of this error within a given level of probability.

From a practical standpoint, the primary requirement for simple random sampling is that each element in the population be clearly and unambiguously identified through the use of a comprehensive sampling frame. This allows the direct, independent and random selection of sample elements, typically through a list in which each element is identified. The most common methods of simple random sampling use a list of population members for a sample frame. Research staff members might number each element in the list sequentially, for example, and select the sample by drawing numbers from a table of random numbers. The numbers pulled from the table correspond to the numbered elements in the sampling frame. The result is a random sample that normally is highly representative of the population from which it was drawn.

If the Public Relations Society of America (PRSA) wanted to survey its members to determine their level of satisfaction with its Programmes and services, a project manager could take a membership list and assign a number to each PRSA member sequentially. The manager would create the sample by randomly drawing numbers assigned to PRSA members. Research staff typically use a table of random numbers for this purpose. A staff member would draw each number until an appropriate sample size was generated. If properly conducted, this random process would produce a probability sample of PRSA members who have a high likelihood of accurately representing the attitudes and opinions of all PRSA membership.

SYSTEMATIC RANDOM SAMPLING

Researchers use an unbiased system to select sample members from a list when they use systematic random sampling. This system allows them to generate a probability-based sample that normally is highly representative of the population from which it was drawn, without some of the inconveniences associated with simple random sampling. Those who use simple random sampling often find the process long and tedious, especially with a large sample and/or population and of manual selection procedures. Researchers who must assign numbers to individual sample elements and draw random numbers from a table to create the sample find the process wearisome. When researchers use systematic random sampling, they develop an uncomplicated system using the total sample size and the size of the population to help them draw a probability-based sample relatively easily.

First, research team members determine the final sample size they need for a study. This is the number of people who will actually complete interviews. Researchers often need to generate a total original sample that is several times larger than is required for their final sample, because of the number of sample elements that cannot be contacted or refuse to participate in a survey. Once researchers determine the total sample size, they determine a sampling interval by dividing the size of the sampling frame (this is the total population) by the desired total sample size. The result is a number (n) which researchers use to generate a sample by selecting every n^{th} element from a sampling frame. Researchers must select the first sample element randomly from the frame to produce a probability sample so they randomly select the first element from within the sampling interval. They complete the sample-selection process by selecting every n^{th} element from the sampling frame. The result is a systematic random sample.

An example helps make systematic random sampling more clear. If corporate personnel managers wanted to survey their classified staff as part of a Programme to improve employee relations, their first step is to determine the final sample size they want for the study. Sample size calculations are discussed later in this chapter, but for this example, let's say that after some careful thinking and a little fun with math, administrators determine they want a final sample size of approximately 400 from the approximately 6,000 employees who work as full- or part-time classified staff. After some additional calculations, researchers determine that an original total sample size of 850 classified staff members would produce about 400 completed surveys from participants.

The projects' directors decide to use a mailing list of classified staff members as a sampling frame because it contains the names and addresses of all classified staff members and has no duplicate listings. They divide the sampling frame (6,000) by the original sample size (850) to determine the sampling interval. The first sample element must be selected randomly, so project managers put the first seven names in the directory on individual pieces of paper, put them in a box and shake it up, and draw a name. If project managers drew the 5th name on the list, they would proceed to draw the sample by starting at Name 5 and selecting every 7th name. Thus, researchers would draw Name 5, Name 12, Name 19, Name 26, and so on. By using the sampling interval (7 in this example), researchers produce a systematic random sample.

Systematic random samples and simple random samples are not exactly the same; however, systematic samples closely approximate simple random samples to produce a probability sample that normally is highly representative. In terms of bias, the greatest danger researchers face when they use systematic sampling is periodicity. Periodicity refers to bias that occurs when a sampling list has a cyclical repetition of some population characteristic that coincides with a sampling interval. If this occurs, the sample elements selected are not generalizable to the population from which they were drawn. Researchers should be careful to inspect population lists before sampling to make sure there are no obvious signs of periodicity. When researchers are careful, the potential for bias in systematic sampling normally is small. Ultimately, researchers use systematic random sampling more than simple random sampling because of its simplicity and usefulness in complex sampling situations.

STRATIFIED SAMPLING

Researchers divide a population into different subgroups, or strata, when they engage in stratified sampling, similar to quota sampling. The key difference between the methods is that investigators use a random, probability-based method to select sample elements when they engage in stratified sampling, whereas they use a nonrandom, nonprobability-based method to select sample elements when they engage in quota sampling. Researchers have two primary reasons for stratification: to control the representativeness of the sample and to use different probability-based selection procedures in different strata. Researchers also may use stratified sampling when they are primarily interested in the key similarities and differences among the strata, when the prior information they have for individual strata is different, or to improve sampling efficiency when research costs differ by strata.

Researchers use two types of stratified sampling: proportional and disproportional. When they use proportional sampling, project managers draw sample members from each stratum in proportion to their existence in the population. The resulting sample proportionally represents individual strata as they exist in a population. Researchers use disproportionate sampling to help ensure the overall sample accurately represents the opinions, attitudes, and behaviours of a significant stratum within the population. Project managers may use disproportionate sampling when strata are too small to be accurately represented in a sample selected through other means.

In this case, research staff may find it necessary to weight the data to obtain unbiased estimates of the total population. This may be necessary, for example, when researchers' use of other probability sampling methods would underrepresent the opinions, attitudes, and behaviors of minority members of a population. When researchers use either proportional or disproportional stratified sampling to their advantage, they can produce highly representative, probability-based samples.

CLUSTER SAMPLING

Researchers select sample elements in groups rather than by individuals when they use cluster sampling. The sample frame consists of clusters rather than individuals, and each cluster serves as a sample element. The clusters researchers use for sampling commonly are preexisting natural groups or administrative groups of the population. These may include geographical designations such as neighborhoods, cities, counties, or zip code areas, for example, or other common groupings such as universities, hospitals, factories, or schools.

Researchers often use cluster sampling to make data collection more efficient. If a metropolitan school district wanted to learn about the attitudes and experiences of its students, it could send interviewers to meet one on one with individually selected student sample members. This process, however, would be expensive and increase the time needed to complete the project. If researchers used schools as sample clusters and randomly selected from among them, less time and travel would be required, and the efficiency of data collection would be increased.

Cluster sampling also is used when a comprehensive list of sample elements is not available. If an organization wanted to sample city residents as part of a community relations Programme, project managers would likely have trouble locating a complete list of all community residents, and the process would be costly and time consuming. If researchers wanted to use cluster sampling, they could create a sampling frame by using city blocks as clusters.

After research staff identified and labeled each block, they could randomly selcct an appropriate number of blocks. Next, researchers would randomly sample dwelling units within each block. Finally, interviewers would randomly sample people living in each dwelling unit and collect data. This sampling process is known as multistage sampling because sampling takes place in diffcrent stages. Researchers sample city blocks in the first stage, followed by dwelling units and individual people.

Researchers' primary concern when using cluster sampling is the potential for increased error relative to other probability-based sampling methods. When investigators use cluster sampling, standard error may increase if sample members' attitudes, behaviors and other characteristics are largely the same, or homogeneous, within each cluster. In this instance, samples selected from within homogeneous clusters will not reflect the diversity of attitudes and behaviors that exists in the larger population. This problem can be countered, in part, by selecting a high number of small clusters and selecting a relatively low number of sample elements from within each cluster.

Cluster samples, along with systematic and stratified samples, are acceptable alternatives to simple random sampling. In each case, sample elements have an equal chance for selection. Ultimately, researchers' choice of a sampling method often depends on the time and money available for a project, the population being sampled, the subject under investigation, and the availability of a comprehensive list of target population members.

HOW BIG SHOULD A SAMPLE BE?

One of the first questions clients, managers, and others involved in a research project typically ask is what is the "best" sample size for a project. Unfortunately, as is the case so often in life and particularly in survey research, the answer typically is a firm "it depends." In fact, the methods researchers use to determine the appropriate sample size for a study can be relatively complicated and even controversial. Research professionals often use different formulas to calculate sample size-in some cases based on different assumptions about population characteristics-and may suggest conflicting sample sizes, as a result. Not surprising, several common misperceptions exist concerning sample size calculations including the following:

Myth 1: Bigger samples are always better. The Literary Digest case demonstrates the fallacy concerning bigger sample sizes. When researchers use probability sampling methods, a mathematically calculated sample size based on an appropriate formula nearly always produces trustworthy results with known ranges of error. Researchers can use simple math to verify this information. When researchers use nonprobability sampling methods, there is no scientific way to determine how well a sample represents a population, or how much error survey results contain. Remember, a large, unrepresentative sample is no more representative than a small, unrepresentative sample. In addition, a representative sample that is unnecessarily large is a waste of resources. A sample's size should be the result of a researcher's purposeful decision-making process, not a number researchers stumble upon as they try to generate the largest sample possible.

Myth 2: As a rule of thumb, researchers should sample a fixed percentage of a population to produce an acceptable sample size. It is not uncommon for those uninitiated in survey research methods to suggest using a fixed percentage of the population to determine sample size. If researchers sampled 10% of a 50,000-person population, for example, they would generate a sample of 5,000 participants. Once again, probability-based sampling methods allow the use of mathematical formulas to calculate sample sizes that normally produce highly trustworthy results with known ranges of error. Arbitrarily sampling a certain percentage of the population is unnecessary and results in an arbitrary sample size.

Such a practice is as illogical as if you ate a certain percentage of the food in your refrigerator because you were hungry. Just as the amount of food you eat should be based on your body's needs (with notable exceptions for mocha almond fudge ice cream and chocolate in any form), so should a study's sample size be based on the requirements of a research project instead of on an arbitrary percentage of a population.

Myth 3: Researchers should base sample sizes on industry standards or "typical" sample sizes used in other research projects. In reality, there is little that is standard about a research project. Although researchers may use familiar formulas to determine the sample size for a study, they should not use these formulas without careful consideration. A project's unique needs, the individual characteristics of a population and sample, and other issues greatly affect sampling decisions. Researchers serve the needs of clients and organizations best when they make thoughtful sample-size decisions, based on the unique requirements of individual research projects.

Having said all of this, we must engage in a small amount of backpedaling. Many public relations students (and some practitioners for that matter) have varying degrees of math phobia and short attention spans when it comes to highly technical or theoretical information. It is necessary to understand a little theory and use a small amount of basic algebra to calculate sample sizes. With this in mind, in this text we use simple sample-size calculations and avoid math when possible. We also try to provide a basic conceptual understanding of these formulas and the concepts they use. In short, we take some shortcuts to make these topics as accessible as possible. The result is that we do not follow our own advice in some instances. Please keep in mind there is more to this sometimes complicated topic than we discuss in this text. If you find these basic concepts and formulas easy to understand, or if you will be involved in research on a regular basis, you should read more on additional aspects of sample-size calculations so you are fully informed.

For the math-challenged among us, we offer our encouragement. Read the next section slowly, draw pictures of the concepts if it helps you understand them, and try the math out yourself. Put in a little effort and you should emerge with a clear understanding of the topic. To explain sample-size calculations, first we provide a conceptual understanding of sample-calculation concepts and processes. Then, we do some basic sample-size calculations, based on the concepts we have explained. Finally, we calculate the amount of error that exists in survey data once researchers have completed a survey.

CALCULATING THE APPROPRIATE SAMPLE SIZE

Anyone can determine the optimal size for a sample with precision, provided they understand a few key concepts based on probability theory and a bell-shaped curve. These concepts include sample distribution and standard deviation, confidence level, confidence interval, and variance. Once you grasp these concepts, it is easy to understand the basis for sample-size calculations; the rest is simply a matter of applying the formulas.

Sample Distribution and Standard Deviation

Sample distribution and standard deviation are the first and, in some ways, most complex concepts to understand. A sample distribution is a grouping or arrangement of a characteristic that is measured for each sample member, and it reflects the frequency with which sample characteristics are assigned to each point on a measurement scale. Almost any characteristic that researchers can measure has a sampling distribution, but in survey research investigators typically study sample members' opinions, attitudes, behaviors, and related characteristics. If we were to chart a sampling distribution, the result would be shaped like a bell provided the sampling distribution was normal. It would be tall in the middle where the average of the sampling distribution is located because most people would be near the average. There would be fewer people toward either edge, or tail, of the bell because fewer people would have characteristics or behaviors so far above or below the average.

If we were practitioners at university health facility, for example, we might conduct a survey to better understand smoking behaviour among students. We could ask a randomly selected student sample to fin out a questionnaire that contained attitudinal and behavioral questions, including a question about the number of cigarettes participants had smoked in the past 7 days. Participants' responses would likely vary greatly. Many students would have smoked no cigarettes in the past 7 days, while other students would have smoked a high number of cigarettes. When we computed students' response to our smoking question, we could use the information to generate a sample distribution. If our research revealed the average number of cigarettes smoked in the past week by participants was 3.5, this number would be placed under the middle of the curve at its tallest point and most participants would be near the average, or mean, in the large part of the bell-shaped distribution. Our sample's smoking distribution would get smaller at its tails because fewer participants would smoke in numbers that were far above or below average.

As we planned our campaign, we would make inferences about the population (all students at our university) based on the responses of our sample. Error occurs when researchers take measurements from a sample and use them to make inferences about a population because there are differences between a sample distribution and a population distribution. We could not determine the exact average number of cigarettes smoked weekly by students at our university, for example, unless we conducted a census by interviewing every student. We have not conducted a census, and, because of this, the responses of our sample will not exactly represent the true responses of the population. In our smoking survey, our sample mean for cigarettes smoked in the last 7 days might be 3.5, whereas the true value for the population might be 3.8. The difference between the opinions and behaviors of the sample, and the opinions and behaviors of the population, is error.

As researchers, we must understand this error, so we use a tool to measure it called standard deviation. Standard deviation is a standardized measure of dispersion (or variation) around a mean. Standard deviation is, essentially, a standardized unit of measurement that researchers use to measure distances from a sampling distribution's midpoint to its outer limits. Think of standard deviation as a simple unit of measurement. Researchers use standard deviation to measure distance from the mean in a bell-shaped curve in the same way a carpenter uses inches to measure the length of a board.

Researchers use standard deviation for various purposes. If the publishers of a book survey 10 people and ask them to read and rate it using a scale of 0 to 10, for example, the text might receive an average rating of 5. If all 10 people who read the book actually rated the text as a 5, the average rating is highly accurate and there is no standard deviation. If 5 people rate the text as a 10, however, and 5 people rate the text as a O, the mean rating still is 5. This time the average rating is not very accurate. No one, in fact, actually gave the text a 5 rating.

The standard deviation would be relatively large because there is a lot of dispersion around the mean. Although the means are the same in each case, they actually are different and standard deviation helps us measure and understand this. Using our smoking survey example, if every participant in our smoking survey said they smoked 3.5 cigarettes in the last 7 days, our mean would be highly accurate and we would have no deviation from the mean. When we ask sample members about their smoking habits, however, we will undoubtedly receive different responses and we can use the mean and standard deviation to understand these responses.

How do standard deviation and sample distribution help us when we calculate sample size? Standard deviation gives researchers a basis for estimating the probability of correspondence between the normally distributed, bell-shaped curve of a perfect population distribution, and a probability-based sample distribution that always contains some error. Researchers call standard deviation measurements "standard" because they associate with, or measure, specific areas under a normal curve. One standard deviation measures about 68% of a normally distributed curve; two standard deviations measure a little over 95% of a normally distributed curve; and three standard deviations measure over 99% of a normally distributed curve. Research professionals use standard deviations to calculate sample sizes because of their instrumental role in measuring the area under a normally distributed curve. In particular, researchers use standard deviations to determine a sample's confidence level, as we will demonstrate.

CONFIDENCE LEVEL

A confidence level is the degree of certainty researchers can have when they draw a inferences about a population based on data from a sample. Basically, it is the level of probability researchers have that a characteristic they find in a sample can be accurately generalized to the population. In essence, the confidence level answers the question, "How confident are we that our sample is representative of the population?" A confidence level of 90% means researchers are 90% confident the sample accurately represents the population.

In the same way, a confidence level of 95% means researchers are 95% confident the inferences they draw about the population from the sample are accurate.

This raises an important question: Are researchers really 90% or 95% confident about the representativeness of the sample, or are they simply guessing, perhaps based on their experience? In fact, researchers' claims of a confidence level are accurate because the confidence level is based on standard deviation. Remember, a standard deviation allows researchers to estimate probability between a normally distributed population curve and a less than perfect sampling distribution because standard deviation measurements associate with specific areas under the curve. A standard deviation of 1.65 measures 90% of a normally distributed curve, a standard deviation of 1.96 measures 95% of a normally distributed curve, and a standard deviation of 2.58 measures 99% of a normally distributed curve. Remember these numbers because we will use them again shortly.

This means that when researchers calculate sample size, they select standard deviations associated with specific areas under a normally distributed curve to provide the desired confidence level. When investigators use 1.65 in the sample-size formula, they calculate a sample size that provides a 90% confidence level; when they use 1.96 in the formula, they calculate a sample size that provides a 95% confidence level; when they use 2.58 in the formula, they calculate a sample size that provides a 99% confidence level.

Most often, researchers use 1.96 standard deviations to calculate sample size, resulting in a 95% confidence level. A confidence level of 95% means our sample statistics will accurately represent the true parameter of a population 95% of the time. Here is another way to think about this: If we conducted a survey of the same population 1.00 times, our sample responses would be accurate in 95 of the 100 surveys we conducted. The 95% confidence level is a standard convention of social science, but researchers can use other confidence levels. In particular, if researchers desire a high degree of confidence when making inferences about a population based on data from a sample, they may choose a higher confidence level. Rarely do researchers use a lower confidence level.

Confidence Interval

A confidence interval is a range or margin of error that researchers permit when making inferences from a sample to a population. As noted, the inferences researchers make about a population based on sample data are not completely accurate. Unless investigators conduct a census, the observed values they collect from a sample (statistics) will not provide completely accurate information concerning a population's true values (parameters).

The population parameter falls somewhere within the range of the confidence interval, although researchers arc never exactly sure where the parameter is located unless they conduct a census. The confidence interval usually is stated as a positive-to-negative range, such as +/-3% error or +/-5% error. A confidence interval of +/-3% has a total error margin of 6%, whereas a confidence interval of +/-5% has a total error margin of 10%. If 57% of registered voters in California express support for a citizens' initiative in a survey with a +/-5% confidence interval, for example, the true population value may be as high as 62% (+5%) or as low as 52% (-5%).

What is an acceptable confidence interval in a survey? As is often the case in survey research, the answer depends on various factors. Many applied public relations and market research surveys have a +/-5% confidence interval, but there is nothing critical about this range of error. Researchers commonly choose smaller confidence levels when they want to reduce the margin of error and increase the precision of the inferences they draw concerning a population. When media organizations poll the public to predict election outcomes, for example, they often use a smaller confidence interval, such as +/-3%. Ultimately, researchers should make confidence interval decisions based on the necessities and challenges of individual research projects.

It may surprise you to know that the confidence level and the confidence interval do not have to add to 100. Those new to research often assume the confidence level and confidence interval must add to 100 because researchers often conduct surveys with a +/-5% error at a 95% confidence level. It is incidental that these numbers add to 100. It is legitimate to conduct a survey with a +/-3% margin of error at a 95% confidence level, for example, or a survey with a +/-2.5% margin of error at a 99% confidence level. In addition, many researchers use a 95% confidence level as a standard and only make adjustments to the confidence interval when calculating sample size. Researchers should make decisions concerning confidence levels and confidence intervals based on the requirements of individual research projects.

Variance

Variance is simply dispersion. When researchers calculate sample size, it helps them to understand how the characteristic or variable they are examining is dispersed throughout a population. If we want to understand the use of public transportation in our community as a way to reduce traffic and pollution, for example, it would be useful to know the percentage of community members who actually use public transportation. In short, we want to know how public transportation use is dispersed throughout our community as a characteristic of the population.

For research purposes, it is useful to consider variance as a simple percentage. Community members who use public transportation, for example, fit into one category that makes up a certain percentage of the population. Community members who do not use public transportation do not belong in the category and make up the remaining percentage of the population. The percentages add up to 100%. Researchers can examine the dispersion of most variables this way because a population can be divided into two categories on the basis of almost any characteristic. This includes, for example, students who smoke cigarettes and students who do not smoke cigarettes; community residents who live in a certain neighborhood and residents who live in other neighborhoods; workers who are employed and workers who are unemployed; people who think coffee is a major food group and people who do not.

Any time researchers examine a variable or characteristic, they want to know its dispersion within a population because they can use this information to help them calculate sample size. Population members who have a characteristic or variable fit into a single category, and researchers use this to distinguish them from the rest of the population. In the formula we examine shortly, the percentage of a population that belongs to a category is expressed as a decimal. The remaining percentage of the population (that does not belong to the category) also is expressed as a decimal and is subtracted from 1. Together, these two numbers add to 1.0 or 100% of the population. Despite the importance of variance, researchers often have to set aside variance percentages when they calculate sample size because percentages only reflect the dispersion of a single characteristic or variable in a population.

Researchers commonly examine multiple variables in a single survey, each with a different percentage of dispersion. Each variable would require a different sample size, which is impractical and unnecessary. Researchers address this problem by using the largest measure of variance available to calculate sample size because, at a minimum, it provides an acceptable measure of dispersion for all variables. To use the largest measure of variance, researchers use .5 (or 50%) as the percentage of a population that belongs to a category. Researchers also use .5 as the percentage for the rest of the population because 1 - .5 = .5 and these percentages add up to 1.0, or 100% of the population. Although it is not necessary for researchers to use .5 and 1 - .5 in every sample-size calculation, this practice is almost always required by the necessities of a multifaceted research project, and so we use it in all of our sample-size calculations.

SAMPLE SIZE CALCULATIONS

Now that you understand standard deviation, confidence level, confidence interval, and variance, you are ready to calculate sample size. What if we want less error (a smaller confidence interval), meaning more confidence in the precision of our survey results? It is easy to adjust the formula to fit the demands of any research situation. In the following calculations, for example, we determine sample sizes based on different confidence levels. We calculate each sample size with a +/-5% confidence interval, but with different confidence levels to show how different confidence levels affect sample size. To change confidence levels, we use standard deviations that correspond to different areas under a normally distributed, bell-shaped curve.

Recall that the standard deviation for a 90% confidence level is 1.65; the standard deviation for a 95% confidence level is 1.96, and the standard deviation for a 99% confidence level is 2.58. Notice that we increase sample size each time we increase the confidence level. The only difference in each calculation is the level of confidence researchers have when they make inferences from a sample to a population.

Here is a basic sample-size calculation using this formula. What if we want less error (a smaller confidence interval), meaning more confidence in the precision of our survey results? It is easy to adjust the formula to fit the demands of any research situation. In the following calculations, for example, we determine sample sizes based on different confidence levels. We calculate each sample size with a +/-5% confidence interval, but with different confidence levels to show how different confidence levels affect sample size. To change confidence levels, we use standard deviations that correspond to different areas under a normally distributed, bell-shaped curve. Recall that the standard deviation for a 90% confidence level is 1.65; the standard deviation for a 95% confidence level is 1.96, and the standard deviation for a 99% confidence level is 2.58. Notice that we increase sample size each time we increase the confidence level. The only difference in each calculation is the level of confidence researchers have when they make inferences from a sample to a population.

ERROR CALCULATIONS

The same information you learned to calculate sample size also helps you calculate the margin of error for a survey, once you have collected data. In most cases, final sample size is not 384 or 1,060 completed interviews, even if this is researchers' targeted sample size. Researchers aiming for a specific sample size typically collect additional interviews for various reasons. Research staff may have to throw out some interviews, for example, because of problems with data collection, such as a survey that is only partially complete.

At other times, researchers may collect a larger sample size so they have a stronger basis from which to make sample subgroup comparisons. Regardless of the reason, researchers can use standard deviation, confidence level, and variance to calculate the margin of error that exists in a survey's results based on their sample size. How do changes in the confidence level affect the margin of error for a sample? In the following calculations, we determine margins of error for surveys with the same sample sizes at different levels of confidence.

ISSUES AND ASSUMPTIONS

The formulas presented here require various assumptions and raise some important issues. We have addressed many of these issues and assumptions in the preceding sections, but readers may need to alter the formula or disregard it completely as the assumptions on which the formula is based change. One of the primary assumptions of all sample size formulas, for example, concerns researchers' use of probability sampling methods. When researchers use nonprobability sampling methods, no sample-size formula will produce an accurate sample size because it is impossible to determine the representativeness of the sample.

One issue we have not addressed concerns the need to correct the formula according to a population's size. Researchers sometimes use sample-size formulas that contain something called finite population correction. Finite population correction is an adjustment factor that is part of a sample-size formula. The appropriate sample size for a population of 1 million people is 384, the same sample size we calculated for a survey with a 95% confidence level and a +/- 5% margin of error.

Is it necessary for researchers to correct for population size? Generally, researchers have no need for population correction unless the size of the population is small and the sample is more than 5% of the total population. In most sample surveys, population correction makes little difference in sample-size calculations and researchers simply exclude a population correction factor because it is unnecessary. In fact, researchers would generally use the same sample size for a survey of registered voters in Chicago, a survey of registered voters in Illinois, or a survey of all registered voters in the entire United States! Although there are important exceptions, once a population reaches a certain size, sample sizes generally remain consistent. For this reason, and to keep our sample calculations simple, the sample size formula we have presented does not include population correction.

Sampling is a powerful tool that helps practitioners obtain accurate information at a reasonable cost. Researchers' selection of a proper sampling method is as important as their selection of a proper research method to the success of a study. Even the most carefully planned and executed study will produce untrustworthy results if you use an improper sampling method.

Although sampling can be complex, it is in your own best interest to learn all you can about the sample-selection procedures used in a study. Few people would buy an automobile without first inspecting the vehicle they are purchasing. Still, a surprising number of practitioners make research "purchases" without ever inspecting one of the most critical elements of their research project, the sampling procedures used in a study.

As demonstrated in this chapter, it is not necessary for practitioners to become sampling experts to understand many important issues related to sampling selection. It is necessary, however, for practitioners to understand basic distinctions in sampling methods and to work with researchers to ensure that the sample used in a study has the greatest chance of accurately representing the attitudes, opinions, and behaviors of the population from which it is drawn.

Chapter 12

Creating Effective Message

In the 1950s and early 1960s, communication experts noticed that mass communication campaigns were having little effect, and many believed the situation hopeless. One scholar caused an uproar with an article calling mass media campaigns essentially impotent, and another published an influential book asserting that information campaigns tended to reinforce existing opinions but rarely changed anybody's minds. These followed on the heels of two other scholars who blamed the receivers of messages for failing to be persuaded by them. This pessimistic view still prevailed a decade later, when a man named Mendelsohn shot back with a more realistic diagnosis and a more optimistic prognosis. His ideas have had an enormous impact on the communication field.

THREE ASSUMPTIONS FOR SUCCESS

Mendelsohn believed campaigns so often failed because campaign designers overpromised, assumed the public was going to automatically receive and be interested in their messages, and blanketed the public with messages that were not targeted properly and were likely to be ignored or misinterpreted. As McGuire wrote later, successful communication campaigns depend on a good understanding of two types of theories: those that explain how someone will process and respond to a message, and those that explain why someone will or will not respond to a message in desirable ways.

After nearly three decades, Mendelsohn's diagnosis still applies. Recent surveys and interviews with public relations professionals have shown consistently that one of the major reasons clients and superiors lose faith in public relations agencies and professionals is overpromising (Bourland, 1993). Overpromising often occurs when Programme planners do not have a good understanding of their publics and of the situation in which Programme messages will be received. People from varied backgrounds and with varied interests are likely to interpret messages differently. Moreover, a good understanding of the problem, the publics, and the constraints affecting the likelihood of change (remember social marketings "price") helps the Programme planner set goals and objectives that can be achieved using the strategies available in the time allotted.

Mendelsohn trio of campaign assumptions are as follows:

1. Target your messages.
2. Assume your target public is uninterested in your messages.
3. Set reasonable, midrange goals and objectives.

On the one hand, Mendelsohn's admonition that message receivers will not be interested in a campaign and that campaigns setting ambitious goals are doomed to failure can cultivate pessimism. Mendelsohn's point, however, is that campaign designers who make his three assumptions can make adjustments in strategy that will facilitate success both in the short term and in the long run. The implication of Mendelsohn's tripartite is that research is necessary to define and to understand the target publics, and that an understanding of theory is necessary to develop strategies that acknowledge the public's likely lack of interest and that point to strategies that will compensate for it. Mendelsohn illustrated his point with an example from his own experience, which, depending on your perspective, could be viewed either as a major success or a dismal failure.

Mendelsohn's campaign tried to increase traffic safety by addressing the fact that at least 80% of drivers considered themselves good or excellent drivers, yet unsafe driving practices killed people every day. Long holiday weekends were especially gruesome. Meanwhile, most drivers ignored the 300,000 persuasive traffic safety messages disseminated each year in the print media.

Mendelsohn's team, in cooperation with the National Safety Council and CBS, developed "The CBS National Driver's Test," which aired immediately before the 1965 Memorial Day weekend. A publicity campaign distributed 50 million official test answer forms via newspapers, magazines, and petroleum products dealers before the show aired. The show, viewed by approximately 30 million Americans, was among the highest rated public affairs broadcasts of all time to that point and resulted in mail responses from nearly a million and a half viewers. Preliminary research showed that almost 40% of the licensed drivers who had participated in the broadcast had failed the test. Finally, 35,000 drivers enrolled in driver-improvement Programmes across the country following the broadcast.

The producer of the Programme called the response "enormous, beyond all expectations." Yet no evidence was provided that accident rates decreased because of the broadcast, and the number of people enrolled in driver improvement Programmes reflected only about .07% of those who had been exposed to the test forms. How was this an "enormous" success? Mendelsohn realized that bad drivers would be difficult to reach because of their lack of awareness or active denial of their skill deficiencies, and he realized that to set a campaign goal of eliminating or greatly reducing traffic deaths as the result of a single campaign would be impossible. As a result, Mendelsohn's team chose more realistic goals in recognition of the fact that a single campaign could not be expected to completely solve any problem.

The goals of the campaign were as follows:

1. Overcome public indifference to traffic hazards that may be caused by bad driving (increasing awareness).

2. Make bad drivers cognizant of their deficiencies (comprehension).
3. Direct viewers who become aware of their driving deficiencies into a social mechanism already set up in the community to correct such deficiencies (skill development).

HOW PEOPLE RESPOND TO MESSAGES

Evaluating Mendelsohn's success illustrates both the pitfalls of dependence on the traditional linear model of the communication process and the advantages of adopting a more receiver-oriented view, commonly known as the domino model or hierarchy of effects theory of persuasion. The domino model acknowledges that campaign messages have to achieve several intermediate steps that intervene between message dissemination and desired behaviour changes.

According to McGuire, the originator of the domino model, effective campaigns need to acknowledge the following steps, which have been modified here to reflect recent research findings and the symmetrical public relations perspective. Each step is a repository for dozens, if not hundreds, of studies that have shown the importance of the step in people's decision making, along with the factors that enhance or compromise the success of campaign messages at each step.

1. *Exposure:* This, unfortunately, is where most public relations Programmes begin and end, with getting the message out. Obviously, no one can be persuaded by a message they have had no opportunity to receive. Simply placing a message in the environment, however, is not enough to ensure its receipt or acceptance. Recall that some 300,000 safe driving messages had been ignored consistently by the target public before Mendelsohn's campaign.
2. *Attention:* Even a paid advertisement broadcast during the Super Bowl will fail if the target publics have chosen that moment to head to the refrigerator for a snack, never to see or hear the spot ostensibly

broadcast to millions. A message must attract at least a modicum of attention to succeed, and campaign designers should not forget the obvious: that complex messages require more attention than simple messages. Production values such as colour can make a difference: Colour can attract attention, communicate emotion and enhance memory ("Breaking Through," 1999; "The Cultural," 1998). Production values, however, do not guarantee success even if they do attract attention. Colour must be used carefully, for example, because the meaning of colour may vary with the context and cultural environment.

Although orange may signify humor, Halloween, and autumn, it also can mean quarantine (United States) or death (Arabian countries). Red can mean danger (United States), sin (United States), passionate love (Austria and Germany), joy and happiness (China and Japan), and death (Africa). Quite a range! As a result, the International Red Cross, sensitive to this issue, uses green in Africa instead of red (Felton, 1998). According to the Y & R Brand Futures Group, blue has become a popular colour to signify the future, because people across cultures associate it with the sky and water, signifying limitlessness and peace.

3. *Involvement (liking or Interest)*: Although research has shown people have an "orienting response" that instinctively draws their attention to sudden changes in sounds or visual effects, other research has shown they stop paying attention if a message seems irrelevant, uninteresting, or distasteful. Messages that seem relevant sustain people's interest, making people more likely to learn from the message. Social marketing theory acknowledges the importance of this step by its placement of the audience, or public, in the center of the planning profile. Everything about the campaign goal—its benefits, costs, and

unique qualities—must be considered from the target public's point of view.

They care much more about how a proposal will affect them than how it will affect your company. The City of Tacoma, Washington, for example, wanted to extend the life of its landfill and promote recycling. A 1995 survey of customers found that customers would recycle more if they did not have to sort and separate items. As a result, the city responded by offering a new commingle recycling Programme that enabled customers to throw all recyclables into the same bin. Recycling increased 300% to 400%, far exceeding the research-based objective of 200% to 300% and earning the city a Silver Anvil Award from PRSA.

4. *Comprehension (learning what):* Sustained attention increases but does not guarantee the likelihood of comprehension. Messages can be misinterpreted. As noted, a cereal promotion suggested over a dozen whimsical ideas for getting a cookie prize, named Wendell and shaped like a person, to come out of the cereal box. Having a cookie for breakfast appealed to children, as did the silly ideas, such as telling him he had to come out because he was under arrest. Unfortunately, one if the ideas—call the fire department to rescue a guy from your cereal box—backfired when some children actually called 911, which confused, alarmed and irritated the rescue teams. The boxes had to be pulled from the shelves in at least one region of the country.

5. *Skill acquisition (learning how):* Well-intentioned people may be unable to follow through on an idea if they lack the skills to do so. Potential voters without transportation to the polls will not vote; intended nonsmokers will not quit smoking without social support; interested restaurant patrons will not come if they cannot afford it; parents interested in a civic betterment Programme win not attend a meeting if

they do not have child care. An effective campaign anticipates a target public's needs and provides the help they require.

The National Fire Protection Association (NFPA), for example, found through a Burke Marketing survey that many people had a passive attitude about fire, believed they had much more time to escape than they really do, and only 16% had developed and practiced a home fire escape plan. As a result, NFPA's 1998 Fire Safety Week promotion focused on teaching students about fire escape planning and practice, with incentives to encourage them to participate in a documented practice drill with their families. Although the Silver Anvil Award-winning campaign generated an enormous amount of publicity, the most dramatic result was that at least 25 lives were saved as a direct result of the families' participation in the promotion.

6. *Persuasion (attitude change):* Although McGuire listed this step following skills acquisition, attitude change often precedes skill development. People who lack the skills to follow through on an idea may tune out the details, figuring it is not relevant for them. Attitude change is another of the necessary but often insufficient steps in the persuasion process. Sometimes, however, attitude change is all that is necessary, particularly if the goal of a campaign is to increase a public's satisfaction with an organization to avoid negative consequences such as lawsuits, strikes, or boycotts. Usually, however, a campaign has an outcome behaviour in mind. In that case, remember that people often have attitudes inconsistent with their behaviors. Many smokers believe smoking is a bad thing but still smoke. Many nonvoters say voting is important and they intend to vote, but they still fail to show up on election day.

7. *Memory storage:* This step is important because people receive multiple messages from multiple sources all day, every day. For them to act on your message, they need to remember it when the appropriate time comes to buy a ticket, make a telephone call, fill out a form, or attend an event. They need to be able to store the important information about your message in their memory, which may not be easy if other messages received simultaneously demand their attention. Key elements of messages, therefore, need to be communicated in ways that make them stand out for easy memorization.
8. *Information retrieval:* Simply storing information does not ensure it will be retrieved at the appropriate time. People might remember your special event on the correct day but forget the location. Reminders or memory devices such as slogans, jingles and refrigerator magnets can help.
9. *Motivation (decision):* This is an important step that many campaign designers forget in their own enthusiasm for their campaign goals. Remember Mendelsohn (1973) admonition that people may not be interested in the campaign? They need reasons to follow through. The benefits need to outweigh the costs. In addition, the benefits must seem realistic and, should be easily obtained. The more effort required on the part of the message recipients the less likely it is they will make that effort. If the message recipients believe a proposed behaviour is easy, will have major personal benefits, or is critically important, they are more likely to act.

The challenge for the Programme planner is to discover what will motivate the target audience successfully, an issue addressed later in this chapter. Elgin DDB of Seattle, when asked to help reduce Puget Sound curbside disposal of grass clippings by 5%, realized motivation would be an important focus. Focus groups and phone surveys indicated the target group, male homeowners aged 25 to 65, had an interest in grasscycling but needed the proper tools to make it easy and practical. As a result, they arranged to recycle consumers' old polluting gas mowers for free at a special event and sell Toro and Ryobi mulch mowers at below the normal retail price, with an additional rebate. With a goal of selling 3,000 mowers, they sold 5,000. They hoped to remove 1,500 gas mowers from the market and ended up recycling approximately 2,600. And, as for their original goal of reducing curbside disposal of grass clippings by 5%? They more than tripled the target amount, reducing grass clippings by 17%, winning a 1999 Silver Anvil Award.

10. *Behaviour:* Success often is measured in terms of behaviors such as sales or attendance figures. Marketing experts, however, know that getting someone's business once does not guarantee long-term success. One study ("Building Customer," 1996) found that keeping customers loyal can boost profits up to 80%. As a result, the Programme planner needs to do everything possible to ensure that behaviour attempts meet with success. Victoria's Secret, for example, wound up with hundreds of thousands of frustrated web browsers when it promoted an online fashion show following the 1999 Super Bowl only to have the technology crash. Anticipating demand and handling unsuccessful attempts in a positive way can help cement relationships for the long term.

11. *Reinforcement of behaviour, attitude or both:* Most people are familiar with the term buyer's remorse, which is what people feel if they have second thoughts about a decision they made. Sometimes buyer's remorse results from a bad experience with an organization, such as an unresponsive telephone operator, quite unrelated to the product or idea that was the focus of a campaign. Programme planners should

anticipate possible reasons for buyer's remorse in a campaign and make follow-up communication part of the campaign to ensure targeted publics continue to feel good about the organization's products or ideas.

12. *Post-behaviour consolidation:* This is the final step in a message receiver's decision-making process. At this point, the receiver considers the campaign messages, the attitudes and behaviours involved, and the successes or failures encountered in implementing the targeted attitudes or behaviors, to incorporate this new information into a preexisting world view. By attending a special event promoting both a company and a cause, such as feeding the homeless, a message recipient may develop a long-term connection with both the company and the cause. Alternatively, target publics may decide they had a fun time but these issues do not take higher priority for future decisions than they did before the campaign. Affecting a targeted public's world view is the most challenging goal for a public relations campaign, but for Programmes focused on building long-term, mutually beneficial relationships, this result also is the most coveted.

McGuire (1989) suggested a success rate of 50% at each stage in a typical mass media campaign would be improbably optimistic. Given that level of attrition, a campaign exposed to 1 million people would gain the attention of 500,000, would hold the interest of 250,000, would be understood as intended by 125,000, would address the necessary skills and needs of 62,500, would be persuasive to 31,250, would be remembered at the time of the communication by 15,625, would be recalled later by 7,813, would be sufficiently motivating to 3,907, would achieve behaviour change among 1,954, would achieve repeat behaviour among 977, and would gain long-term "consolidation" among 489. No wonder campaign designers in the 1950s and 1960s thought campaigns were doomed to failure. The good news, however, is that this pessimistic view assumes each step has an equal chance of success, each step is equally important to the campaign, and the steps must proceed in the order delineated by McGuire's matrix. Fortunately, these assumptions do not always apply.

If we think back to Mendelsohn (1973) campaign, in which 50 million people were exposed to promotions regarding the CBS National Driver's Test, 30 million viewed the Programme to become aware of the hazards of unsafe driving, nearly 40% of licensed drivers failed the test, and approximately 35,000 drivers enrolled in driver improvement Programmes, should we consider Mendelsohn's campaign a success or a failure? The campaign achieved close to .1% success throughout the hierarchy of effects.

Given Mendelsohn's points about assuming the target is uninterested, the need for targeting the audience, and the need to set reasonable goals, we must consider the situation before assigning credit or blame. Bad drivers are not likely to be interested in being told their driving is deficient; indeed, they are likely to be defensive. Everyone thinks everyone else is the bad driver. In fact, Mendelsohn found that 80% of drivers thought they were good drivers, yet almost half of licensed drivers failed the National Driver's Test. That means that one of every two bad drivers either didn't know or would not acknowledge their deficiencies. So Mendelsohn was correct, even understated, on the first point. As for targeting the audience, the CBS National Driver's Test did not broadcast exclusively to bad drivers.

It had to find them among all other viewers of the Programme, some of whom would not be licensed drivers, would not be old enough to drive, or would be safe drivers. As a result, the campaign could not reasonably expect, nor would it desire, all 50 million people exposed to the campaign to enroll in driver improvement Programmes. Indeed, if that many people signed up for class, there would not have been enough teachers to serve them all. If 40% of the drivers who watched the Programme took the test and failed it in the privacy of their own homes, many of them probably changed their attitudes about their own driving and perhaps took some extra precautions the next time they drove, regardless of whether they enrolled in a formal driver improvement Programme. Finally, the 35,000 drivers who did sign up for formal Programmes represented a 300% increase, in a 3-month period, over the previous annual enrollment in the Programmes.

Any public relations agency promising 50 million exposures and 50 million behaviors would be dismissed as naive and absurd. Any public relations agency promising a 300% increase in targeted behaviors, particularly for a challenging behaviour to change, probably also would be dismissed as arrogant and unrealistic. So from Mendelsohn we can learn that the definition of success depends on the viewer's perspective. Defining success in terms of desired receiver-oriented outcomes is more appropriate than defining success in terms of source-oriented outputs such as reach or impressions. Promising clients huge exposure can tempt them to expect more impressive behavioral outcomes than would be realistic. With such dangers in mind, McGuire (1989) explained various fallacies that can doom a campaign, along with principles for counteracting challenges along the way.

COMMON PROBLEMS

McGuire noted three fallacies that dog campaign designers with an insufficient grasp of persuasion theory.

1. The attenuated effects fallacy. Clients and agencies alike want to assume that exposure will produce success in terms of reputation, sales, or other desirable outcomes. The likelihood of continued success along each successive decision-making step, however, is probably less than 50% in a mass market campaign, making the final outcome likely to be less than .1% of the original number exposed to the campaign, as demonstrated.
2. The distant measure fallacy. Sometimes Programme planners report results for attitude change as if they represent behaviour change, or they may report

changes in awareness as a representation of attitude change. If a Programme hopes to achieve behaviour change, it must measure behaviour, not attitudes, as an outcome. Using "clip counts" as an indicator of awareness, by collecting the amount of publicity accumulated, misrepresents campaign effects.

3. The neglected mediator fallacy. Well-meaning Programme planners can make unwitting mistakes if they assume elements that enhance success at one step will continue to enhance success at every step. For example, using Nancy Reagan as a spokesperson for the Just Say No antidrug Programmes of the 1980s helped the campaigns achieve tremendous exposure nationwide. But Nancy Reagan's credibility among the targeted audience of at-risk adolescents was not high. Likewise, having police officers deliver messages to school children in the DARE to Say No to Drugs campaigns might get the children's attention, but it would do little to provide them with the skills needed to face possible ostracization from their peers. A spokesperson more relevant to their own needs and interests is important to such a campaign.

McGuire also offered several recommendations designed to help maximize success at each step. Even if a campaign cannot achieve 300% increases in behaviour, as Mendelsohn's campaign did, it probably can do better than .1% of those initially exposed to a Programme message if the designer successfully implements the following principles.

1. The compensatory principle. The good news is that sometimes things can balance out such that something working against your campaign at one step may work in favor of it at another step. If a simple, graphics-heavy message on television gets people's attention but communicates little information about a complex issue, a companion message, perhaps in a medium such as print or web-

based technologies more amenable to careful consideration, can provide the necessary details. Not everyone will pursue the details, but if the initial message piques the public's interest, more people probably will pay deeper attention to the companion message than would have done so otherwise. If a political figure helps a campaign achieve exposure but is irrelevant to the ultimate target public, a campaign can include more appropriate message sources for different targeted publics.

2. The golden mean principle. Usually, a moderate amount of something, rather than extreme levels, has the maximum effect. This principle seems like common sense but can be difficult to apply because it can be challenging to determine what levels of humor or fear, for example, seem extreme to the target public. Simi larly, the campaign designer needs to know what level of complexity makes a message incomprehensible, versus what level of simplicity makes the message boring. The golden mean principle, therefore, illustrates why pretesting is vital to message development.
3. The situation weighting principle. According to McGuire, achieving the hierarchy of effects is not as difficult as it may seem at first glance, because some steps will probably be easier to achieve than others. For example, publicity campaigns continue to hold such popularity because they often reach enough people who already have the interest and motivation to follow through on a message about a new product or service opportunity.

Most people will not be interested, but if enough interested people read a well-placed piece on a new restaurant, they will need little additional impetus to get them to the restaurant, as long as the location is easy to remember. They already may possess the skills (transportation and money), the attitude (liking to eat out at that type of restaurant), and the motivation (perhaps an anniversary or birthday dinner is coming up). Likewise, people who want to do something they never thought possible may jump at the opportunity if a campaign addresses their needs (the skill development step).

The result, according to the domino model and Mendelsohn assumptions, is that a well-researched, carefully targeted campaign will make more dominos fall without going awry.

Acknowledging People Are Not Always Logical

Because the domino model is such a useful campaign planning tool, it is the most popular theory of persuasion among public relations Programme planners. In fact, Ketchum Public Relations has fashioned a Public Relations Effectiveness Yardstick. The Yardstick approximates the hierarchy of effects for easy application, by combining the steps of the domino model into three levels of effect.

The first level, called the basic level, measures outputs, or exposure in McGuire terminology, such as total placements and number of impressions. The second level, called the intermediate level, measures outgrowths, such as whether target audiences have received messages directed at them, whether they have paid attention to them, whether they have understood them, and whether they have retained them. This corresponds to the steps of attention, comprehension, interest and memory storage in McGuire's model. The third level, coed the advanced level, measures public relations outcomes, such as opinion, attitude, or behaviour change.

The domino theory, however, has one important limitation: It incorporates an assumption the recipients of campaign messages will process them in a logical way, carefully considering the veracity of campaign messages to evaluate whether they wish to perform the proposed behaviour. The truth is people are not always logical, and we do some things not because they seem right but because they feel good. As a result, it is important to consider another theoretical perspective on persuasion that explicitly acknowledges our logical lapses.

The most popular alternative to the hierarchy of effects theory is called the elaboration likelihood model (ELM). Developed by Petty and Cacioppo using tightly controlled experiments with limited samples of college students, this theory has its detractors and should be applied with respect for its limitations. Its basic principles, however, provide a useful framework for public relations Programme application, regardless of how the scholars sort out the details. According to the ELM, people process messages differently depending on their level of involvement with the issue. In this way, the ELM dovetails with Grunig and Repper situational theory of publics. People uninterested or uninvolved in a topic will not process messages deeply, but those more interested will be more likely to elaborate, or think more carefully about, the message.

The result is that the campaign designer can think broadly of two routes to persuasion. The first route is called the central approach, and emphasizes logic and careful consideration. The second route is called the peripheral approach, and forgoes logical arguments in favor of more emotionally or heuristic-based strategies. These strategies include elements such as likable, attractive, powerful, credible sources. According to the ELM, decisions achieved using the central approach are more likely to last, whereas decisions achieved using the peripheral approach are more likely to fade, or decay. The peripheral approach, however, can achieve changes more quickly because less thoughtful consideration is necessary from the message recipients.

The central approach requires a larger investment of energy from the message recipient, making it more likely to succeed if recipients are highly involved or interested in the topic. If it succeeds it has longer lasting effects because people feel more invested in a decision that took more effort to make and that is based on facts instead of on surface cues. The peripheral approach is more appropriate for low-involvement issues or among target publics who do not care much about the issue. Again, it requires research to determine the extent to which target publics feel involved and ready to participate in thoughtful decision making.

McGuire called the ELM an alternative route to persuasion because the ELM model's central approach follows all the steps in the domino model, whereas the peripheral approach bypasses several steps, concentrating on elements such as attention, liking, and motivation to the exclusion of elements such as attitude change and skill development. Both the central approach and the peripheral approach require that the Programme planner understand what will attract and hold message recipients' attention, along with what will motivate them to follow through the hierarchy of effects necessary to achieve behaviour change.

FINDING THE RIGHT MOTIVATING STRATEGY

To help campaign designers sort through the possible strategies for motivating target publics, McGuire has created a matrix that summarizes hundreds of scientific studies on attitudes and persuasion into 16 categories. A modified version of McGuire's matrix is presented here to help the public relations professional. Managers may notice that the top half of the chart, labeled cognitive theories, roughly corresponds to the central approach of the ELM theory, whereas the bottom half of the chart, labeled affective theories, roughly corresponds to the peripheral approach.

The top and bottom halves of the chart are divided again, to acknowledge that sometimes people are motivated by the need for stability, because utter chaos would make life too unpredictable and uncomfortable, and sometimes people are motivated by the desire to grow, such as by the desire to become smarter, or more successful, or more independent, or more happy.

The most effective campaign probably will combine various strategies from the matrix to address the needs and interests possessed by different target publics or to address the challenges presented at different steps in the persuasion process. For example, a campaign might use an affective (emotionally based) strategy to pique the public's interest in an issue and follow that with a more logically based message to deepen the public's understanding of the issue. Remember that virtually no effective campaign will forgo emotional appeals as part of its strategic mix. A dry recitation of information attracts little attention, interest, or motivation except from the most dedicated target publics. Again, research and pretesting are required to determine which among the following strategies is most appropriate for a given public relations Programme or campaign.

LOGICAL STRATEGIES

The first half of McGuire dynamic theories matrix focuses on primarily logic-based appeals. On the whole, logical appeals serve as useful strategies for publics who have an interest in a topic and some motivation to ponder it. For issues they care less about or feel defensive about, rational arguments may not work. Evan logic-based arguments include some affective elements, appealing in positive ways to make target publics think better of themselves or in negative ways to encourage them to avoid thinking less of themselves. As a result, they include a range of positive and negative strategies, as follows:

1. *Consistency:* People desire to have consistency in their lives. If campaigns demonstrate two conflicting beliefs, they will feel cognitive dissonance, meaning discomfort from the contradictions in their belief system, which they will want to resolve. The consistency-based message is one of the most popular campaign strategies, because it offers a straightforward way to communicate that the public is mistaken for disagreeing with the client's point of view. The Family Violence Protection Fund, for example, challenged its target public that "if the noise coming from next door were loud music, you'd do something about it," implying that if the noise is coming from something much more serious such as spousal abuse, there's no excuse for domestic violence and no excuse for failing to report it. The

idea that the reader would intervene for something trivial but bothersome, yet not for something so serious, aims to create dissonance by making the reader feel selfish.

2. *Noetic or attribution:* Sometimes the campaigner prefers to take a more positive approach to people's desire for consistency. The noetic approach relies on highlighting an association that gives the target public and the organization some common ground on which to share their perspectives, to encourage the target public to view the organization or its proposed behaviors in a more favorable light. One use for attribution theory is to point out a simple association between two things the public may not have connected previously, such as CARE, a social assistance organization, and Starbucks coffee.

   Working Assets long distance service has used the strategy to appeal to consumers who favor nonprofit causes such as Greenpeace, Human Rights Watch, and Planned Parenthood. Of course, communication managers should use such strategies carefully. Appealing to consumers who favor Greenpeace and Planned Parenthood can alienate others who despise those organizations. Another use is to attribute the cause of a problem to a desired issue instead of an undesired issue. For example, some businesses might prefer to attribute the reason for a problem, such as diminished salmon runs, to dammed-up rivers instead of to a complex variety of environmental factors. In this way an organization can deflect blame from its own environmental practices to one cause.

3. *Categorization:* A popular strategy among political campaigners in particular, the categorization approach responds to people's desire to organize their world into sensible categories such as good and bad, or real and unreal. If the campaign designer can change the way people view a situation, it may change the way they evaluate issues relevant to the

situation. For example, a moderate Republican challenging a Democrat for office may apply the label "liberal," or "tax and spend" to the Democrat to evoke a reliable response from targeted segments of the electorate, but the same Republican can fall victim to a more conservative Republican challenger who may relabel the moderate Republican as "too liberal" or as "tax and spend" to associate him or her more with Democrats than with Republicans. Such strategies, however, can stretch the truth or ethical boundaries and should be used with care. One candidate in a Pennsylvania Senate race, Rick Santorum, went so far as to relabel the "problem" for the state's gun-control opponents as his rival, Harris Wofford. Santorum's direct mail piece suggested Wofford should be "targeted" to rid Pennsylvania of the gun control problem. The piece, with Wofford's name imprinted in the center of a target, not only looked as if it was meant for real target shooting, but it even was offered for sale as such.

4. *Inductional:* This approach can be called the coupon approach because it endeavors to arrange a situation to induce the desired behaviour without changing an attitude first. Instead, the campaign follows the behaviour change with an appeal to change corresponding attitudes. For example, people might attend a rock concert benefiting the homeless out of a desire to hear the music and see the stars. Once at the concert, they might receive a pitch to support the targeted charity. 5. Autonomy. This strategy appeals to people's desire for independence. Particularly in the United States, individualist-minded publics do not want to be bossed around. Appealing to their desire to be self-sovereign sometimes can help an organization develop a convincing message. Organizations that believe their own sovereignty is under attack often resort to this

strategy, hoping targeted publics will share their outrage. For example, Voters for Choice told readers of the New York Times that "you have the right to remain silent," displaying a tombstone with the name of Dr. David Gunn, who had been killed for practicing abortion, "but your silence can and will be used against you by anti-choice terrorists." Sometimes the strategy can work with an ironic twist, in an attempt to convince people that giving up some freedom, such as by following the rules in a wilderness park, actually will gain them more freedom by ensuring they can enjoy the peace and quiet themselves.

6. *Stimulation:* Sometimes the right thing to do seems boring, and some excitement makes it seem more appealing. As a positive type of appeal, stimulation strategies appeal to people's curiosity or their desire to help create or preserve something with an exciting payoff, such as a wilderness area that can offer outdoor adventures. A group of police officers in Washington state, for example, although visiting middle schools with a serious antidrug message, have transformed themselves into rap stars to deliver their message with rhythm instead of force. As they chant about things students should not do or "you're busted!" the students gyrate and yell the punch line back to the officers. The message gets through.
7. *Problem solver:* Another favourite campaign strategy, the problem solver approach simply shows a problem and demonstrates the favored way to solve the problem. Not enough people can afford to go to college; give to the United Negro College Fund. Not enough children have safe homes; be a foster parent. Use of this strategy assumes the target public will care enough about the problem to respond, which is a big assumption to make. Recall Mendelsohn advice to assume the opposite, that the audience is uninterested. Campaigns that neglect to confirm this

assumption through research risk failure. When the assumption holds, however, the results can be impressive. It worked for Beaufort County, South Carolina, which had to persuade voters to approve a 1% sales tax increase to pay for improving a dangerous 13-mile stretch of road and bridges when the measure had failed by a 2-to-1 margin twice before. The carefully coordinated Silver Anvil Award-winning campaign overwhelmed the vocal opposition in a 58% to 42% victory when White retirees, young workers, employers, and older African-Americans became familiar with the problem, that "The Wait Is Killing Us," and mobilized in support of the measure.

8. *Teleological:* Just as noetic theories (creating a positive association) offer the opposite strategy from consistency approaches (creating an apparent contradiction that requires resolution), teleological approaches offer the positive alternative to problem solver approaches. Teleological means heaven like, and the approach relies on showing what the world would look like if a problem already had been solved. This is a useful strategy for incumbent candidates for political office who wish to show their service has made a positive difference for their constituents. In other cases, the target public is shown the ideal result of implementing a desired behaviour, along with a script advising how to make the ideal result become reality.

Affective Strategies

The second half of McGuire dynamic theories matrix focuses on more emotionally based appeals. On the whole, emotional appeals serve as useful nudges for undecided or uninterested target publics. For issues that require complex consideration, however, or for which a target public has a deeply held view that counters the sponsoring organization's view, emotional appeals can accomplish little or, even worse, backfire. They, too, include a range of positive and negative approaches, as follows:

9. *Tension-reduction (fear appeals)*: This strategy attempts to produce tension or fear in the message recipient, which makes the target public uncomfortable and in need of a solution that will reduce the tension. It is the emotional parallel to the consistency-cognitive dissonance approach, which aims to create or highlight a contradiction in the target public's beliefs and behaviors they will want to resolve. The tension-reduction strategy is particularly popular among health campaigners, who try to scare the public into more healthy habits.

   The problem with fear appeals, however, is they can backfire badly if not applied with precision. One weakness in fear appeals is a failure to resolve the tension in the message. Threatening a target public with a dire outcome (usually death) linked to a behaviour, such as drug use or eating habits, without showing how the problem can be fixed and how the situation might look with the problem resolved, can make the target public resent the message and the messenger. Another problem is the use of extreme or unrealistic levels of fear, such as the Partnership for a Drug-Free America's admonition equating the use of marijuana with Russian roulette. Because the production of fear appeals is filled with so many pitfalls and the effects of fear appeals are so difficult to predict, they are best avoided. Although appropriate in some situations, such appeals must be well researched. Clients who cannot be dissuaded from using a fear appeal simply must build a large pretesting budget into the project.

10. *Expressive:* Just as noetic strategies take the opposite tack as consistency strategies and teleological approaches reflect the mirror image of problem-solver approaches, the expressive approach takes a positive

twist on the tension-reduction approach. The expressive appeal acknowledges that a target public may find the organization's undesired behaviour desirable. For example, many drug users perceive real benefits to the use of drugs, such as escape from reality or peer acceptance. From a social marketing point of view, these benefits are important to acknowledge, along with the real perceived costs of physical and mental discomfort associated with "saying no" to drugs.

Expressive strategies probably have the greatest potential for making difficult behaviour-change campaigns effective, but they are rarely used because they do not reflect the campaign sponsor's perspective. Various theories, however, ranging from co-orientation theory to excellence theory to social marketing theory, all lend strong support to the value of the expressive approach. Unfortunately, clients often design campaigns using strategies more persuasive to themselves than to their target publics.

11. *Ego defensive:* The ego-defensive approach sets up a situation in which the target public will associate smartness and success with the desired attitude or behaviour, whereas failure is associated with the refusal to adopt the message. This approach can be used in both a positive and a negative application. For example, the Business Alliance for a New New York produced messages promising that "you don't have to be a genius to understand the benefits of doing business in New York. (But if you are, you'll have plenty of company.)" The Illinois Department of Public Health and Golin/Harris International focused on making safe-sex decisions "cool" in awkward situations. Research designed to ensure that the appeal would not backfire included mall intercepts of 200 teens, a 33-member teen advisory panel, feedback from high-risk adolescents via state-funded organizations, and message testing using

quantitaive and qualitative methods. On the other hand, the Partnership for a Drug-Free America produced messages offering "ten ugly facts for beautiful young women," in an attempt to make use of cocaine seemego threatening. Again, the danger of ego-defensive appeals is they need to seem realistic to the target public and, therefore, require considerable pretesting.

12. *Repetition:* If you simply say the same thing over and over enough times, sometimes it will get through. According to McGuire (1989), three to five repeats can help a message get through, especially if the message is presented in a pleasant way. Many campaign designers interpret the three-to-five rule as a magic bullet guaranteeing a message will be successfully propelled into waiting target publics. Repetition, however, constitutes a useful supplemental strategy for an otherwise well-designed campaign, instead of a sufficient strategy in itself.
13. *Assertion:* The emotional parallel to autonomy appeals, the assertion strategy focuses on people's desire to gain power and status. A popular appeal for low-involvement issues or products, the assertion appeal promises increased control over others or a situation in return for adopting the proposed attitude or behaviour.
14. *Empathy:* Empathy strategies appeal to people's desire to be loved. Although most applications of the empathic strategy focus on how target publics can achieve personal acceptance from others, this approach can appeal to people's altruism and desire to feel good for helping others they care about. A simple but eloquent American Red Cross appeal, for example, notes that "when you give blood, you give another birthday, another anniversary, another day at the beach, another night under the stars, another talk with a friend, another laugh, another hug, another chance."

15. *Identification:* People aspire to feel better about themselves and frequently aspire to be like someone else. Often they look to other role models who embody positive characteristics. Campaigns commonly use this to create positive associations between a proposed idea or product and a desirable personality such as Michael Jordan. Negative associations also can be made, but as with most negative appeals they require careful pretesting to avoid failure.
16. *Bandwagon:* Making an idea seem contagious can make the idea seem even better. If 2,000 community leaders and neighborhood residents have signed a petition favoring the construction of a new city park, shouldn't you favor it, too? Mothers Against Drunk Driving has made use of this strategy by encouraging people to tie red ribbons on their car antennas during the winter holidays to publicly state their support for sober driving. The strategy does not do much to change strongly held opinions, but it can sway the undecided and serve as a useful reminder and motivator for those in agreement with a campaign message.

Diffusion of Innovations

Another popular theory that is a variation on the domino model provides useful guidance for campaign designers hoping to promote the adoption of an innovation. Innovations can be products such as a new computing tool or ideas such as recycling or changing eating habits. According to diffusion of innovations theory (Rogers, 1983), people considering whether to adopt an innovation progress through five steps that parallel the hierarchy of effects in the domino model.

The innovation-decision process follows the way an individual or decision-making unit passes from a lack of awareness to use of the new product or idea. The likelihood of someone making progress through the steps depends on prior conditions such as previous experiences, perceived needs, the norms of the society in which the target public lives, and the individual's level of innovativeness.

The steps include knowledge, persuasion, decision, implementation, and confirmation. Innovations are evaluated on the basis of their relative advantages, which Rogers called compatibility, complexity, trialability, and observability. Simply put, an innovation is more likely to be adopted if it seems to have clear benefits that are not difficult to harvest, particularly if giving it a try is not especially risky.

Diffusion of innovations theory teaches that most innovations occur according to a fairly predictable S-curve cycle. First, a few brave souls give the new idea a try, and then the innovation picks up speed and becomes more broadly accepted. Finally, most people likely to adopt the innovation do so, and the rate of change slows down again. Campaigns advocating relatively innovative ideas or products benefit from tailoring their messages according to where the innovation is on the S-curve.

Campaigns advocating adoption of an innovation should consider that people who are more innovative will have different needs and interests than people less innovative. According to diffusion of innovations theory, campaigners can think of five broad target publics: innovators, who are the first 2.5% to adopt a new product or idea; early adopters, who are the next 13.5%; the early majority, who represent 34% of the total potential market; the late majority, who represent another 34%; and laggards, who are the final 16%. People who fit in each of these categories have characteristics in common with each other.

According to diffusion of innovations theory, people associate mainly with people who share key characteristics with them (called homogeneous), but they learn new things from people who are slightly different (called heterogeneous). People who are completely different will probably not be able to relate well with the target public and will have less persuasive potential.

Inoculation

Inoculation theory looks like the mirror image of diffusion of innovations theory. The idea behind inoculation is to address potential trouble before it starts so that potential problems never pick up speed to create a crisis. Just as a flu shot can prevent a full-blown attack of the flu bug, a small dose of bad news early can prevent an issue from turning into a full-blown crisis. For example, political candidates expecting bad news to hit the media can present the news themselves, from their own perspective. Taking away the element of surprise or confrontation makes the news less sensational and, therefore, less damaging.

Theories explaining how and why message recipients make decisions in various circumstances demonstrate that purely informational messages and messages that appeal mainly to the client instead of the message recipient can doom a communication Programme. Remember that if the target public already shared the organization's point of view perfectly, a communication Programme probably would not be necessary.

Because the goal of a public relations Programme is to increase the degree to which a target public and an organization share common perspectives and priorities, the organization controlling the message needs to make overtures inviting collaboration with the target public, instead of expecting the target public to invite the organization's perspective into their lives. Making a change is not the target public's priority. Understanding how and why message receivers think the ways they do can greatly enhance the communication professional's ability to build constructive relationships with them by pinpointing the strategies target publics find relevant, credible, and compelling.

Index

A

B

F

G

H

I

J

K

L

M

N

O

P

Q

R

S

T

U

V

W

Y

Z